THE YOGA OF DELIGHT,
WONDER, AND ASTONISHMENT

SUNY Series in Tantric Studies
Paul Muller-Ortega, Editor

THE YOGA OF DELIGHT, WONDER, AND ASTONISHMENT

A Translation of the Vijñāna-bhairava
with an Introduction and Notes by
Jaideva Singh

Foreword by Paul Muller-Ortega

State University of New York Press

First published in U.S.A. by
State University of New York Press, Albany

Printed in the United States of America
Published in India by Motilal Banarsidass, Delhi, 1979

For information, address State University of New York
Press, State University Plaza, Albany, N.Y., 12246

Production by Diane Ganeles
Marketing by Theresa A. Swierzowski

Library of Congress Cataloging in Publication Data

ISBN 0-7914-1073-0

ISBN 0-7914-1074-9

10 9 8 7 6 5 4 3

Dedicated

With Profound Respect to
Svāmī Lakṣmaṇa Joo
Who unsealed my Eyes

BLESSING

For centuries India has been a spiritual light to the world, and today that light is spreading even more widely in the West. The spiritual teaching of India has come down from very ancient times. It has remained pure and unadulterated despite many invasions and the reigns of out-siders belonging to different religious faiths.

Among these ancient teachings of India the Tantra scriptures have the unique, in fact, the highest place. In them one finds not only means for knowing the nature of the highest reality, but also techniques to experiencing it. Today, looking for peace and truth, seekers all over the world are becoming interested in the teachings of the Tantras. But unfortunately, many teachers who have gathered wrong understanding of the sublime teachings of the Tantras, have been teaching and writing anything about them. As a result seekers are improperly guided, and remain ignorant of the real knowledge and yogic techniques which the Tantras have to offer.

Therefore it is high time to publish translations of the ancient and authoritative works which explain the true nature of the yogic practices of Tantric Shaivism. However, this job has to be done by scholars with a thorough knowledge of the subject. It is a matter of great joy that the *Vijñāna Bhairava,* one of the most highly honoured Tantra treatises of Kashmir Shaivism, is now coming to light and becoming available to English-speaking readers. It has been translated, annotated and explained by no less a personage than Shri Jaideva Singh, who has had the opportunity to study with the great teachers of Kashmir Shaivism. He is rich not only in years, but in knowledge too and therefore worthy of doing this work. Among his many English works are two other books of Kashmir Shaivism: the translations and annotations of the *Pratyabhijñāhṛdayam* and the *Śiva Sūtras*. May God grant him many years to serve Him by bringing out more books of Kashmir Shaivite philosophy to help spread in the world this invaluable knowledge of the ancient teachings of the Truth. He deserves to be praised for his love and interest in this philosophy.

Let Lord Bhairava bless the translators, editors, publishers, printers and others who have helped in the revival of His words and also those who would read them.

SWAMI MUKTANANDA
GANESHPURI

CONTENTS

FOREWORD

It is a happy occasion that this book comes before the public as part of the ongoing program of publication by SUNY Press in the Tantric Studies Series. The *Vijñāna-bhairava (VBh)* is one of the foundational, revealed texts of tantric Shaivism. It is praised as the venerable *Shaivopanisad,* the precious and esoteric compendium which sings of the omnipresence of Shiva and of his all-pervasive availability. In its short compass, the *VBh* gathers up a treasure-house of secret, yogic methods for experiencing the extraordinary and paradoxical reality of unbounded consciousness which is called Bhairava or Śiva.

This book joins two other translations by Jaideva Singh, published in the Tantric Studies Series, of foundational texts of the non-dual Shaivism of Kashmir. It is no exaggeration to say that Singh's life-work of investigation into one of the most esoteric traditions of the Hindu Tantra may be credited with contributing greatly to the current vogue in Kashmir Shaiva and Tantric studies. He opened up access to this tradition by translating and annotating five of its fundamental texts.

Singh first presented to the public a translation of the *Pratyabhijñāhṛdayam* (1963), recently reissued in a second edition by SUNY Press as *The Doctrine of Recognition* (1990). This was followed in subsequent years by four other translations and annotations of crucial texts of the Kashmir Shaiva tradition: the *Śiva-sūtras* (1979), the *Spanda-kārikās* (1980), the *Parātriṃśikā-vivaraṇa* (1988), and the present book, the *Vijñāna-bhairava* (1979). The *Parātriṃśikā-vivaraṇa* was recently reissued by SUNY Press as *A Trident of Wisdom* (1989). This intense labor of scholarship amply demonstrates Singh's deep commitment to making accessible to the modern reader the vision of reality contained in these texts.

THE VIJÑANA-BHAIRAVA

The *Vijñāna-Bhairava* is a work of very great importance. Abhinavagupta's (ca. 950–1014 C.E.) respect for it is evidenced in his having termed it *Śiva-vijñāna-upaniṣad,* the "Esoteric Teaching for the direct knowledge of Śiva." Although it is a relatively brief text of 163 ślokas, each of its verses (from verse 24 on) represents a compressed description of a particular meditation method (*bhāvanā* or *dhāraṇā*) for entering into the experience of Śiva. While the dating of such a text is problematic at best, it is at least prior to the ninth century C.E. and is perhaps even several centuries older than that. First published in the Kashmir Series of Texts and Studies as Volume No. VIII in 1918, the KSTS edition incorporates the fragment of a commentary by Kṣemarāja which unfortunately breaks off at verse 18. The remaining commentary is attributed to Shivopādhyāya, an eighteenth century author who is clearly not reliable.

The emphasis of this rich text is on the direct, personal experience of the Supreme rather than on any ritualistic or external performances. Its close relationship with the Kaula environment is evidenced in a statement at the end of the text by the Goddess that as a result of Bhairava's exposition, she now understands the essence of the *Rudra-yāmala-tantra (RYT)*.

The *VBh* is one of the bliss-saturated texts of tantric Shaivism. Its essential teaching centers on the omnipresence and all-pervasiveness of the extraordinary consciousness which it calls Śiva. Its yogic methods hint at a profound secret: it requires but a subtle shift of attention to bring this astonishing reality into view. If the yogin can turn within, away from the external forms of reality, unexpected transformations will occur in his awareness. This shift will open, as it were, a chink in the apparently impregnable smoothness of the ordinary world. Through this chink there will stand revealed the *ekarasa,* the unitary and uncontainable reality of Bhairava which overflows into the awareness of the practitioner. Thus, the *VBh* places an overwhelming emphasis on the various methods by means of which this experience will become actual. It teaches the numerous, secret keys or gestures of attention that will reveal infinity. These yogic rearrangements of perception are called *dhāraṇā*-s or *bhāvanā*-s, and they employ (among other things) the breath and its cycles and spaces; mantras; the placing of attention on different parts of the body; powerful contemplations; and many other techniques. Moreover, true to its tantric provenance, the *VBh* discovers the reality of Bhairava in unexpected and even apparently bizarre places.

The *VBh* links itself to the mysterious *Rudra-yāmala-tantra* in its opening and closing verses. This attribution brings to mind a similar connection of the so-called *Parātriṃśikā* verses (commented on by Abhinavagupta in his *PTv* and *PTlv*) which are said to form the last part of the *RYT*. Some scholars argue that the *RYT* is merely a "convenience" or "ghost" title and that no such actual text ever existed. In their study of tantric literature, Goudriaan and Gupta demonstrate that while there are two separate published texts that link themselves to the *RYT*—an *Uttara-tantra* and an *Anuttara-tantra*—neither text is linked with the verses commented upon in the *PTv* and *PTlv*. There are as many as fifty other texts which claim to derive from this mysterious Tantra of which perhaps the earliest are precisely the *Parātriṃśikā* verses and the *Vijñāna-bhairava* (Goudriaan and Gupta, *HTŚL*, pp. 47–48).

While the *VBh* antedates the tradition that has come to be called Kashmir Shaivism, it is especially in the texts of this tradition that it is interpreted and referred to as an authoritative and sacred source. One can find scattered verses of the *VBh* quoted in the works of Abhinavagupta, as well as in those of his great disciple and interpreter, Kṣemarāja. The interested reader is encouraged to consult the previous volumes in the SUNY Press Tantric Studies Series as well as the many important publications in the SUNY Press Shaiva Traditions of Kashmir Series for information about the non-dual Shaivism of Kashmir.

DHĀRANĀ AS YOGIC METHOD

The *VBh* constitutes an extended collection of 112 meditational methods—*dhāraṇā-s* or *bhāvanā-s*—for approaching the omnipresent and paradoxical reality of Śiva. As one scans the great variety of yogic methods it compiles, one is immediately struck by the contrast in tone between this text and the earlier classical expositions of Yoga in the *Yoga-Sūtra* and its commentaries. While equally serious in its yogic intent, the *VBh* has an almost playful and experimental approach which seems anchored in the confidence that one can finally never stray for very long from the reality of Śiva. Such a reality is everywhere, and within it—at its Heart—there is a power which operates continuously to reveal it. Moreover, because it is grounded in the essentially tantric realization of the omnipresent purity of consciousness, the text has the freedom to explore as meditational methods domains that might have been puritanically disdained by the earlier yogic traditions of the classical period. All things, all experiences, all moments are bathed in the unassailable purity of the absolute consciousness. It requires but a shift of attention, a subtle refocussing of energies, and that extraordinary reality comes into view.

It is important to emphasize that the *VBh* functions within the tradition as an advanced text. Later interpreters certainly understood that the reception of the initiatory impulse of *śaktipāta* from a qualified preceptor was a prerequisite for the successful application of its *dhāraṇās*. On the backdrop of such an essential initiation — which sets in motion the *sādhanā* of the practitioner — each *dhāraṇā* was then seen as a doorway that gives access to the blissful reality of Bhairava.

In the traditional progression of *sādhanā,* Śiva first becomes accessible in the enstatic state of *turīya,* which the advanced yogin stabilized by gaining proficiency in the *nimīlana* or closed-eyed *samādhi.* Contrary to earlier yogic notions, for the *Tantra* the journey of consciousness does not terminate in this introvertive condition. Indeed, the tantric practitioner will attempt to entice the absolute consciousness out of its severe and self-enclosed state. The *sādhaka* wishes to activate a dancing blissfulness within the initial, flat voidness of pure, contentless consciousness. The *VBh* prescribes certain secret and subtle gestures of awareness which unfold and magically expand the experience of *samādhi.* One cannot resist quoting here the foundational text of the *Śiva-sūtras* (I.12) which insists that: *vismayo yogabhūmikaḥ,* the levels or stages of Yoga constitute wonder. The Yoga of the *VBh* is wonder-filled, it is the Yoga of astonishment — *camatkāra,* the Yoga of delight, of the delightful play of the *śakti,* the play of consciousness within itself. The *VBh* is an initiatory manual which instructs the practitioner in the intricacies of this advanced sport of *Śiva.*

Māyā, the cosmic, creative illusion functions to create a veil which conceals and obscures the underlying reality known as the *śivanāndarasa,* the nectarean taste of the blissfulness of Śiva. Nevertheless, there are cracks in this veil, places where the ultimate reality shines through. Although the methods of the *VBh* resist summarizing—they display a fascinating variety of yogic technique—there are, nevertheless, powerful recurring themes: *śūnya* or emptiness; *nirvikalpa,* which contrasts the nondual space of emptiness between and behind thoughts with the notion of *vikalpa,* dual, polarizing thought; *madhya,* the space or interval; *śakti,* the great power; *ānanda,* the inherent and impeccable blissfulness. If there is one of these themes that seems most fundamental in the *VBh,* it might be that the taste of Śiva may be had in the *madhya,* the middle or interval: the interval between two thoughts, between two breaths, between two states of consciousness — waking and sleep, for example; between two sensations; between any two experiences whatsoever. Through this crack in the ordinariness of things, the practitioner gains a glimpse of the Heart, of the extraordinary state of nondual consciousness.

To this may be attributed the highly experiential tone of the text. It does not contain a sustained philosophical argument. Rather, it is an instructional guide that continuously invites the practitioner to look more deeply and more subtly at her own experience. The blissful and shattering realizations that the practitioner will undergo as a result of its methods serve as its only form of justification or proof.

As it prescribes these methods the *VBh* seems to speak to us to say: Look into the place of voidness. Locate it and lose yourself in it. Releasing all thoughts, emotions, and feelings, go beyond all that arises within you to locate the powerful darkness, the space in between, the interval. Allow yourself to yield to this precious space. At first, all will be lost in a potent nirvāṇic amnesia of self and world. But gradually, where no foothold appeared to be possible, deep in the *nirvikalpa,* the yogin will locate the wordless, silent pulsation of consciousness, the continuous self-englobing as consciousness implicately enfolds on itself. This is the *saṃghaṭṭa,* the self-embrace of Śiva and Śakti. From this there emerges a power, a vibration, a pulsation within which the yogin bathes and from which s/he takes nourishment and refreshment. Attuning to this *śakti,* the yogin will be led ever inward to experience the opening of the great spaces of the Heart.

Then, suddenly, this inwardness will reverse itself. During everyday situations—listening to the notes of a song, to the flow of breath; or, in the midst of powerful emotions such as fear, anger, or great happiness; or, as waking yields to sleep; there may occur a sudden, flashing expansion, a surging efflorescence of consciousness, which is the manifestation of Bhairava. The *Śiva Sūtras* state (I.5): *udyamo bhairava*—Bhairava is the surging expansion. Thus, many of the methods in the text address the advanced yogin who has long cultivated an inward and enclosed *samādhi.* They urge him to another, more daring stance of openness to the hidden presence of Śiva flashing from the most unexpected of places. These methods cultivate the open-eyed *samādhi* that will result in the *bhairavīmudrā* in which the yogin bathes in all moments in the perception of unbounded consciousness. Thus, the advanced *sādhanās* prescribed in the *VBh* advise an alternation of introvertive states—in which Śiva is discovered as concealed in the innermost depths—with extrovertive conditions which reveal the discovery of Śiva everywhere. In this way, the *sādhanās* of the *VBh* emulate the essential pulsation of the *rudrayamala,* of the expansion and contraction of the Rudradyad as they embrace in the Heart of reality.

THE FLOWING HEART

According to the tradition, it is the Heart which serves as the source of the nectarean bliss of Śiva. From this Heart, the revealed scriptures of the Shaivite tradition are said to come forth like waves or currents of transforming and blissful knowledge. The *tantra*-s and *āgama*-s transcribe the revelatory dialogue that takes place in the Heart between Bhairava and the Goddess. This pair is termed the *saṃghaṭṭa,* the spiralling and fecund self-embrace of the absolute consciousness. In philosophical terms, the *prakāśa,* the great light of consciousness, is continuously encompassing itself. This self-encompassing is termed the *vimarśa:* the self-referential, self-consciousness of the *prakāśa*. From this embrace, there issues forth the rumbling vibration which is the *spanda*. As this *spanda* takes shape it impels the dialogue between Bhairava and the Goddess and this intimate dialogue issues forth as the secret knowledge that the ultimate reality has of itself.

This knowledge embodies itself as the *āgama*-s and *tantra*-s which serve as the textual foundation for all forms of medieval Shaivism, including the tradition of non-dual Shaivism of Kashmir. In this domain of immense numbers of texts, it is not surprising that various and conflicting lists have come down to us. For Abhinavagupta, the premier exponent and intellectual synthesizer of these revealed texts in the Kashmiri tradition, the *Mālinī-vijaya-tantra* was the most authoritative. In this branch of Shaivism, we encounter a traditional list of eleven tantra-s which usually includes the *Svacchanda,* the *Vijñāna-bhairava,* the *Ucchuṣma-bhairava,* the *Ānanda-bhairava,* the *Mṛgendra, Matañga, Netra, Naiśvāsa, Svāyambhuva* and *Rudra-yāmala*.

BHAIRAVA

The form of Śiva encountered in the *VBh* and in many of the other revealed texts of the non-dual Shaivism of Kashmir is called Bhairava. Representations of this god show a form of dread and terror. A sinister, fanged face often surmounted by writhing and venomous serpents conveys the fury of the god of death, who is also paradoxically the god of transformation and release. In the *VBh,* it is Bhairava who is the interlocutor who instructs the Goddess in the multifarious and secret techniques for liberation.

The term Bhairava derives from the root bhī, to be afraid, and the related adjective, bhīru, fearful, timid. By a curious process of inversion, Bhairava comes to mean that which is frightful, terrible, horrible. It is Śiva in the form of Bhairava who punishes the creator god, Brahmā, for the sin of arrogance by cutting off one of his heads with the nail of his left thumb. Because he is now guilty of the sin of brahminicide, Bhairava is condemned to wander, begging for alms and carrying Brahmā's skull which remains attached to his hand. The skull finally drops off when Bhairava expiates his sin by entering the precincts of the holy city of Banaras.

Many powerful tantric themes are densely packed into the figure of Bhairava. The skull-bearing transgressor of *dharma* who is fearful and terrible resonates with the yogic and tantric cremation-ground culture of heterodox and transgressive groups who sought power through control of and possession by hordes of frightening goddesses.

At the same time, and especially as a result of the later interpretive strategies of Abhinavagupta, the term Bhairava (or Bhairavatā, or Bhairavasvarūpa) transcends its mythic and personified identity and comes to stand for the Ultimate itself, the huge abyss of the unbounded and uncontainable light of consciousness. To attain Bhairava in this yogic sense is to enter into the experience of this all-encompassing and nondual reality of ultimate consciousness.

Thus, in the hands of this authoritative expositor of the Tantra, these older conceptions become the synthetic Trika-Kaula which, permeated with a thoroughgoing nondualism, transforms these older cults of controlled possession into a yogic if left-handed Tantra. Dominated by an overarching inquiry into the nature of the power of Ultimate consciousness, of Bhairava conjoined with the Goddess, Abhinavagupta's writings transmute the external goddesses into the mechanisms of the ultimate reality of Śiva, and the secret ritual into an occasion for the recognition by consciousness of its true identity as Śiva. We can see many reflections and anticipations of these themes in the *VBh*.

THE RUDRA-DYAD

In the light of these ideas if the textual-historical connection of the *VBh* to the *RYT* is unimaginatively dismissed, there is the risk of missing the deep symbolic import of such an attribution. From the symbolic point of view, when the *Vbh* says that it is the essence of the *RYT* it alludes to its own textual myth of origin. The *rudra-yāmala* or Rudra-dyad contains one of the deep symbolic clues to an understanding of the *Vbh*. In the *PTlv* Abhinavagupta tells us (comm. on verses 5–9a, p. 5):

> Therefore, the phoneme *Ḥ*, the *visarga*, or Emissional Power is termed the *Rudra-yāmala*, the Rudra-dyad, because it consists of both the supreme Śiva and *śakti*, of the rest and activity which constitute the Union of Bhairava with his beloved.

Similarly, in the *TĀ* (3.68–69) Abhinavagupta says:

> The twinned form of Śiva and *śakti* is known as the union. It is termed the power of bliss because the entire universe is emitted by it. That reality which is higher than the highest and the lowest, is called the Goddess, that reality is the essence, the Heart, the supreme Emissional Power of the Lord.

The text arises out of the *saṃghaṭṭa* or union of Śiva and Shakti. It sings of the extraordinary reality which dances hidden at the Heart of all things. In her initial question to Bhairava, the Goddess asks him to reveal his own essential nature to her. In his response, Bhairava first praises her question as pertaining to the very essence of the Tantra and then dismissively disdains all descriptions of the *sakala* or composite form of the Ultimate as insubstantial and phantasmagoric. Instead he praises the *niṣkala* or transcendent aspect of the Supreme. In return, the Goddess beseeches Bhairava to teach her the method by which she may gain an understanding of this transcendent and blissful nondual reality.

EMBODIED BLISS

The one who experiences this embodied enlightenment is said to dwell in a universal bliss, the *jagadānanda*, as s/he abides in the *bhairavīmudrā*, the spiritual posture in which consciousness is simultaneously completely introverted and completely extroverted. This posture describes the inner state of the one who has achieved embodied enlightenment, the *jīvanmukta*. It describes the tasting of the nectar of the bliss of Śiva which is discovered by the *jīvanmukta* both at the innermost depths of his being, as well as in the outermost limits of sensory experience. Indeed, the *bhairavīmudrā* is important because it represents the fullest possible stretch of awareness. In this condition what the *jīvanmukta* tastes in the innermost depths of consciousness is identical to that which is found as the essence of all sensory experiences of the so-called objective world. Using the methods of the *Vbh,* the practitioner finds the way to entice the divine pulsation of consciousness into revealing itself to her at all times, in all experiences, and under all circumstances.

Abhinavagupta ecstatically sings the praises of this state in the *PTv* (comm. on 32b, pp. 270–271):

> That in which everything shines and which shines everywhere, O awakened ones, is the one brilliant quivering gleam, the Supreme Heart. That which is the abode of the origin of his own world, expanding and contracting at the same time, he rejoices in his own Heart. He should worship the vibrating Heart which appears as cosmic manifestation; thus the Heart should be worshipped in the heart, in the *suṣumnā* passage where one will encounter the great bliss of the pair of Śiva and Śakti.

Like the serpent entwined around the *liṅga,* the spiralling embrace of consciousness with itself always first implodes centripetally into the dark star, the great void at the Heart of all things. Here nothing that is not infinity itself can gain a foothold. Here all defining limitations and identifying, intrinsic characteristics of individuality are bewilderingly and fiercely stripped away. Who dares to enter into this abyss—which is the intimate abode of the deepest embrace of Śiva and of Śakti—must truly be a renunciate, must have courageously abandoned himself to the sacrificial yielding of all things into the all-consuming fire of Śiva.

Yet the dark star of the Heart is also the illuminating, perpetual supernova always joyfully exploding centrifugally outward. At the highest level, it does so through the all-encompassing vibration of the supreme *mantra* of consciousness, the great, thundering *OM,* which is also the *mahāmantra AHAM*. In this primordial cry, Śiva perpetually announces the realization of recognition, *Śivo'ham*—"I am Śiva," or again, "It is Śiva which is the great *I AM,* the great 'I' consciousness of reality." This great *mantra* then fractures itself through the four levels of speech, reducing and congealing the hyperfluidity of the ultimate light as it approaches ever closer to human knowability. The interplay of the titanic, gorgeous, and perhaps even (from one perspective) horrifying forces that perpetually dwell at the Heart of things is the true domain of the Tantra. The perennial intent of the tantric practitioner is the fascinated emulation of this great play of Śiva and Śakti.

The *VBh* invites the practitioner to discover the continuous occurrence of this play at the intimate core of life. It prescribes the methods by which the *sādhaka* can come to embody the paradoxical totality of these unimpeded forces within a transformed human life. Thus, the text itself arises as part of the play, the great dialogue, the blissful intercourse of this divine pair. Bhairava, the horrific, skull-bearing, trident-carrying god, sweetly instructs the Great Mother of the Universe in the many and utterly secret—*atirahasya*—methods of the Tantra. These methods allow the practitioner to validate experientially the intellectual teaching of the omnipresence of Shiva.

Thus, the Tantra rejects the dry vistas of traditional philosophical debate which seek only the re-presentation of the Ultimate through conceptual truths. It rejects as well the self-enclosing renunciation of traditional Indian monasticism which seeks protectively to isolate the monk from the imagined strain of worldliness. Transcending the dualities and distinctions of conventional thought and morality, the Tantra demonstrates an outward gesture of embracing delight in all of reality. The tantric hero pushes outward into adventurous, spiritual exploration, into savoring and delighting the experience of so many varieties of the blissful *ekarasa,* the unitary taste of consciousness. In this way, the tantric hero delights in all, even the bitterness and suffering of the ordinary world yield under the piercing scrutiny of the yogin to reveal to him their essential measure of blissfulness. In this way s/he becomes the great dancer, the one who relishes the nectar, the taste of the *śivanāndarasa*.

Jaideva Singh died at the age of 93 on May 27, 1986. Convinced as he was that Kashmir Shaivism represents the most profound expression of the ancient wisdoms of India, he would have been delighted at the current expansion of interest and study of tantric Shaivism. The present SUNY edition of his translation of the *VBh* continues his life's labor in the dissemination of knowledge about this tradition.

Paul E. Muller-Ortega

PREFACE

Vijñānabhairava is a very ancient book on *Yoga*. It closely follows the basic principles of Śaivāgama. It contains 112 types of *yoga*. There is hardly any other book on yoga which has described so many ways of approach to Central Reality that is present in each man as his essential Self. It is both extensive, and intensive in the treatment of the subject of *yoga*.

An English translation of this excellent work is being provided for the first time. The text that has been adopted is mainly the one that is published in the Kashmir Series of Texts and Studies. At a few places, however, slightly different readings yielding better sense have been incorporated as suggested by Svāmī Lakṣmaṇa Joo.

Each verse of the Sanskrit text has been printed in both Devanāgarī and Roman script. This is followed by an English translation and a number of expository notes which will go a long way in elucidating the main idea of the verse.

A long Introduction explaining the basic principles of the *yogas* described in the text has been provided in the beginning. A glossary of technical terms has also been added at the end.

Since the *yogas* recommended in the book are based on the tenets of the non-dualistic Śaiva Philosophy, the reader will do well to read the author's Introductory Portion of either the Pratyabhijñāhṛdayam or the Śiva-sūtras before taking up the study of the present book.

I express my sincerest gratitude to Svāmī Lakṣmaṇa Joo who has kindly taught this book to me word by word. My thanks are also due to Shri Dinanath Ganj who has kindly helped me in the preparation of the index to important Sanskrit words and the alphabetical index to the verses.

Varanasi

JAIDEVA SINGH

INTRODUCTION

IMPORTANCE OF VIJÑĀNABHAIRAVA

There have been, in India, two main ways of approach to Reality or the Essential Nature of Self, viz., Vivekaja mārga and Yogaja mārga—the path of distinction or discrimination and the path of union or integration. Pātañjala yoga and Śāṅkara Vedānta have adopted the Vivekaja mārga by which the Puruṣa or Ātmā (the Self) is isolated from Prakṛti (in the case of Pātañjala Yoga) or from Māyā (in the case of Vedānta). The word Yoga does not mean union in Patañjali's system; it means *samādhi* or intense abstract meditation (as Vyāsa puts it in his commentary, 'yuji samâdhau'). Śaivāgama has adopted the Yogaja mārga in which the goal is not isolation of the Self from Prakṛti or Māyā but the integration of the individual Self to the Universal Self or Bhairava and the realization of the universe as the expression of His Śakti or spiritual Energy. The ideal of Śaivāgama is not the rejection of the universe but its assimilation to its Source.

Vijñānabhairava is an excellent exposition of the *yogaja mārga*. Hence its importance. It has been referred to as Āgama,[1] Śivavijñānopaniṣad,[2] and Rudrayāmalasāra[3] by Abhinavagupta. Yogarāja has referred to it as Śaivopaniṣad.[4] Kṣemarāja has referred to it at many places in his commentary on Śiva-sūtras.

It is clear that it has been acknowledged by the great exponents of Śaivāgama as a very authentic work on yoga.

THE TEXT

Vijñānabhairava has been published in the Kashmir Series of Texts and Studies with an incomplete commentary of Kṣemarāja, and complete commentaries of Śivopādhyāya and Bhaṭṭa Ānanda.

In the above text, the following remark appears on page 16, after the 23rd verse, "ita uttaraṁ Śrī Śivopādhyāyakṛtā vivṛtiḥ"

1. I.P.V.V. I, p. 207. 2. I.P.V.V. II, p. 405. 3. I.P.V.V., p. 285.
4. *Vivṛti Paramārtha-sāra.*

i.e. "after this, the commentary is by Śivopādhyāya. "Even in the life-time of Śivopādhyāya, the full commentary of Kṣemarāja was not available. It is not known whether Kṣemarāja did not live to complete his commentary, or whether his commentary after the above verse has been lost. All that can be said is that it has not been so far traced."

Śivopādhyāya is greatly influenced by Śāṃkara Vedānta. So his commentary is not reliable. Bhaṭṭa Ānanda is even more avowedly a follower of Śāṃkara Vedānta. His commentary is, therefore, even far more removed from the original intention of the text. In the preparation of the present edition, these commentaries have not been translated.

THE DATE OF VIJÑĀNABHAIRAVA AND THE COMMENTARIES

Vijñānabhairava is a part of the ancient Tantras. It is held in high esteem in Śaivāgama. Abhinavagupta calls it Śiva-vijñāna-upaniṣad.

The text of Vijñānabhairava claims to be the quintessence of Rudrayāmala Tantra which means union of Rudra with His Śakti (Spiritual Energy). The authentic text of Rudrayāmala Tantra is not available. So it is not possible to say how far the text of Vijñānabhairava corresponds to that of Rudrayāmala Tantra.

Tantras contain descriptions of ritual practices, sacred formulae (*mantras*). mystical diagrams (*yantras*), gestures (*mudrās*), postures (*āsanas*), initiations (*dīkṣā*), *yoga* or mystic practices. Vijñānabhairava is purely a manual of mystic practices in accordance with Śaivāgama.

In the present state of our knowledge, it is impossible to give the exact date of Vijñānabhairava. The earliest reference to it is found in Vāmananāth's Advayasampatti-vārttika. It is likely that Vāmananātha may be the same as Vāmana, the celebrated writer on Poetics who flourished during the reign of King Jayāpīda of Kashmir (779—813 A.D.) If that be so, then it can be easily said that Vijñānabhairava was very well known in the 8th century A.D. Perhaps, it may have been compiled a century earlier.

So far as the commentators are concerned, Kṣemarāja flourished in the 10th century A.D. In the colophon of his commentary, Bhaṭṭa Ānanda mentions the date of the completion of the commentary according to which he flourished in the 17th century A.D.

Śivopādhyāya says in the colophon of his commentary that it was finished during the reign of Sukhajīvana. This means that he flourished in the 18th century A.D.

THE SIGNIFICANCE OF VIJÑĀNABHAIRAVA

Vijñānabhairava consists of two words, *vijñāna* and *bhairava*. We have first of all to understand the esoteric significance of Bhairava. Kṣemarāja in his *Udyota* commentary gives a description of the esoteric meaning of Bhairava. The sum and substance of it is that Bhairava is an acrostic word consisting of the letters, *bha*, *ra*, and *va*; *bha* indicates *bharaṇa* or maintenance of the universe; *ra* indicates *ravaṇa* or withdrawal of the universe; *va* indicates *vamana* or projection i.e., manifestation of the universe. Thus Bhairava indicates all the three aspects of the Divine.

This has been clarified by Abhinavagupta in Tantrāloka III, verses 283—285 in which he describes the three aspects of the Divine as *sraṣṭā* (manifester of the universe), *viśvarūpatā*, Bhairava in His cosmic essence in whose consciousness the entire universe differentiated in six ways (*ṣadadhvā*) is reflected, and Bhairava as *praśama* in whose flame of *mahābodha* (universal consciousness), everything is dissolved.

While Bhairava has three aspects, He from the point of view of the mystic, is that Ultimate Reality in which *prakāśa* i.e. Light of Consciousness and *vimarśa* or Eternal Awareness of that Light are indistinguishably fused. In other words, Bhairava is parama Śiva in whom *prakāśa* and *vimarśa*, *Śiva* and *Śakti*, *Bhairava* and *Bhairavī* are identical. Bhairava or Parama Śiva embraces in Himself transcendence and immanence, Śiva and Śakti. It is this Bhairava that is the goal of the seeker.

The *svarūpa* or essential nature of Bhairava is *vijñāna* or *bodha* or *mahābodha*, *cit* or *caitanya* the main characteristic of which is *svātantrya* or absolute freedom revealing itself in *icchā*, *jñāna*, and *kriyā*. It is to this Vijñānabhairava that the seeker of spiritual life has to be integrated.

The entire manifestation consisting of subject and object is a mere reflection in this *vijñāna*. Just as a city in a mirror appears as something different from the mirror, though it is nothing different from the mirror, even so the universe though appearing different from *vijñāna* is nothing different from it.

In verses 2 to 6 of *Vijñānabhairava*, the *Devī* mentions certain well known statements about Bhairava and wants to know His *parāvasthā*—highest state or essential nature. Bhairava categorically rejects the various well known opinions about His highest state and pithily but with luminous clarity states in verses 14 and 15 what His essential nature consists in :

"Parāvasthā (the highest state) of Bhairava is free of all notions pertaining to direction (*dik*), time (*Kāla*), nor can that be particularized, by some definite space (*deśa*) or designation (*uddeśa*). In verity that can neither be indicated nor described in words. One can be aware of that only when one is completely free of all thought-constructs (*vikalpas*). One can have an experience of that bliss in his own inmost Self (when one is completely rid of the ego, and is established in *pūrṇāhantā* i.e. in the plenitude of the divine I—consciousness).

That state of Bhairava which is full of the bliss of non-difference from the entire world (bharitākārā) is alone *Bhairavī* or *Śakti* of Bhairava."

That state is *Vijñāna*—a state of consciousness which is *nirvikalpa*, free of all thought-constructs. This Vijñānabhairava is the goal of man.

Parādevī or Bhairavī is only the *Śakti* (Power or energy) of Bhairava. Just as there is no difference between fire and its power of burning, even so there is no difference between Bhairava and Parādevī. Parādevī has been called *Śaivī mukha* or means of approach to Śiva.

DHĀRAṆĀS OR YOGA PRACTICES

The Devī now enquires, "By what means can this highest state be realized ?" In reply to this, Bhairava describes 112 *dhāraṇās*.

In Patañjali, the word *dhāraṇā* is used in a somewhat limited sense viz; 'fixation of mind on a particular spot.' In Vijñānabhairava it is used in the wide sense of fixation or concentration of mind or *yoga*. The word *yoga* is used both in the sense of communion (with the Divine) and the means (*upāya*) for that communion. So 112 types of *yoga* or means of communion with Bhairava have been described in this text.

Unfortunately, no word has been profaned so much in modern times as *yoga*. Fire-walking, acid-swallowing, stopping the heart-beat, etc. pass for *yoga* when really speaking they have nothing to do with *yoga* as such. Even psychic powers are not *yoga*. *Yoga* is awareness, transformation of the human consciousness into divine consciousness.

Vijñānabhairava mentions 112 *dhāraṇās* or types of *yoga*. It is a book on *yoga*, not on philosophy, but its system of *yoga* can be better understood if one is acquainted with its metaphysical background. The reader would be well advised to go through the author's Introduction either in *Pratyabhijñāhṛdayam* or *Śiva-sūtras* in order to get an idea of the metaphysics on which the present *yoga* system is based.

The means of communion with Bhairava have been classified under four broad heads in *Śaivāgama*, viz., *anupāya*, *śāmbhava*, *śākta* and *āṇava*. These have been described in detail by the author in the Introduction to the *Śiva Sūtras*. In this book, in the notes under each *dhāraṇā* it has been indicated whether it is *āṇava* or *śākta* or *śāmbhava*. *Anupāya* literally means 'no means', 'without any means' which has, however, been interpreted by Jayaratha as *Iṣat upāya* i.e. very little means. Just a casual hint by the *guru* or the spiritual director is enough for the advanced aspirant to enter the mystic state. Such a rare case is known as that of *anupāya*. *Āṇava*, *śākta* and *śāmbhava* are definite techniques. These are, however, not watertight compartments. The aspirant has to pass from the *āṇava* to *śākta* and finally from the *śākta* to the *śāmbhava* state.

Vijñānabhairava has utilized all the traditional techniques of *yoga*-postures, *mudrās* or gestures, development of *prāṇaśakti*, awakening of *kuṇḍalinī*, *mantra japa* or recital of words of power or sacred formulae, *bhakti* (devotion) *jñāna* (realization through understanding), meditation, *bhāvanā* (creative contemplation). It even uses certain techniques of very non-formal nature, e.g., looking vacantly at the dark night, high mountains, watching the condition of consciousness in a see-saw movement, the condition of consciousness before falling asleep, intently looking at a vase without partition, etc. It has recommended one hundred and twelve *dhāraṇās ad modum recipientis* (according to the mode of the recipients) keeping in view the fitness or competence of the aspirants so that any technique that may suit a particular aspirant may be adopted by him.

The ultimate goal recommended by the text is identification with Bhairava—undifferentiated universal consciousness which is the heart (*hṛdaya*), nectar (*amṛta*), Reality *par excellence* (*tattva* or *mahāsattā*) essence (*svarūpa*), Self (*ātman*), or void (*śūnyatā*) that is full. This involves the following processes:

(1) Perfect interiorization so that one is absorbed in the heart of the Supreme.

(2) Passing from *vikalpa* or the stage of differentiating, dichotomizing thought-construct to *nirvikalpa* stage of thought-free, non-relational awareness.

(3) Disappearance of the limited pseudo-I or ego which is only a product of *Prakṛti* and the emergence of the Real Universal I (*pūrṇāhantā*) which is divine.

(4) Dissolution of *citta* or the individual mind into *cit* or universal Consciousness.

This is the essence of *yoga* according to *Vijñānabhairava*.

IMPORTANT BASES OF THE DHĀRAṆĀS RECOMMENDED

The important bases of the *dhāraṇās* recommended in the text are the following:

1. *Prāṇa*:

Indian thought believes that between the body and the mind or between the material or physical energy and mental energy, there is *prāṇa* which is an intermediary link between the two. The word *prāṇa* has been variously translated as the vital force, biological energy, bio-plasma, etc. It has been a moot point in western Philosophy and Psychology as to how mind which is psychic in nature affects the body which is physical or material in nature. According to Indian Philosophy, between the body and *manas* or mind, there is *prāṇa* which serves as a link between the two. *Prāṇa* is not mind; it is insentient, but it is not like gross physical energy. It is subtle biological energy which catches the vibrations of the mind and transmits them to the nerves and plexuses and also physical vibrations to the mind. By controlling the mind one can control the *prāṇa*, and by controlling the *prāṇa*, one can control the mind.

According to Śaivāgama, *prāṇa* is not something alien to *saṁvit* or consciousness, but the first evolute of *saṁvit* (consciousness) *Prāk saṁvit prāṇe pariṇatā*. In the process of creation *saṁvit* or consciousness is at first transformed into *prāṇa*. So *prāṇa* is a phase of consciousness itself.

The word *prāṇa* is used both in the general sense of *prāṇanā* or *prāṇa-śakti* or life-principle or life-force and in the specific sense of various biological functions. This life-force expresses itself in breath. *Prāṇa* or the life-force cannot be contacted directly. It is only through breath that *prāṇa* or life-force can be influenced. So the word *prāṇa* is generally used for breath also though sometimes the word *vāyu* (as *prāṇa-vāyu*) is added to it. In this context the word *prāṇa* is used for the breath that is exhaled, and *apāna* is used for the breath that is inhaled. The word *prāṇa* is thus used in three senses—(1) in a general sense of *prāṇa-śakti* or life-force, (2) in a specific sense according to the various biological functions, and (3) in the sense of breath.

The breath is associated with inhalation and exhalation. The very first *dhāraṇā* (described in verse 24) utilizes the two poles of respiration, viz. 1 *dvādaśānta*—a distance of twelve fingers from the nose in the outer space where *prāṇa* or exhalation ends and *hṛt* or the centre inside the body where *apāna* or inhalation ends. One has to concentrate on these two points. After some practice, he will realize the state of Bhairava

Similarly, verses 2,3,4,5,6,7 etc. describe how *prāṇa* can be utilized in various ways for realizing the nature of Bhairava.

Several *dhāraṇās* utilize the awakening of *prāṇa-śakti* in the *suṣumnā* for the realization of spiritual perfection. It is by the efflorescence of *prāṇaśakti* in the *suṣumnā* or the medial channel of *prāṇa* in the interior of the spinal column that *kuṇḍalinī* awakens when one has the experience of the union of the individual consciousness with the universal consciousness. Verses 35, 38, 39 etc. refer to such *dhāraṇās*. Notes on these verses should be carefully read.

Uccāra is the natural characteristic of *prāṇa*. *Uccāra* means expression in the form of *nāda* or sound-subtle, inarticulate, or unmanifest and moving upward. The unmanifest, inarticulate sound or *nāda* is known as *varṇa*. Abhinavagupta says:

उक्तो य एष उच्चारस्तत्र योऽसौ स्फुरन् स्थित: ।
अव्यक्तानुकृतिप्रायो ध्वनिर्वर्णः स कथ्यते ॥

(Tantrāloka V, 131)

"From the uccāra of the general *prāṇa*, there vibrates an imperceptible, inarticulate sound which is known as *varṇa*."

Svacchanda Tantra says:

नास्योच्चारयिता कश्चित्प्रतिहन्ता न विद्यते ।
स्वयमुच्चरते देव: प्राणिनामुरसि स्थित: ॥ (VII, 50)

"There is none who sounds it voluntarily, nor can any one prevent its being sounded. The deity abiding in the heart of living creatures sounds it himself.

Abhinavagupta gives the following description of this *nāda*:

एको नादात्मको वर्ण: सर्ववर्णाविभागवान् ।
सोऽनस्तमितरूपत्वादनाहत इहोदित: ॥"

(Tantrāloka VI, 217)

"There is one *varṇa* in the form of *nāda* (sound vibration) in which lie all the *varṇas* (letters) latently in an undivided form. As it is ceaseless, it is called *anāhata* i.e. unstruck, natural, spontaneous, uncaused. As all the varṇas (letters) originate from this *nāda*, therefore, is it called *varṇa* proleptically. Vide verse 38 of the text.

How are we to know about this inarticulate sound ? In the following verse, Abhinavagupta throws a hint as to how we can form an idea of it.

सृष्टिसंहारबीज च तस्य मुख्यं वपुर्विदुः ॥
(Tantrāloka V. 132)

"The *sṛṣṭi bīja* and *saṃhāra bīja* are its main forms". In the words of Jayaratha main forms mean *pradhānam abhivyakti-sthānam* i.e. the *sṛṣṭi bīja* and *saṃhāra bīja* are the main spots of its revelation. *sa* is the *sṛṣṭi bīja* or the mystic letter denoting expiration and *ha* is the *saṃhāra bija* or the mystic letter denoting inspiration.

In verses 155 and 156 of Vijñānabhairava is given the process by which this *nāda* expresses itself in the breath of every living creature. "The breath is exhaled with the sound *sa* and then inhaled with the sound *ha*. Thus the empirical individual always recites this *mantra haṃsaḥ* (verse 155). Throughout the day and night he (the empirical individual recites this *mantra* 21,600 times. Such a *japa* (recitation) of the goddess is mentioned which is quite easy to accomplish; it is only difficult for the ignorant." (verse 156).

This *haṃsaḥ mantra* is repeated by every individual automatically in every round of expiration-inspiration. Since the repetition is automatic, it is known as *ajapā japa* i.e. a repetition of the *mantra* that goes on spontaneously without anybody's effort. This *haṃsaḥ* (I am He i.e. I am Śiva or the Divine) is the *ādi prāṇa* i.e. initial *prāṇa* which is the first evolute or transformation of consciousness.

There are two ways in which this *prāṇic mantra* can be utilized for the awakening or rise of *Kuṇḍalinī*. One is *anusandhāna* or prolonged mental awareness of this automatic process which has been referred to above. Another way is conscious *japa* or recitation or repetition of this *mantra* as *so'ham* or simply *aum* (ओम्). This requires a further elucidation.

In the descending arc of the creative activity from consciousness to inconscient matter or in other words from the conscious creative pulsation of the Divine *Śakti* known as *parāvāk* or *vimarśa* at the highest level down to *vaikharī* or gross speech at the level of the living being, there is a movement downward from the centre of Reality to the periphery in the successive form of *parāvāṇī*, (the spiritual logos in which the creative process is in the form of *nāda*), *paśyantī* (*vāk-śakti*, going forth as seeing, ready to create in which there is no difference between *vācya* (object) and *vācaka* (word), *madhyamā* (*śabda*) in its subtle form as existing in the *antaḥkaraṇa* prior to its gross manifestation), *vaikharī* (as gross, physical speech). This is the process of *sṛṣṭi* or the outward movement or the descending arc. In ordinary *japa* (muttering of *mantra* or sacred formula), the process is just the reverse. In this the sound moves from *vaikharī* through *madhyamā* towards *paśyantī* and *parāvāṇī*.

Ordinarily, *japa* starts in *vaikharī* form (vocal muttering). It depends entirely on the will and activity of the person who does the *japa*. After constant practice of *japa* for some years, an extraordinary thing happens. A time comes when the *japa* does not depend on the will and activity of the reciter any longer. It now goes on automatically inwardly without any effort on the part of the reciter. It becomes an *ajapājapa*. When this proceeds for a long time, the *prāṇa* and *apāna* currents that normally move in a curvilinear way on the *iḍā* and *piṅgalā* channels become equilibrated; the *kuṇḍalinī* now awakens; the equilibrated current now flows upward in the *suṣumnā* i.e. in the interior of the spinal column. This upward movement is known as *uccaraṇa*. *Prāṇa* and *manas* are so closely associated that *manas* also acquires upward orientation along with it.

As the *kuṇḍalinī* rises, there is the experience of *anāhata nāda*-automatic, unstruck sound. The *kuṇḍalinī* passing through the various *cakras* finally joins the *Brahmarandhra*, and then *nāda* ceases; it is then converted into *jyoti* (light).

2. *Japa* :

This has already been described in connexion with the *sādhanā* or spiritual praxis of *prāṇa* above. The praxis of japa has been mentioned in verses 90, 145, 155, 156, etc. *Praṇava japa* leading to the development of the various *śaktis* or manifestation of spiritual stages is recommended in verse 42. This is explained under a separate head.

3. *Bhāvanā* :

In Tantrasāra, Abhinavagupta gives an excellent exposition of *bhāvanā*. Man's mind manifests itself in all kinds of *vikalpas* or thought — constructs. *Vikalpa* is the very nature of mind. If that is so, the aspirant should mentally seize one *Śuddha* or pure *vikalpa*, viz. of the highest I-consciousness, of the real Self as being *Śiva*. He has to practise the *bhāvanā* of this pure *vikalpa*. *Bhāvanā* is creative contemplation. Imagination plays a very large part in it. One has to imagine oneself with all the faith and fervour at his command that he is Śiva. This *śuddha vikalpa* eliminates all other *vikalpas*, or thoughts and a time comes when the *śuddha vikalpa* also ceases. Then the empirical, psychological self is dissolved, and one is landed in one's real, metempirical, metaphysical Self.

Abhinavagupta traces the following steps to Bhāvanā. A *sadguru* or Self-realized spiritual director initiates the aspirant into the mysteries of the *āgama*, into the irrefutable conviction of the essential Self being *Śiva*. The second step consists in *sat-tarka*. *Sat-tarka* in this context does not mean logic-chopping, but training the mind in harmonious consonance with the truth of the essential Self being Śiva. This culminates in *Bhāvanā*. *Bhāvanā* is the power of spiritual attention, a total dedication of the mind to one central thought, a nostalagia of the soul, a spiritual thrust towards the source of one's being.

Bhāvanā is finally metamorphosed into *śuddha vidyā* whereby the psychological I is swallowed up into the essential metaphysical I. Verse 49 lays down the *bhāvanā* of the essential Self. In a few other verses also, the verb form of *bhāvanā*, e.g. *bhāvayet*, *bhāvyaḥ*, etc. has been used. The *bhāvanā* of *laya* or dissolution of the various *tattvas* in a regressive order, of the gross into the subtle, of the subtle into the subtler, of the subtler into the subtlest, etc. is recommended in verse 54.

4. *Śūnya (void)* :

Contemplation of *śūnya* or void is another basis of *dhāraṇā* recommended. Verses 39, 40, 45, 58, 122, etc. refer to the contemplation of the void. Contemplation over *śūnya* or the void is explained in some detail under a separate heading.

5. *Experience of Vastness or Extensive Space* :

Experience of a vast, extensive space without any trees, etc. has no definite, concrete object as *ālambana* or support for the mind. In such a condition, the *vikalpas* or thought-constructs of the mind come to a dead stop, and supersensuous Reality makes its presence felt. Verse 60 of the text describes this state.

6. *Intensity of Experience*:

Even in the intensity of sensuous experience, one can have the experience of the Divine, provided one is careful to track the joy felt on such occasions to its source. The text gives several examples of the intensity of experience.

The first one is of the joy felt in sexual intercourse mentioned in the verses 69-70. It should be borne in mind that this example is given only to illustrate the intensity of experience in union. From physical union, one's attention has to be directed to spiritual union. This does not advocate sexual indulgence. The notes on these verses should be carefully read. The mystic experience of Tao in Chinese esotericism is described in a similar strain. The following lines will amply bear it out. "Thou knowest not what is love, nor what it is to love. I will tell thee; love is nothing other than the Rhythm of Tao.

I have said it to thee, it is from Tao that thou comest; it is to Tao that thou shalt return. Woman reveals herself to thy eyes and thou thinkest that she is the end towards which the Rhythm leads thee, but even when this woman is thine and thou hast thrilled with her touch, thou feelest still the Rhythm within thee unappeased and thou learnst that to appease it thou must go beyond. Call it love if thou wilt; what matters a name ? I call it Tao.

The beauty of woman is only a vague reflection of the formless beauty of Tao. The emotion she awakens in thee, the desire to blot thyself out in her beauty...believe me, it is nothing else than the rhythm of Tao, only thou knowest it not.....Seek not thy happiness in a woman. She is the revelation of Tao offering itself to thee, she is the purest form in Nature by which Tao manifests; she is the Force which awakens in thee the Rhythm of Tao – but by herself she is only a poor creature like thyself. And thou art for her the same revelation as she is for thee. It is the expression of Tao who has no limit nor form, and what thy soul desires in the rapture which the vision of it causes thee, this strange and ineffable sentiment, is nought else than union with that Beauty and with the source of that Beauty—with Tao.

Thy soul has lost its beloved Tao with whom it was formerly united and it desires reunion with the Beloved. An absolute reunion with Tao—is it not boundless Love ? To be so absolutely one with the Beloved that thou art entirely hers and she entirely thine—a union so complete and so eternal that neither life nor death can ever separate thee, so peaceful and pure that Desire can no longer awake in thee, because the supreme happiness is attained and there is only peace, peace sacred calm and luminous. For Tao is the Infinite of the soul, one, eternal and all-pure."

(Quoted in Mother India of January, 1979 from Arya, June, 1915).

Sex is an example of the joy of intensive experience derived from *sparśa* or contact.

Verse 71 which describes the intensive experience of joy at the sight of a friend or relative is an example of the pleasure of *rūpa* or visual perception. Verse 72 gives an example of the joy of *rasa* or taste and verse 73 gives an example of the joy of *śabda* or sound.

7. *Mudrās and Āsanas* :

Various *mudrās* are recommended as helpful in *dhāraṇās*. *Mudrā* is a technical term meaning a particular disposition and control of the organs of the body as a help in concentration. Various *mudrās* for this purpose are described in verse 77.

Āsana means posture. Several *āsanas* are helpful in *dhāraṇā*. Such examples are given in verses 78, 79 and 82.

The following concepts have to be clearly grasped in order to be able to understand the *dhāraṇās* recommended in Vijñānabhairava.

Kṣobha :

The word *Kṣobha* means mental agitation, disquiet, turmoil, Verse 74 says that wherever there is *tuṣṭi* or mental satisfaction or joy, there the mind should be fixed. In all such joys or intensive experience, it is implied that the fixation of the mind should be without *kṣobha* or mental agitation. When one is deeply moved by some beautiful object e.g. a beautiful woman, the attitude should be "This beautiful tabernacle houses Śiva who is my own essential Self." It is this attitude which leads to the right *dhāraṇā* based on aesthetic experience. If one's mind is agitated by such experience and he is carried away by sense-pleasure, he cannot have the proper *dhāraṇā*. He will be unable to utilize that experience for yogic purposes. As Spandakārikā puts it : "यदा क्षोभः प्रलीयेत तदा स्यात् परमं पदम्" (I, 9)

"When the mental turmoil disappears, it is only then that the highest state is attained."

This mental turmoil is caused because of our identification of our Self with the mind-body complex and its claimant and clamorous deṣires. When one is convinced that the mind-body complex is not the Self, but rather the Divine presence within the mind-body complex is the Self who is Śiva, then every attractive object is considered to be only the expression of Śiva Himself, then the mental turmoil ceases and the mind is fixed on Śiva whose expression that object happens to be.

Vikalpa :

A *vikalpa* is a thought-construct. *Vikalpas* are various mental counters through which man carries on the business of life. *Vikalpas* may refer to various things of the external world like tree, flower, river, etc. or various images, fancies, etc. of the mind. In *vikalpa* mind sets a limit to one particular thing or idea, and differentiates it from the rest; mind constructs a 'particular' by means of thought which it marks off from the rest of the world or from other ideas. Each *vikalpa* has two aspects; the positive aspect consists of the idea that is selected, and the negative consists of the rest that are set aside or rejected. *Vikalpas* are concerned with particulars. Secondly, *vikalpas* are relational i.e. there is always a subject-object relationship in *vikalpas*. Reality is non-relational, there is no object outside Reality. Therefore *vikalpas* are unable to grasp Reality.

There is, however, one *śuddha* or pure *vikalpa*, viz., the 'thought that I am Śiva'. By the *bhāvanā* or creative contemplation of this *vikalpa*, all other *vikalpas* are eliminated. Finally this *vikalpa* also disappears and one is landed in a *nirvikalpa* or thought free state which denotes the awareness of Reality.

MADHYAVIKĀSA (THE DEVELOPMENT OF THE MIDDLE STATE) :

When the *prāṇa* or exhalation arising from the centre of the body does not return from the *dvādaśānta*(a distance of 12 fingers in the outer space) for a split second and the *apāna* or inhalation arising from the *dvādaśānta* does not return from the centre for a split second, this is known as *madhyadaśā*. By intensive awareness of this *madhyadaśā*, there is *madhya vikāsa* or the development of the middle state.

The *madhya vikāsa* can occur through several means, either by one-pointed awareness of the pauses of *prāṇa* and *apāna* (vide verse 25) or by means of the dissolution of all *vikalpas* (vide verse 26) or by retention of *prāṇa* and *apāna* (vide verse 27) or by *vikalpa-kṣaya*, *Śakti-saṅkoca* and *śakti-vikāsa*, etc. as recommended in the 18th *Sūtra* of *Pratyabhijñāhṛdayam* or in the gap between two thoughts when one thought ceases and another is about to arise as recommended in *Spandakārikā*. (III, 9).

Sūtra 17 of *Pratyabhijñāhṛdayam* says: "मध्यविकासाच्चिदानन्दलाभः" which means "By the development of the *madhya* (middle or centre) is there acquisition of the bliss of *Cit* "

What is this *madhya* (middle or centre) ? *Kṣemarāja* explains it in the following way in his commentary on the above *sūtra*.

"*Saṁvit* or the Universal Consciousness is the centre of every thing, for everything depends on it for its existence. In the empirical order *saṁvit* is at first transformed into *prāṇa*. Assuming the role of *prāṇaśakti*, resting in the planes of *buddhi*, body etc. it abides principally in the *madhya nāḍī*, in the innermost central channel of *prāṇa* in the spinal column. When the *prāṇaśakti* in the central channel develops or when the central Universal consciousness develops in any other way, one acquires the bliss of universal consciousness and becomes liberated while living."

So *madhya-vikāsa* means the development of the metempirical or universal consciousness. In such a state *citta* or the individual empirical consciousness is transformed into *citi* or the the met-empirical consciousness.

ŚŪNYA :

The word *śūnya* means void, a state in which no object is experienced. It has, however, been used in various senses in this system.

Madhyadhāma or the central channel in the interior of the spinal column has generally been called *śūnya* or sometimes even *śūnyātiśūnya* (absolute void). The word *śūnya* occurring in the verse No. 42 of Vijñānabhairava has been interpreted as *unmanā* by Śivopādhyāya. In verse 61 *madhya* has been interpreted as *śūnya* by Śivopādhyāya. Kṣemarāja has interpreted *śūnya* as māyā and *śūnyātiśūnya* as *mahāmāyā* in his commentary on VII, 57 in Svacchanda Tantra. At some places, Śiva is said to be *śūnya* or *śūnyāti-śūnya*.

The main philosophical sense of *śūnya*, however, is given in the following verse quoted by Śivopādhyāya in his commentary on verse 127 of Vijñānabhairava :

"सर्वालम्बनधर्मैश्च सर्वतत्त्वैरशेषत: ।
सर्वक्लेशाशयै: शून्यं न शून्यं परमार्थत:" ॥

That which is free of all supports whether external existents like jar or flower or internal existents like pleasure, pain or thought, that which is free of all *tattvas* or constitutive principles, of the residual traces of all *kleśas*, that is *śūnya*. In the highest sense, it is not *śūnya* as such (i.e. as non-existence)". *Avidyā*, *asmitā*, *rāga*, *dveṣa*, and *abhiniveśa* i.e. primal ignorance, the feeling of I-ness, attraction, repulsion and fear of death are considered to be *kleśas*.

Sivopādhyāya has further given a long quotation from *Vimarśa-dīpikā* which means that Śiva is full and free and fundamental ground of all that is known as void, from whom all the *tattvas* arise and in whom they are all dissolved. Since *Śiva* or the foundational consciousness cannot be described in words or any determination of thought, therefore, is He called śūnya.

The most explicit explanation of *śūnya* is given in Svacchanda Tantra in the following verse :

"अशून्यं शून्यमित्युक्तं शून्यं चाभाव उच्यते ।
अभावः स समुद्दिष्टो यत्र भावाः क्षयं गताः ।
सत्तामात्रं परं शान्तं तत्पदं किमपि स्थितम्" ॥

(IV. 292–293)

"That which is said to be *śūnya* (void) in this system is not really *śūnya*, for *śūnya* only means absence of objects. That is said to be *abhāva* or absence of existents in which all objective existents have disappeared. It is the absolute Being, that state which abides as transcendent and absolute peace."

Kṣemarāja in his commentary on the above explains *aśūnya* or non-void as *cidānandaghana—parama—śivatattvam* i.e. *parama Śiva* (absolute Divine Reality) who is a mass of consciousness and bliss, *mahāsattā* as *prakāśātmaiva hi sarveṣām bhāvābhāvānāṃ sattā* i. e. the Light of Universal Consciousness, the Reality which is the source of both existents and non-existents and *abhāva* as *na vidyate bhāvaḥ sarvaḥ prameyādi prapañco yatra* i. e. that in which the manifestation of all objective phenomena ceases. The core of the meaning of the word *śūnya* is that in which there is no objective existent.

ŚŪNYA—ṢAṬKA (THE GROUP OF SIX ŚŪNYAS) :

Svacchanda Tantra recommends contemplation over six voids (IV 288—290). The first *śūnya* which is known as *ūrdhva śūnya* or higher *śūnya* is the stage of *śakti*; the second is the *adhaḥ* or the *śūnya* which is the region of the heart; the third is the *madhya* or the middle *śūnya* which is the region of throat, palate, middle of the eye-brows, forehead and *brahmarandhra*. The fourth *śūnya* is in *vyāpinī*, the fifth in *samanā* and the sixth in *unmanā*. These have to be contemplated as void and rejected. Finally the aspirant has to pass over to *Parama Śiva* who is the subtlest and the highest void, free of all conditions (*sarvāvasthā-vivarjitam*), who is *śūnya* only in the sense that he is transcendent to all manifestation and defies all characterization by the mind. The other voids are *sāmaya* i.e. meant to be abandoned. It is only in the highest *śūnya* i.e. *parama śiva* that the mind should finally rest. The other *śūnyas* are means for the attainment of the highest *śūnya* (*paraśūnya-pada-prāpti-upāyabhūtāḥ*).

Vyāpinī, samanā, etc. are explained under *praṇava* and its *śaktis*.

PRAṆAVA AND ITS ŚAKTIS :

The word *praṇava* is interpreted in various ways—(1) *praṇūyate* —the Supreme Self that is lauded by all, (2) *prāṇān avati*—that which protects the vital forces, (3) *prakarṣeṇa navīkaroti*—that which renovates every thing, renews the soul as it were. There are various kinds of *praṇava*—*śākta praṇava, śaiva praṇava* and Vedic *praṇava*. It is used as *mantra* which means a sacred formula which protects one by reflection (*mananāt trāyate iti mantraḥ*).

The Vedic *praṇava* is *auṁ* which is repeated as a powerful *mantra*. Svacchanda Tantra describes in detail the various *śaktis* or energies of *auṁ*. It tells us how by the recitation of *auṁ*, there is the upward functioning of *prāṇa* (the life force) and ascension of *Kuṇḍalinī*.

In *Sāivāgama*, it is maintained that universal consciousness (*saṁvid*), in the process of manifestation, is at first transformed into *prāṇa* or life force and that is how life starts. On the arc of ascent, by the proper recitation of *auṁ, prāṇa* again becomes pure consciousness (*saṁvid*) while the empirical consciousness (*citta*) returns to its essence, the absolute consciousness (*citi*).

Dhāraṇā No. 19 described succinctly in verse 42 and touched upon briefly in verses 154-156 of Vijñānabhairava tells us how the *uccāra* or upward movement of *praṇava*, from gross utterance, to subtle vibration (*spandana*) and finally to mental reflection, leads us on to Śiva-consciousness. A detailed description of this *dhāraṇā* is given below :

By a long practice of true and concentrated *uccāra* of *auṁ* the energy of breath is introverted in the form of *madhya śakti* or middle energy known as *haṁsa* or *kuṇḍalinī* which rises in eleven successive movements without the least effort of the will. These movements are given below :

1 to 3 : The first three movements consist in the recitation of

a, u, m—'A' is to be contemplated in the navel, 'u' in the heart, 'm' in the mouth.

A, u, and m are recited in the gross form. The time taken in the recitation of each of these is one *mātrā* or mora.

4. After this appears *bindu* which is nasal resonance indicated by a point in ॐ and which symbolises concentrated energy of the word. The phonemes rest in it in an undivided form. It is a point of intense light. Since there cannot be any gross utterance of the *mantra* after *auṁ*, the *bindu* becomes from this stage an activity which operates by itself. Henceforward, there is no utterance but only the rise of the *prāṇic* energy in a subtle form of vibration (*spandana*) which becomes subtler and subtler as it proceeds onwards. The energy of the *bindu* appears as a point of light in the middle of the eye-brows. The subtlety of the *prāṇic* energy in *bindu* measured in terms of time would be $\frac{1}{2}$ of a *mātrā* or mora. The time occupied in uttering a short vowel is called a *mātrā*. Kṣemarāja in his commentary on the fifth verse of Vijñānabhairava says that *bindu* is a point of light which is identified in an undivided form with all objective phenomena.

5. Now *bindu* is transformed into *nāda* (subtle, inarticulate sound), and the predominance of objectivity inherent in it gradually disappears. It then assumes the form of *ardhacandra* (half-moon) and appears in *lalāṭa* or the forehead. The subtlety of its vibration consists in $\frac{1}{4}$ of a *mātrā* or mora.

6. After this, when objectivity inherent in *bindu* completely disappears, the energy assumes the form of a straight line and appears in the upper part of the forehead. The subtlety of its vibration consists in 1/8 of a *mātrā*. It is known as *nirodhikā* or *nirodhinī* (lit., that which obstructs). It is so-called, because it prevents the undeserving aspirants from entering the next stage of *nāda* and the deserving ones from slipping into dualism.

7. *Nāda*. It is a mystical resonance and extends from the summit of the head and expands through the *suṣumnā* i.e. the central channel. It is *anāhata* i.e. spontaneous sound, not produced by percussion and is inarticulate. It never sets i.e. it always goes on sounding in all living creatures.

The subtlety of its vibration consists in 1/16 of a *mātrā*.

8. *Nādānta*—This is an aspect of energy beyond *nāda*. It is extremely subtle and resides in *brahmarandhra* which is a little above the top of the head. The subtlety of its vibration consists in 1/32 of a *mātrā*.

After the experience of this station, the sense of identification of the Self with the body disappears.

9. Śakti or Energy in itself. There is a feeling of *ānanda* or bliss in this stage. Its *mātrā* is 1/64. Śakti is said to reside in the skin.

10. The next stage is that of *vyāpinī* or *vyāpikā*. It is all-penetrating energy and fills the cosmos. Kṣemarāja says that in this the limits of the body are dropped and the *yogi* enjoys the experience of all pervasiveness like the sky. It is said it is experienced at the root of the *śikhā* or tuft of hair on the head. Its *mātrā* is 1/128.

11. *Samanā*—When the *vyāpinī* stage is reached, all spatial and temporal limitations have been overcome, and all objectivity has disappeared. Then the stage of *samanā* is reached which is only *bodha* or the energy of illumination which is, as Kṣemarāja puts it, only an activity of thinking without any object of thought. (*mananamātrātmaka—karaṇarūpa-bodhamātrāvaśeṣe samanā* com. on V. 5 of V.B.) *Samanā* resides in the *śikhā* or tuft of hair on the head. Its *mātrā* is 1/256. It is through this *śakti* that *Śiva* carries on the five acts of manifestation, maintenance and withdrawal of the universe and veiling of Self and revealing of Self through grace.

If the *yogī* who has reached the stage of *samanā* directs his attention towards the universe, he acquires the supernormal powers of omnipresence, omniscience, etc., but if he is indifferent towards these powers, and directs his attention to still higher realm of existence, he reaches *unmanā śakti* and is then united with *parama Śiva*—Absolute Reality.

The *yogī* who rests contented in *samanā śakti* has only *ātma-vyāpti* which is explained by Kṣemarāja as *śuddhavijñānakevalatā* i.e. the isolation of pure consciousness. (Svacchanda Tantra p. 246). He cannot attain *Śivavyāpti* which is the state of identification with *parama-Śiva*.

13. *Unmanā*. The stage above *samanā* is *unmanā*. It is the ultimate energy beyond all mental process. Kṣemarāja explains

it thus—*unmanam-utkrāntam-utkarṣam ca manaḥ prāptaṁ yatra tadunmanam* i.e. '*unmanā* is that state in which *manas* or mental process is transcended and it reaches its highest excellence. *Unmanā* is the highest *śūnya* (void), not *śūnya* in the popular sense, but in the sense of the disappearance of all objectivity. It is *Sattāmātram* which, as Kṣemarāja explains, is the Light of Universal Consciousness which is the fount and source of every thing.

According to some it is to be contemplated in the last part of the tuft of hair on the head, and its *mātrā* is 1/512. According to Svacchanda Tantra, however, it is *amātra*, without any measure, for being outside the province of *manas* (mentation), it is beyond time.

As has been said above, the *yogī* whose consciousness rises only upto *samanā* has *ātmavyāpti* only i.e. he has an experience of the pure Self completely freed of limitations of *māyā* and *prakṛti*. But this is not the highest goal of man according to Śaivāgama. According to it, the highest goal is *Śiva-vyāpti* or *Śivatva-yojanā*—identification with *Śiva* who is all-inclusive. It is only by rising to the stage of *unmanā* that one can be identified with the *svātantrya-śakti* (absolute freedom) of *parama Śiva*.

Manas (mental process) is characterized by *saṁkalpa*—determinate thought and purpose, and the knowledge obtained by *saṁkalpa* is in a successive order being in time whereas *unmanā* which is above thought-process and is identified with *svātantrya-śakti* knows all things simultaneously (*manaḥ kramato jnāñam, unmanaṁ yugapat sthitam, vindate hyatra yugapat sarvajnādi-guṇān parān*. Svacc. Tantra V. 394-395).

CONCLUSION :

Vijñānabhairava gives the quintessence of all the *dhāraṇās* in the following verse :

"मानसं चेतना शक्तिरात्मा चेति चतुष्टयम् ।
यदा प्रिये परिक्षीणं तदा तद् भैरवं वपुः ।।" (838)

Citi, the dynamic universal consciousness in its descent towards manifestation assumes four forms for appearing as a limited individual viz; (1) *Cetanā* which, as Sivopādhyāya explains in his commentary, means *buddhi* in this context (2) mānasa—*manas* with its characteristic activity of *saṃkalpa* or thought-constructs (3) *śakti* which, in this context, means *prāṇaśakti* which constitutes the support of the body and empirical life, and (4) *ātmā* which, in this context, means *jīvātmā*, the ego or the empirical self conditioned by the above three.

This is the arc of *nimeṣa* or *avaroha*-descent of the dynamic universal consciousness (*citi*) into individual human life. It is only at the human stage that *unmeṣa* or *adhyāroha*—ascent towards the higher life is possible. When the above four are dissolved (*parikṣīṇam*) into *cit* (the Higher Universal Divine Consciousness), it is only then that one attains to *bhairava*—consciousness.

Kṣemarāja in his commentary on 21st *śūtra* of section III of the *Śiva-śūtras* quoting this verse says, *Avikalpakarūpeṇa . . . saṃvedanena. . . samāviśet. Kīdṛk ? magnaḥ śārīraprāṇādipramātṛtāṃ tatraiva citcamatkārarase majjanena praśāmayan.*

"One has to enter the divine consciousness by thought-free, non-relational awareness. How? By dissolving the personal self consisting of the body, prāṇa, etc. in the savoury sap of the Universal Divine Consciousness."

The chrysalis of the ego has to split before one can enter the *sanctum sanctorum* of the Divine Presence. In the words of Kaṭhopaniṣad *Yogaḥ prabhavāpyayau* Yoga is both dissolution and emergence—both death and rebirth. One has to die to live. It is a divine filiation and cannot be described in any human language, for it is reality of a different dimension. In the beautiful words of Dr. Anand K. Coomaraswamy, "The condition of deification is an eradication of all otherness." It is for this consummation that 112 *dhāraṇās* have been described in *Vijñānabhairava*.

VERSE 1

श्रीदेव्युवाच

श्रुतं देव मया सर्वं रुद्रयामलसम्भवम् ।
त्रिकभेदमशेषेण सारात्सारविभागशः ॥१॥
अद्यापि न निवृत्तो मे संशयः परमेश्वर ।

Śrī devy uvāca:
Śrutaṃ deva mayā sarvaṃ rudrayāmalasambhavam /
Trikabhedam aśeṣeṇa sārāt sāravibhāgaśaḥ // 1
Adyāpi na nivṛtto me saṃśayaḥ parameśvara /

TRANSLATION

Bhairavī,[1] the *śakti* of Bhairava[2] says (uvāca) O *deva*[3] (divine one) who in manifesting the universe and treating it as your play are my very self, I have heard in toto all the scriptures which have come forth from the union of Rudra[4] and his pair śakti[5] or which are the outcome of Rudrayāmala Tantra, including the Trika together with its divisions.[6] I have heard the Trika which is the quintessence of all the scriptures and also all its further essential ramifications.[7]

But O supreme Lord, even now my doubt has not been removed.

NOTES

1. Bhairava is the word used for Supreme Reality. Its synonym is Parama Śiva. Bhairava means the terrible one who destroys the ego. The word Bhairava consists of three letters *bha*, *ra* and *va*. The hermeneutic etymology of Bhairava gives the following interpretation:

'Bha' indicates *bharaṇa*—maintenance of the universe; 'ra' indicates 'ravaṇa'—withdrawal of the universe; 'va' indicates 'vamana—projecting or letting go of the universe i.e. manifestation. Thus, Bhairava indicates all the three aspects of the

Divine, viz., sṛṣṭi (manifestation), sthiti (maintenance) and saṃhāra (withdrawal).

Bhairavī is the śakti of Bhairava. The works of Āgama or Tantra are generally written in the form of a dialogue between Bhairava and His śakti Bhairavī or between Śiva and His consort Pārvatī or Śivā. In all these works, Bhairavī or Śakti puts a question in the form of inquiry and Bhairava or Śiva answers the question raised.

This is the Indian way of saying that these scripture, are a revelation. A relevant question arises in this connexion, "Bhairavī or Śakti of Bhairava is non-different from Bhairava; then what is the sense in a dialogue between the two ? It requires two to enter into a dialogue, but when Bhairava and Bhairavī are non-different, (i.e. are not two), how can there be a dialogue between them ?" The answer is that *anugraha* or grace is one of the five aspects of Bhairava (sṛṣṭi, sthiti, saṃhāra, tirodhāna, anugraha). His *anugraha* is represented by His śakti. In order to extend His grace to humanity, He reveals certain fundamental spiritual truths which may be inapprehensible to man in his present stage of evolution. All these truths lie in a latent form at the *parāvāk* level where object and word, truth and its manifestation, idea and its expression are in an indistinguishable unity. In order that these truths may be available to man, the *anugraha* (grace) aspect of the Supreme Divine assumes the role of Devī or Bhairavī who puts questions from the *paśyantī* level and receives answers at that level. Both the questions and the answers are transmitted in *vaikharī* form (human language) in order that man may be able to comprehend them. The dialogue between Bhairava and Bhairavī is a methodological device for revealing truths existing at the parāvāk level in *vaikharī* or human language. A dialogue containing questions and answers is the most realistic and lively form of bringing home to the listener or reader subtle truths which are not easy of comprehension.

2. The word in Sanskrit is *uvāca* which is past tense and means 'said', but as the question is perennial and the answer contains eternal truth, it is taken in the sense of present tense. The *parāvāk* level is beyond the category of time. So the division of past, present, future, month, year, etc. cannot be applied to it.

At the *paśyantī* level, the *parā* level appears anterior. Therefore the truth of *parā* level is expressed at the *paśyantī* level in past tense. Time is relative only to limited beings. To the Divine, there is no division of time. In his case, it is eternal now.

3. The word *deva* is derived from the root *div* which has many meanings, to manifest, to play, etc. Kṣemarāja in his commentary on this word says, "विश्वावद्योतनक्रीडनादिसतत्त्व स्वात्मन्" "O my very Self whose nature it is to display His sport in the form of the manifestation of the universe. The *devī* calls *deva* as 'my very Self', because the *devī* is not different from the *deva.*

4. Rudra: Bhairava or Śiva is called Rudra, because *ru* stands for *ruk* (disease), and *dra* stands for *drāvi* (melter, dissolver). As Kṣemarāja puts it *Rudra* is *samastarugdrāvi.* Rudra is one who dissolves all the ills (of life).

5. Yāmala means 'pair.' Kṣemarāja says "Rudratacchakti-sāmarasyātmano yāmalāt" i.e. Yāmala connotes the union of Rudra and His Śakti i. e. *prakāśa* and *vimarśa.* It is in this aspect that the highest scripture is revealed. He quotes the following verse in support of his statement:

अदृष्टविग्रहाच्छान्ताच्छिवात्परमकारणात् ।
ध्वनिरूपं विनिष्क्रान्तं शास्त्रं परमदुर्लभम् ॥

"The most inaccessible scripture has come out in the form of word from Śiva who is the supreme source, who is free of all division and agitation and whose form is invisible.

Rudrayāmala is also the name of an ancient Tāntrika work which has not yet been properly edited.

6. *Trikabhedam*: Kṣemarāja explains this in the following words: "त्रिकस्य परादिशक्तित्रयसारनरशक्ति-शिवात्मनस्तत्त्वत्रयस्य भेदो ज्ञान-क्रियाप्राधान्येतरादिप्रतिपादनेन भिद्यमानता यत्र ।"
Trika denotes the triple divisions of *Śakti*, viz; parā (phase of highest identity, transcendent), *parāpara* (identity in difference; intermediate), and *apara* (immanent). This expresses itself in the triple division of *Śiva*, *Śakti* and *nara* (*jīva*--living creatures). This division is further complicated by the fact that in *apara* or *nara* level, only *kriyā* (activity) is predominant, in *parāpara* or

Śakti level and in *para* or Śiva level both jñāna and kriyā (knowledge and activity) are predominant.

It should be borne in mind that the sphere of *nara* extends from *prithivī tattva* to *māyā tattva*; the sphere of *śakti* extends from śuddha *vidyā* upto *Sadāśiva* and the sphere of *Śiva* includes only *Śiva* and *Śakti*.

7. *Sārāt-sāravibhāgaśaḥ*: Trika is the *sāra* or quintessence of all the scriptures. In support of this Kṣemarāja quotes the following verse:

> वेदादिभ्यः परं शैवं शैवाद्वामं तु दक्षिणम् ।
> दक्षिणात्परतः कौलं कौलात्परतरं त्रिकम् ॥

"The (dualistic) Śaiva system is superior to the *vedas* and other scriptures, the system pertaining to the left-handed path is superior to the (dualistic) Śaiva one: the system pertaining to the right-handed path is superior to the left-handed one; the *Kaula* system is superior to the right-handed one and Trika is superior to the *Kaula* system. "Since *Trika* is superior to every other system or scripture, it has been designated as *sāra*, the quintessence of all philosophical systems and spiritual praxis.

The (dualistic) *Śaiva* system is characterized by external rituals. In *vāma* or left-handed path, the emphasis is laid on Self-consciousness in the midst of sensuous experience of form, sound, touch, taste and smell. In *dakṣiṇa* or right-handed path, emphasis is laid on meditation. In *Kaula* system, the emphasis is laid on the realization of universal consciousness. In *Trika*, the ideal is not only the realization of the essential or divine Self but also *jagadānanda* in which the world is realized as the bliss of the Divine made visible.

What is *sārāt-sāravibhāga* i. e. further essential ramification of the above quintessence ? This is what Kṣemarāja has to say on his point.

तत्रापि सिद्धामालिन्युत्तरादिक्रमात् ज्ञानप्रकर्षोपदेशोत्कर्षात् उत्कृष्टम् The correct reading is तत्रापि सिद्धानामकमालिन्युत्तरादिक्रमात् ज्ञानप्रकर्षोपदेशक्रमात् उत्कृष्टम्। Even here (i. e. even in Trika) there is the successive gradation of high, higher and highest on the basis of the teaching of successive preeminence of *jñāna* (gnosis). *Siddhā* emphasizes *Kriyā* (rituals and active meditation); *Nāmaka* emphasizes *jñāna* (knowledge); Mālinī emphasizes both *jñāna* and *Kriyā.* These constitute further division in *Trika.*

THE ORDER OF PRESENTATION OF THE SUBJECT MATTER

From the first verse beginning with 'Śrutaṃ deva' upto the seventh verse, ending with 'chindhi saṃśayam', the *devī* enumerates her doubts. From 'sādhu, sādhu,' a part of the seventh verse upto the 21st verses ending with *Śivaḥ priyo*, Bhairava briefly answers her questions. Then from the 22nd verse, beginning with *Deva, deva* upto the 23rd verse, ending with *brūhi bhairava,* the *Devī* requests Bhairava to expound to her the means by which one can realize the Highest Reality.

In answer to the above inquiry from 24th upto 138th verse, Bhairava expounds to her 112 *dhāraṇas* or types of yoga by which one can realize the Highest Reality. After this, the *Devī* raises a few more questions, and *Bhairava* answers them. Finally, the *Devī* expresses her satisfaction over the answers and becomes united with *Bhairava.*

VERSES 2-4.

किं रूपं तत्त्वतो देव शब्दराशिकलामयम् ॥ २ ॥
किं वा नवात्मभेदेन भैरवे भैरवाकृतौ ।
त्रिशिरोभेदभिन्नं वा किं वा शक्तित्रयात्मकम् ॥ ३ ॥
नादबिन्दुमयं वापि किं चन्द्रार्धनिरोधिकाः ।
चक्रारूढमनच्कं वा किं वा शक्तिस्वरूपकम् ॥ ४ ॥

Kiṃ rūpaṃ tattvato deva śabdarāśikalāmayaṃ // 2
Kiṃ vā navātmabhedena bhairave bhairavākṛtau /
Triśirobhedabhinnaṃ vā kiṃ vā śaktitrayātmakam // 3
Nādabindumayaṃ vāpi kiṃ candrārdhanirodhikāḥ /
Cakrārūḍham anackaṃ vā kiṃ vā śaktisvarūpakam // 4

TRANSLATION

Oh God, from the point of view of absolute reality, what exactly is the essential nature of Bhairava ? According to

Bhairava Āgama (Bhairave[2]), (1) does it consist of the energies of the multitude of letters (*śabdarāśikalāmayam*[3]) ? or (2) does it consist of nine different forms(*navātmabhedena*)[4] for the realization of the essential nature of Bhairava (*Bhairavākṛtau*) ? (3) or does it consist of the specific *mantra* that unites in an integral form the three divisions as delineated in Triśirobhairava[5] (*triśirobhedabhinnam*) (4) or does it consist of three *Śaktis*[6] (presiding over the previously mentioned three *tattavas*) ? (5) or does it consist of *nāda* (power of *mantra* inseparably present as *vimarśa* in all the words) ? or of *vindu* (power of *mantra* inseparably present in all the objects of the universe as *Prakāśa*[7] (6) or does it consist of *ardhacandra*, *nirodhikā*[8] etc ? (7) or does it consist of some mysterious power residing in the *Cakras* (energy centres in the body) ? or the vowel-less sound of *ha*?[9] (8) or does it consist of purely *Śakti* ?[10]

NOTES

1. 'Bhairavākṛtau' does not mean 'Śiva of terrible form.' 'Bhairavākṛtau' means *Bhairavasvarūpāya*. It is a locative case in the sense of *nimitta* (purpose). So 'Bhairavākṛtau' means for the realization of the *svarūpa* or essential nature of *Bhairava*.

2. 'Bhairave' here means in Bhairava Āgama, according to Bhairava Āgama.

3. The first question of the *Devī* is: The world consists of objects. Each object is denoted by a word (*Śabda*). *Śabda-rāśi* is the multitude of words which is according to the Sanskrit language, from 'a' (अ) to 'kṣa' (क्ष). *Kalā* means the *vimarśa* or creative energy of the Divine. These energies are *anuttara*, *ānanda*, *icchā*, *jñāna* and *kriyā*. By these are created the various letters from 'a' to '*kṣa*'. These letters give rise to the various *tattvas* (constitutive principles) of which the universe is constituted. For detail, see the author's translation of Śiva Sūtras. Note No. 10 under *Sūtra* 7 of the II section.

The letter '*A*' indicates *Prakāśa* or *Śiva*, the letter '*Ha*' indicates *vimarśa* or *Śakti*. Thus *Aham* includes all the letters of the Sanskrit alphabet. This *Aham* or 'I' denotes the Highest

Reality in which there is complete union of *Śiva* and *Śakti*, and which includes the entire subjective and the objective world.

The Divine in His aspect of non-manifestation is known as *Parama Śiva* or Bhairava or Parama Brahma, in His aspect of manifestation, the Divine is known as *Śabda Brahma*. In this first question, the Devī wants to know whether *Vijñāna* or *Bodha Bhairava* is *Śabda Brahma*.

4. The second question of the Devī is whether the essential nature of the Supreme is of nine forms (navātma) of *mantras*. These as described in Netra Tantra are the following:

(1) Śiva, (2) Sadāśiva, (3) Īśvara, (4) Vidyā, (5) Māyā, (6) Kalā, (7) Niyati, (8) Puruṣa, (9) Prakṛti. According to others, these are (1) Śiva, (2) Śakti (3) Sadāśiva, (4) Īśvara (5) Śuddha Vidyā, (6) Mahāmāyā (7) Māyā, (8) Puruṣa (9) Prakṛti. These are nine forms from the point of view of *tattvas* (constitutive principles). From the point of view of mantra, the nine forms are 1. ह् 2. र् 3. क्ष् 4. म् 5. ल् 6. व् 7. य् 8. ण् 9. ऊँ (णूँ)

5. Triśirobhairava is the name of a *Tantra* work which is now lost. It summarizes the entire manifestation under three broad categories viz., *Śiva*, *Śakti* and *Nara* (*jīva* or living being). In the third question, the Devī wants to know whether the nature of the Supreme consists of the integral combination of these three categories as symbolized by the *mantra sauḥ* (सौः). This specific *mantra* is known as *Parabīja*, *Hṛdaya bīja* or *Prāsāda*. *Sa* (स) of this *mantra* symbolizes the *tattvas* from earth to māyā (31 tattvas of Śaiva philosophy); *au* (औ) symbolizes *Śuddha vidyā*, *Īśvara* and *Sadāśiva* and the two dots of the *visarga* (:) symbolize Śiva and Śakti. For details, see the author's Note No. 2 under the first Sūtra of the Second section of the Śiva-sūtras. Now of the three categories of Nara, Śakti and Śiva the '*S*' (स्) of the mantra Sauḥ (सौः) covers Nara, *au* (औ) covers *Śakti*, and the *visarga* (ḥ) covers Śiva. So the 31 *tattvas* of Śaiva Āgama are covered by *Nara;* the three *tattvas* viz., *Śuddha vidyā*, *Īśvara* and *Sadāśiva* are covered by *Śakti*, and the other two *tattvas* are covered by *Śiva*.

6. In the fourth question, the Devī wants to know whether the nature of the Supreme consists of the three *Śaktis-Parā* (transcendent in which there is no distinction of *Śiva* and *Śakti*), *Aparā*

(immanent) and *Parāparā* (Intermediate between the two) presiding over the categories or principles mentioned above (in Note 5). The *svātantrya śakti* (severeign power) of the Divine is known as *parā* (transcendent), that very *Śakti* wishing to create a universe of successive order is known as *parāparā* (both *para* and *apara*) and appearing as a universe of successive order is known as *aparā* (immanent).

7. Nāda in this context means the *vimarśa* present in all the words (*vācaka*) and *vindu* means the *prakāśa* present in all the objects (*vācya*).

As Kṣemarāja puts it in his commentary, *Yadi vā sarvamantra-cakra-sāmānyavīryātmaka-viśvavācyāvibhāga — prakāśarūpavindu aśeṣavācakāvibhāga-vimarśa-parāmarśamayanādātmakam.*

In the fifth question, the Devī wants to know whether the essential nature of Bhairava is *nāda-vindu—vindu* which symbolizes light or *prakāśa* (Śiva) and which is present in an undivided form in all objective phenomena and *nāda* which symbolizes *vimarśa śakti* that is present in an undivided form in all the words (which signify objective phenomena).

8. In the sixth question, the *Devī* wants to know whether the essential nature of *Bhairava* consists of *ardhacandra nirodhikā* etc. which are a further proliferation of *nāda-vindu.* Nirodhikā in the plural (*nirodhikāḥ*) is meant to express 'et cetera'. The 'et cetera' refers to *nādānta*, *śakti*, *vyāpinī*, *samanā*, and finally *unmanā*.

Vindu (a point) which is present as undivided light in all objective phenomena (*vācya*) is transformed into *nāda* (interior sound). As has been said above, *Vindu* is concerned with objective phenomena (*vācya*). When it is transformed into *nāda*, the predominance of objectivity is slightly diminished, then arises the stage of *ardhacandra* where śakti appears in a curved form like demimoon. After that when the curved nature of all objectivity ceases completely, then arises *nirodhikā*, of the form of a straight line. *Nirodhikā* means obstructer. This energy is so called because she obstructs undeserving aspirants from entering into *nāda*, and prevents the deserving ones from straying away into the state of difference. When the pervasion of *nāda* by letter begins to abate, then the next stage of energy is known as *nādānta* which is characterized by extremely subtle sound and which means the termination of the stage of *nāda*. When the stage of *nāda* ceases completely, then the next stage is that of *Śakti* which is characterized by a sensation of spiritual delight. When that sensation of delight is not confined within the limit of the body, but expands all round like the sky, then that stage is known as *Vyāpinī* (i. e. all-pervasive).

When the idea of all positive and negative existents ceases completely and only *manana* or the faculty of mentation remains, then the stage of *samanā* is achieved.

Finally appears the *unmanā* stage which transcends all mentation, which achieves Śiva-consciousness and is characterized by the consciousness of unity of the entire cosmos. Here there is the unison of *Śiva* and *Śakti*. This is the stage of *Parama Śiva* who is *niṣkala* or transcendent.

The first question is concerned with *mātṛkā*, the second and third are concerned with *mantra*, the fifth and sixth are concerned with *mantra-vīrya* or power of *mantra*. The fourth is concerned with the three *Śaktis* of the Divine.

9. In the seventh question, the Devī wants to know whether the essential nature of Bhairava is some mysterious power present in the *cakras* (energy-centres)in the form of letters or is it *anacka* i. e. vibrating as vowel-less *ha* in the form of *prāṇakuṇḍalinī*. *Prāṇāśakti* present in *Suṣumnā* ceaselessly and spontaneously goes on vibrating as *ha* in a vowel-less form. This is known as *anacka kalā* of *prāṇāśakti*. It is known as *anāhata nāda* i. e. a vibration without any stroke or blow. It goes on vibrating spontaneously. No body produces it and nobody can prevent it from vibrating. It is known as *haṃsa* or *prāṇakuṇḍalinī*.

10. In the eighth question, the *Devī* wants to know whether the essential nature of the Supreme is pure changeless Energy (*Śakti*).

Cakrārūḍha may also mean "Is it Kuṇḍalinī situated in the *mūlādhāra cakra*" or "Is it the *Aham* or the divine I-consciousness resting on the collective whole (*cakra*) of letters beginning with 'a' and ending with 'ha'' '?

VERSES 5-6

परापरायाः सकलम् अपरायाश्च वा पुनः ।
पराया यदि तद्वत्स्यात् परत्वं तद्विरुध्यते ॥ ५ ॥
नहि वर्ण-विभेदेन देहभेदेन वा भवेत् ।
परत्वं, निष्कलत्वेन, सकलत्वे न तद्भवेत् ॥ ६ ॥
प्रसादं कुरु मे नाथ निःशेषं छिन्धि संशयम् ।

Parāparāyāḥ sakalam aparāyāśca vā punaḥ/
Parāyā yadi tadvat syāt paratvaṃ tad virudhyate// 5
Nahi varṇavibhedena dehabhedena vā bhavet/
Paratvaṃ, niṣkalatvena, sakalatve na tad bhavet// 6
Prasādaṃ kuru me nātha niḥśeṣaṃ chindhi saṃśayam//

TRANSLATION

(The Devī puts a further question)

Is the nature of *parāparā śakti* (transcendent-cum-immanent Energy) and *aparā śakti* (immanent Energy) *sakala* i.e. consisting of parts or is the nature of *parā śakti* (transcendent Energy) also *sakala* ? If the nature of *parā śakti* (transcendent Energy) is also sakala, then it would be incompatible with transcendence.[1]

Paratva or transcendence cannot be consistent with the division of letters and colour or of bodies (*na hi varṇavibhedena, dehabhedena vā bhavet paratvam*) ; paratva or transcendence consists only in indivisibility (*niṣkalatvena*); it (transcendence) cannot co-exist with *sakala* (a composite of parts) (*sakalatve na tad-bhavet*).[2] Oh Lord bestow your favour on me, and remove my doubt completely.

NOTES

1. *Parā, parāparā, aparā.*

Svātantrya śakti, the Absolute Sovereign power of Parama Śiva is *parā* i. e. transcendent. Every thing at that level is in the form of *saṃvit* or consciousness. This is the level of absolute non-dualism (*abheda*). This is *parama Śiva's parā śakti*.

Where there is *bhedābheda* i. e. both identity and difference or identity in difference that is known as *parāparā śakti*. Just as an elephant or a city seen in a mirror is both identical and different from the mirror, even so is the position of *parāparā śakti*, Where everything appears as different from each other, that is the level of *aparā śakti*.

2. There can be *Sakalatva* or aspect of division in *parāparā* and *aparā*. If *sakalatva* or divisibility is assumed to be an aspect of *parā* also, then that would be incompatible with the very nature of *parā* which is completely transcendent to division. In Parātriṃśikā, etc (p. 124) does the *sakala* aspect which has been described for the meditation of certain *mantras* concern only *aparā devī* and *parāparā devī* or also *parā devi* ? If it concerns *parā devī* also, then it would be flagrant contradiction in terms, for by its very definition *parā* is *niṣkala* or transcendent to division or parts. How can *sakala* go with *niṣkala* ? This is what the *Devī* wants to know.

VERSES—7-10

भैरव उवाच

साधु साधु त्वया पृष्टं तन्त्रसारमिदं प्रिये ॥ ७ ॥
गूह्नीयतमं भद्रे तथापि कथयामि ते ।
यत्किञ्चित्सकलं रूपं भैरवस्य प्रकीर्तितम् ॥ ८ ॥
तदसारतया देवि विज्ञेयं शक्रजालवत् ।
मायास्वप्नोपमं चैव गन्धर्वनगरभ्रमम् ॥ ९ ॥
ध्यानार्थं भ्रान्तबुद्धीनां क्रियाडम्बरवर्तिनाम् ।
केवलं वर्णितं पुंसां विकल्पनिहतात्मनाम् ॥ १० ॥

Bhairava uvāca
Sādhu sādhu tvayā pṛṣṭaṃ tantrasāram idam priye// 7
Gūhanīyatamam bhadre tathāpi kathayāmi te/
Yatkiñcit saklaṃ rūpam bhairavasya prakīrtitam// 8
Tad asāratayā devi vijñeyaṃ śakrajālavat/
Māyāsvapnopamaṃ caiva gandharvanagarabhramam// 9
Dhyānārtham bhrāntabuddhīnāṃ kriyāḍambaravartinām/
Kevalaṃ varṇitam puṃsāṃ vikalpanihatātmanām// 10

TRANSLATION

Bhairava said

Good! Good! Dear one, you have put questions which pertain to the very quintessence of Tantra. Though, the matter is most esoteric, oh auspicious one, yet shall I explain it to you. Whatever has been declared to be the composite form (*Sakala*)[1] of Bhairava, that oh goddess should be considered as insubstantial (asāratayā), as phantasmagoria (lit. as the net of Indra), as magical illusion (māyā), as dream, as the mirage of a town of *Gandharvas*[2] in the sky. The *sakala* aspect of Bhairava is taught, as a prop for meditation, to those who are of deluded intellect, who are interested in ostentatious performance of rituals, it has been declared for those people who are a prey to dichotomising thought-constructs (*vikalpanihatātmanām*).[3]

NOTES

1. All manifestation from gods down to the mineral is known as *sakala. Sakala* is the sphere of *māyā tattva*. It consists of *bheda*—difference or division. The essential nature of Bhairava cannot be known by means of *sakala* which consists of difference and division.

2. *Gandharvas* are said to be celestial musicians who are believed to have their town in the sky which is entirely imaginary even so is the *sakala* form of *Bhairava*.

3. If the reading is taken as *vikalpanihitātmanām* it would mean 'who are established in dichotomising thought-constructs'.

VERSE 11-13

तत्त्वतो न नवात्मासौ शब्दराशिर्न भैरवः ।
न चासौ त्रिशिरा देवो न च शक्तित्रयात्मकः ॥ ११ ॥
नादबिन्दुमयो वापि न चन्द्रार्धनिरोधिकाः ।
न चक्रक्रमसंभिन्नो न च शक्तिस्वरूपकः ॥ १२ ॥
अप्रबुद्धमतीनां हि एता बालविभीषिकाः ।
मातृमोदकवत्सर्वं प्रवृत्त्यर्थमुदाहृतम् ॥ १३ ॥

Tattvato na navātmāsau śabdarāśir na bhairavaḥ/
Na cāsau triśirā devo na ca śaktitrayātmakaḥ// 11
Nādabindumayo vāpi na candrārdhnirodhikāḥ/
Na cakrakramasambhinno na ca śaktisvarūpakaḥ// 12
Aprabuddhamatīnāṃ hi etā bālavibhīṣikāḥ/
Mātṛmodakavatsarvaṃ pravṛttyarthaṃ udāhṛtam)// 13

TRANSLATION

In reality, Bhairava is neither of the form of nine (*navātma*), nor a multitude of letters (*śabdarāśi*) nor of the three heads (*triśirā*) nor of three *śaktis*, nor consisting of *nāda* and *bindu*, nor of *ardhacandra*, *nirodhikā*, etc., nor is His essence concerned with the piercing of the (six) *cakras*, nor does *śakti* or Energy constitute His essence.[1]

(Then why have these been described by the scriptures as Bhairava's essence at various places ?)

The above concepts are used for those whose intellect is not yet mature enough to grasp Reality (in its highest aspect), Just as a bogy is used to frighten away children from their obstinacy for getting some worthless or undesirable thing. These concepts play the same role as the bonbon of the mother. They are meant to induce the aspirants to tread the path of righteousness and spiritual practices in order that they may ultimately realize the nature of *Bhairava* which is non-different from their essential Self.[2]

NOTES

1. For the explanation of the various alternatives given above see the notes under the verses 2-4.

2. As a bogy is used to frighten away children from their obstinacy for getting a worthless and undesirable thing, even so these concepts are used for dissuading men from sense-pleasures. As mothers offer a bonbon to children to induce them to pursue a right course, even so these concepts are used to induce men, to tread the path of righteousness.

VERSES 14-17

दिक्कालकलनोन्मुक्ता देशोद्देशाविशेषिणी ।
व्यपदेष्टुमशक्यासावकथ्या परमार्थतः ॥ १४ ॥
अन्तः स्वानुभवानन्दा विकल्पोन्मुक्तगोचरा ।
यावस्था भरिताकारा भैरवी भैरवात्मनः ॥ १५ ॥

तद्वपुस्तत्त्वतो ज्ञेय विमलं विश्वपूरणम् ।
एवंविधे परे तत्त्वे कः पूज्यः कश्च तृप्यति ॥ १६ ॥
एवंविधा भैरवस्य यावस्था परिगीयते ।
सा परा, पररूपेण परादेवी प्रकीर्तिता ॥ १७ ॥

Dikkālakalanonmuktā deśoddeśāviśeṣiṇī/
Vyapadeṣṭum aśakyāsav akathyā paramārthataḥ// 14
Antaḥ svānubhavānandā vikalponmuktagocarā/
Yāvasthā bharitākārā bhairavī bhairavātmanaḥ// 15
Tad vapus tattvato jñeyaṃ vimalaṃ viśvapūraṇam/
Evaṃvidhe pare tattve kaḥ pūjyaḥ kaśca tṛpyati// 16
Evaṃvidhā bhairavasya yāvasthā parigīyate/
Sā parā, pararūpeṇa parā devī prakīrtitā// 17

TRANSLATION

[If the *sakala* aspect of Bhairava does not reveal His essential nature, then what is His *niṣkala* aspect by knowing which one may have an idea of His *parāvasthā* (the highest state).

Bhairava now describes the *niṣkala* (transcendent) aspect of the Supreme in the above four verses].

Parāvasthā (the highest state) of *Bhairava* is free (*unmukta*) of all notions pertaining to direction (*dik*), time (*kāla*), nor can that be particularized (*aviśeṣiṇi*) by some definite space (*deśa*) or designation (*uddeśa*). In verity (*paramārthataḥ*) that can neither be indicated (*vyapadeṣṭum aśakyā*) nor described in words (*akathyā*)[1].14

[Then is it impossible to have any experience of her? Bhairava anticipates this question and answers that in the following verse].

One can be aware of that only when one is completely free of all thought-constructs (*vikalponmukta-gocarā*). One can have an experiencc of that bliss in his own inmost self (when one is completely rid of the ego, and is established in *pūrṇāhantā* i.e. in the plenitude of the divine I-consciousness).[2]

That state of *Bhairava* which is full of the bliss of non-difference from the entire universe (*bharitākārā*)[3] is alone *Bhairavī* or *Śakti* of *Bhairava*. 15

That should, in verity, be known as His essential nature, immaculate (*vimalaṃ*)[4] and inclusive of the entire universe (*viśvapūraṇam*). Such being the state of the highest Reality, who can be the object of worship, who is to be satisfied with worship.[5]16.

That *niṣkala* state of *Bhairava* which is celebrated in this way is alone the highest state. That is declared as *parā devī*, the highest goddess, *parā* or highest not only in name, but because that is actually her highest form (*pararūpeṇa*).17

NOTES

1. Kṣemarāja in his commentary (*vivṛti*) says that *vyapadeṣṭum aśakyā* (cannot be indicated) hints at the fact that she cannot be talked about even in *madhyamā* (subtle) speech (*madhyamājalpā-viṣayā*), and *akathyā* (indescribable in words) hints at the fact that she can far less be described in ordinary human language (*vaikharyāpyavyāvarṇīyā*).

2. The 14th verse hints at the highest state of Bhairava in a negative way. It transcends direction, time, space and designation. It cannot be characterized or described in any human language.

The 15th verse hints at that state in a positive way. It says that though it is beyond description, it is not beyond experience (*anubhava*). There are two indispensable conditions (both of which are interconnected) under which one can have an experience of it. (1) It can be within the range of experience if one can rid oneself of all thought-constructs (*vikalponmuktagocarā*). The activity of mind consists in all kinds of thought-constructs. When one can get rid of thought-constructs, the mind is stilled. In that hour of silence emerges the essential Reality from behind the veil. It is the mind that acts as a veil, a barrier, a screen. Mind is the slayer of the Real. Truly has it been said "Be still, my heart, and know." (2) If one can get rid of the ego, the false, artificial 'I' and take a plunge in his inmost essential Self, he will have the experience of a delight which beggars description, a peace that passeth all understanding (*antaḥ svānubhavānandā*). Truly has it been said "He saveth life who loseth it."

This is *śāmbhava yoga*. Though the *parāvasthā* (highest state) of Bhairava cannot be described, it can be experienced.

3. That state of Bhairava is plenary state, a universal, all pervasive delight of creativity (*bharitākārā*). It is this which is His *śakti* or *Bhairavī* which is not exclusive of the universe but inclusive of it. It is only when we miss the whole and cling to the part, the *sakala* aspect of *Bhairava* that we stumble.

4. Kṣemarāja says in his commentary that *Bhairava's* essential nature has been characterized as *vimala* (immaculate) because though it manifests the universe on its own screen, it is not veiled by it (*svabhityābhāsita-jagadanācchāditam*).

5. When the essential nature of Bhairava is recognized as our own inmost self, the distinction between the worshipper and the worshipped disappears and there dawns a sense of non-dualism.

VERSES 18-19

शक्तिशक्तिमतोर्यद्वत् अभेदः सर्वदा स्थितः ।।
अतस्तद्धर्मधर्मित्वात् पराशक्तिः परात्मनः ।। १८ ।।
न वह्नेर्दाहिका शक्तिः व्यतिरिक्ता विभाव्यते ।
केवलं ज्ञानसत्तायां प्रारम्भोऽयं प्रवेशने ।। १९ ।।

Śakti-śaktimator yadvad abhedaḥ sarvadā sthitaḥ/
Atas taddharmadharmitvāt parā śaktiḥ parātmanaḥ// 18
Na vahner dāhikā śaktiḥ vyatiriktā vibhāvyate/
Kevalaṃ jñānasattāyām prārambho'yam praveśane// 19

TRANSLATION

Since there is always non-difference between *Śakti*[1] and possessor of śakti (*śaktimān*) therefore being endowed with His (i.e. *Śaktiman's*) attributes *Śakti* becomes the bearer of the same attributes.[2] Therefore being non-different from *para* (the highest i.e. *Bhairava*) she is known as parā (the highest i.e. *Bhairavī*). 18

The burning power of fire is not accepted as separate from fire even after full consideration (even so the *parāśakti* is not separate from *Bhairava*). Only it is described in a distinct way as a preliminary step for the listener towards its knowledge (lit., towards entry into its knowledge)[3] 19

NOTES

1. Śakti means power, capacity to effect something.

2. Just as Bhairava has the attributes of omniscience, omnipotence, etc., even so His *Śakti Bhairavī* has the same attributes.

3. The power of burning of fire is not anything separate from fire. Only it is described separately so that one may get acquaintance with fire after which one can find out its other attributes. Even so *parāśakti* is not anything separate from *para* (the supreme). Parāśakti is described separately so that she may prove as a first step towards the realization of *para* or *Bhairava*.

VERSES 20-21

शक्त्यवस्थाप्रविष्टस्य निर्विभागेन भावना ।
तदासौ शिवरूपी स्यात् शैवी मुखमिहोच्यते ।। २० ।।
यथालोकेन दीपस्य किरणैर्भास्करस्य च ।
ज्ञायते दिग्विभागादि तद्वच्छक्त्या शिवः प्रिये ।। २१ ।।

Śaktyavasthāpraviṣṭasya nirvibhāgena bhāvanā /
Tadāsau Śivarūpī syāt śaivī mukham ihocyate // 20
Yathālokena dīpasya kiraṇair bhāskarasya ca /
Jñāyate digvibhāgādi tadvac chaktyā Śivaḥ priye // 21

TRANSLATION

When in one who enters the state of *Śakti* (i.e. who is identified with *Śakti*), there ensues the feeling of non-distinction (between *Śakti* and *Śiva*), then he acquires the state of *Śiva*, (for) in the *āgamas* (*iha*), she (*śakti*) is declared as the door of entrance (into *Śiva*) (Lit., *Śakti* is like *Śiva's* face)[1] 20. Just as by means of the light of a lamp, and the rays of the Sun, portions of space, etc.[2] are known[3] even so, Oh dear one, by means of *Śakti* is *Śiva* (who is one's own essential Self) cognized (i.e. re-cognized). 21

NOTES

1. Just as one recognizes a person by his face, even so one recognizes *Śiva* by His *Śakti* who is like His face.

2. Et cetera included forms, figures.

3. There are three points suggested by this simile (1) Just as the flame of the lamp is not different from its light; just as the rays of the sun are not different from the sun, even so *śaktī* is not different from *Śiva.* (2) Just as through the lamp or the sun, objects of the world are perceived, even so through *Śakti* the universe is known. (3) Just as to perceive the light of the lamp, another lamp is not required; just as to perceive the sun, another sun is not required; they are known by their own light. Even so, *Śiva* is known by His *Śakti* who is not different from him.

VERSES 22-23

श्रीदेव्युवाच
देवदेव त्रिशूलाङ्क, कपालकृतभूषण ।
दिग्देशकालशून्या च व्यपदेशविवर्जिता ।। २२ ।।
यावस्था भरिताकारा भैरवस्योपलभ्यते ।
कैरुपायैर्मुखं तस्य परादेवी कथं भवेत् ।। २३ ।।
यथा सम्यगहं वेद्मि तथा मे ब्रूहि भैरव ।

Śrī Devī uvāca
Devadeva triśūlāṅka kapālakṛtabhūṣaṇa /
Digdeśakālaśūnyā ca vyapadeśavivarjitā // 22
Yāvasthā bharitākārā bhairavasyopalabhyate /
Kair upāyair mukhaṃ tasya parā devī katham bhavet // 23
Yathā samyag ahaṃ vedmi tathā me brūhi Bhairava /

TRANSLATION

[Now that the essential nature of *parādevī* (Supreme goddess or *Śakti*) has been hinted at, Bhairavī wants to know how that essential nature can be realized.]

O God of all gods, bearing the emblem of the trident,[1] and having cranium as your ornament,[2] how can that Supreme goddess (the Highest *Śakti*) who transcends all notions of direction, space and time and all manner of description be known? By what means can that complete state of *Bhairava* which is full of the bliss of non-difference from the universe (*bharitākārā*) be realized? In what way is the *parādevī* (the Highest *Śakti*) said to be the door of entrance into *Bhairava*? Please tell me in the *Vaikharī* form (in human language) that which I know fully well at the parā level[3] or please instruct me in such a manner that I may understand it fully.

NOTES

1. Bearing the emblem of the trident (*triśūla*). Bhairava is said to be bearing the trident, because the three spikes of the trident represent *icchā* (will), *jñāna* (knowledge) and *kriyā* (activity) which are the main characteristics of *Bhairava*.

2. Bhairava is generally represented as having a cranium bowl in his hand. This *kapāla* or cranium-bowl symbolizes the universe consisting of words and objects which betoken *Bhairava's svātantrya* (absolute freedom) and *caitanya* (supreme consciousness).

3. Being the *parā śakti* (Highest *Śakti*) of *Śiva*, she already knows the truth at the *parā* (highest) level, but she wants *Bhairava* to tell it to her in the *Vaikharī* form (gross speech, human language). *Vedmi*—I know is present tense. If she knows, why does she request Bhairava to tell it to her ? The explanation is that she knows it at the *parā* level, at the transcendental level, now she wants its exposition at the empirical level.

[Dhāraṇā 1]

VERSE 24

श्रीभैरव उवाच

ऊर्ध्वे प्राणो ह्यधो जीवो विसर्गात्मा परोच्चरेत् ।
उत्पत्तिद्वितयस्थाने, भरणाद्भरिता स्थितिः ।। २४ ।।

Ūrdhve prāṇo hy adho jīvo visargātmā paroccaret /
Utpattidvitayasthāne bharaṇād bharitā sthitiḥ // 24

TRANSLATION

Bhairava says:

Parā devī or Highest *Śakti* who is of the nature of *visarga*[1] goes on (ceaselessly) expressing herself upward (ūrdhve) (from the centre of the body to *dvādaśānta*[2] or a distance of twelve fingers) in the form of exhalation (*prāṇa*) and downward (*adhaḥ*) (from *dvādaśānta* to the centre of the body) in the form of inhalation (*jīva* or *apāna*).[3] By steady fixation of the mind (*bharaṇāt*)[4] at the two places of their origin (viz., centre of the body in the case of *prāṇa* and *dvādaśānta* in the case of *apāna*), there is the situation of plenitude (*bharitāsthitiḥ* which is the state of *parāśakti* or nature of *Bhairava*).[5]

NOTES

1. Visargātmā—who is of the nature of *visarga*. The word visarga means letting go, projection or creation, i.e. who is creative. The creative function of the Divine includes two movements-outward and inward or centrifugal and centripetal. In living beings, the outward or centrifugal movement is represented by expiration or exhalation; the inward or centripetal movement is represented by inspiration or inhalation. *Parā* or *parā devī* or *Parā śakti* is designated as *Visargātmā*, because it is by this rhythm of centrifugal and centripetal movement that she carries on the play of life whether in the macrocosm or the microcosm. This movement is known as *uccāra* or *spandana* or ceaseless throb of *Parādevī*.

In Sanskrit, *visarga* is represented by two points or dots one above the other. One point in this case is *dvādaśānta* where *prāṇa* ends and the other is the *hṛt* or centre of the body where *apāna* ends. It is because of these two points also that Parāśakti is known as visargātmā.

2. Dvādaśānta—literally meaning 'end of twelve' indicates the point at a distance of 12 fingers from the tip of the nose in the outer space where expiration arising from the centre of the human body, and passing through the throat and the nose ends. This is known as *bāhya dvādaśānta* or the external *dvādaśānta*.

3. The *apāna* or inhalation is called *jīva*, because it is the inhalation or return movement of the breath that is responsible for life.

4. *Bharaṇāt* here means by close observation or one-pointed awareness. Awareness of what ? Śivopādhyāya in his commentary clears this point in the following way:

"Bharaṇāditi — *nityonmiṣadādyasphurattātmabhairavīyaśakty-upalakṣaṇāt*. i.e. *bharaṇāt* here means by an intent awareness of that who by implication is the ever-risen initial flash of the *śakti* of *Bhairava*.

5. The dhāraṇā or the yogic practice referred to in this verse is the following:

There are two points or poles between which respiration goes on constantly. One of these is *dvādaśānta* in the outer space where *prāṇa* or exhalation ends and the other *hṛt* or the centre inside the body where *apāna* or inhalation ends. At each of these points, there is *viśrānti* or rest for a split second. The breath does not actually stop there totally but remains in the form of a throb of *śakti* in suspended animation and then again the breathing process starts. One should contemplate over the *śakti* that appears in the period of rest and should remain mindful of it even while the breathing process starts. By constant practice of this *dhāraṇā*, he will realize the state of plenitude of *Bhairava* (*bharitā sthitiḥ*).

As this practice is without any support of *vikalpa*, it is *Śāmbhava upāya.*

There is another important interpretation of this *dhāraṇā*. In inhalation, the sound of *ha* is produced; in exhalation, the sound *saḥ* is produced; at the junction point in the centre the sound of *ṃ* is added. So the whole formula becomes 'Haṃsaḥ'. The *parādevī* goes on sounding this formula or *mantra* ceaselessly in every living being. *Hṛdaya* or the centre is the starting point of the sound *ha* and *dvādaśānta* is the starting point of the sound *saḥ*. By contemplating over these two points, one acquires the nature of *Bhairava.* This would be an *āṇava upāya*. *Śaḥ* represents *Śiva*; *ha* represents *Śakti; ṃ* represents *nara.* So in this practice, all the three main elements of Trika philosophy, viz, *Śiva*, *Śakti* and *Nara* are included.

[Dhāraṇā 2]

VERSE 25

मरुतोऽन्तर्बहिर्वापि वियद्युग्मानिवर्तनात् ।
भैरव्या भैरवस्येत्थं भैरवि व्यज्यते वपुः ॥ २५ ॥

Maruto'ntar bahir vāpi viyadyugmānivartanāt /
Bhairavyā bhairavasyettham bhairavi vyajyate vapuḥ // 25

TRANSLATION

Of the breath (exhalation or *prāṇa*) arising from the inner i.e. the centre of the body (*hṛt*) there is non-return for a split second from the *dvādaśānta* (a distance of twelve fingers from the nose in the outer space), and of the breath (inhalation or *apāna* arising from *dvādaśānta* i. e. the outer space, there is non-return for a split second from the centre of the body (*hṛt*).[1] If one fixes his mind steadily at these two points of pause, one will find that Bhairavī the essential form of Bhairava is manifested at those two points.[2]

NOTES

1. The pause of prāṇa in the *dvādaśānta* is known as *bahiḥ kumbhaka* or external pause. The pause of the *apāna* in the internal centre of the body is known as *antaḥ kumbhaka* or internal pause By the *anusandhāna* or one-pointed awareness of these two pauses, the mind becomes introverted, and the activity of both *prāṇa* and *apāna* ceases, and there is the upsurge of *madhya daśā* i. e. the path of the *madhya nāḍī* or *suṣumnā* becomes open.

2. If one mentally observes the above two pauses, he realizes the nature of Bhairava. This is *āṇava upāya* inasmuch as this process involves the *dhyāna* or meditation on the two *kumbhakas* or pauses of *prāṇa* and *apāna*.

[Dhāraṇā 3]

VERSE 26

न व्रजेन्न विशेच्छक्ति-र्मरुद्रूपा विकासिते ।
निर्विकल्पतया मध्ये तया भैरवरूपता ॥ २६ ॥

Na vrajen na viśec chaktir marudrūpā vikāsite /
Nirvikalpakatayā madhye tayā Bhairavarūpatā // 26

TRANSLATION

When the middle state develops by means of the dissolution of all dichotomising thought-constructs[1] the *prāṇa-śakti* in the form of exhalation (*prāṇa*) does not go out from the centre (of the body) to *dvādaśānta*,[2] nor does that *śakti* in the form of inhalation (*apāna*) enter into the centre from *dvādaśānta*. In this way by means of Bhairavī who expresses herself in the form of the cessation of *prāṇa* (exhalation) and *apāna* (inhalation), there supervenes the state of Bhairava.[3]

NOTES

1. In this dhāraṇā, *prāṇa* (exhalation) and *apāna* (inhalation) cease and *madhya daśā* develops i.e. the *prāṇaśakti* in the *suṣumnā* develops by means of *nirvikalpabhāva* i. e. by the cessation of all thought-constructs; then the nature of Bhairava is revealed.

Śivopādhyāya in his commentary says that the *nirvikalpa bhāva* comes about by *Bhairavī mudrā* in which even when the senses are open outwards, the attention is turned inwards towards inner *spanda* or throb of creative consciousness which is the basis and support of all mental and sensuous activity, then all *vikalpas* or thought-constructs cease. The breath neither goes out, nor does it come in, and the essential nature of Bhairava is revealed.

2. *Dvādaśānta* means a distance of 12 fingers in the outer space measured from the tip of the nose.

3. The difference between the previous *dhāraṇā* and this one lies in the fact that whereas in the previous dhāraṇā, the *madhya daśā* develops by one-pointed awareness of the pauses of *prāṇa* and *apāna*, in the present *dhāraṇā*, the *madhya daśā* develops by means of *nirvikalpa-bhāva*.

Abhinavagupta has quoted this *dhāraṇā* in Tantrāloka v.22 p. 333 and there also he emphasizes *nirvikalpa-bhāva*. He says that one should fix one's mind with pointed awareness on the junction of *prāṇa*, *apāna* and *udāna* in the centre, then *prāṇa* and *apāna* will be suspended; the mind will be freed of all *vikalpas*, *madhya daśā* will develop, and the aspirant will have the realization of his essential Self which is the nature of Bhairava.

Śivopādhyāya says that since this *dhāraṇā* takes the help of *madhyadaśā*, it may be considered to be an *āṇava upāya*. But the development of *madhyadaśā* is brought about by *nirvikalpa-*

bhāva in this *dhāraṇā*. From this point of view, it may be considered to be *śāmbhava upāya*.

[Dhāraṇā 4]

VERSE 27

कुम्भिता रेचिता वापि पूरिता या यदा भवेत् ।
तदन्ते शान्तनामासौ शक्त्या शान्तः प्रकाशते ॥ २७ ॥

Kumbhitā recitā vāpi pūritā vā yadā bhavet /
Tadante śāntanāmāsau śaktyā śāntaḥ prakāśate // 27

TRANSLATION

When the *Śakti* in the form of exhalation (*recitā*) is retained outside (at *dvādaśānta*), and in the form of inhalation (*pūritā*) is retained inside (at the *hṛt* or centre), then at the end of this practice,[1] the *Śakti* is known as *Śāntā*[2] or tranquillized and through *Śakti Śānta Bhairava*[3] is revealed.

NOTES

1. By means of continuous practice of *kumbhaka* or retention of breath in the above way, physical and mental tranquillity is experienced, and *madhya daśā* is developed. The sense of *bheda* or difference between *prāṇa* and *apāna* disappears. That is why this *prāṇa śakti* is known as *śāntā*.

2. On account of the disappearance of *bheda* or difference between *prāṇa* and *apāna* the *Śakti* is known as Śāntā or which in this context means 'subsided', 'ceased'.

3. *Bhairava* (the divine self) is called *Śānta* (peaceful) because He transcends all the limits of name and form and in Him there is no trace of difference or duality.

This *dhāraṇā* is a variety of *Āṇava upāya*.

[Dhāraṇā 5]

VERSE 28

आ मूलात्किरणाभासां सूक्ष्मात् सूक्ष्मतरात्मिकाम् ।
चिन्तयेत्तां द्विषट्कान्ते शाम्यन्तीं भैरवोदयः ॥ २८ ॥

Āmūlāt kiraṇābhāsāṃ sūkṣmātsūkṣmatarātmikām/
Cintayet tāṃ dviṣaṭkānte śyāmyantīm Bhairavodayaḥ// 28.

TRANSLATION

Meditate on the Śakti[1] arising from the *mūlādhāra cakra*[2], scintillating like rays (of the sun), and getting subtler and subtler till at last she dissolves in *dvādaśānta*.[3] Thus does *Bhairava* become manifest.[4]

NOTES

1. *Śakti* here refers to *prāṇaśakti* that abides as *prāṇakuṇḍalinī* in the interior of the body. *Kuṇḍalinī* lies folded up in 3½ folds in *Mūlādhāra*.

2. *Mūlādhāra cakra* is situated in the spinal region below the genitals. A *cakra* is a centre of *prāṇic* energy located in the *prāṇamaya kośa* in the interior of the body. This *dhāraṇā* refers to the rise of *Kuṇḍalinī* which goes in a flash into *dvādaśānta* or *Brahmarandhra* (the *cakra* at the top of the head) and dissolves in it. This is known as *cit-kuṇḍalinī* or *akrama kuṇḍalinī* i.e. *kuṇḍalinī* that does not pass successively through the *cakras* but goes directly to *Brahmarandhra*.

3. *Dviṣaṭkānte* (twice six) means *dvādaśānta* at the end of 12 fingers. This *dvādaśānta* refers to *Brahmarandhra* which is at a distance of 12 fingers from the middle of the eye-brows (*bhrūmadhya*).

4. In *dvādaśānta* or *Brahmarandhra*, *Kuṇḍalinī* gets dissolved in *prakāśa* or light of consciousness abiding in *Brahmarandhra*. In that *prakāśa* is revealed the nature of Bhairava.

Inasmuch as this *dhāraṇā* depends on the *bhāvanā* of *prāṇa śakti*, this is *āṇava upāya*. Netra Tantra, however, takes it a *Śāmbhava upāya*. (VIII, p. 200).

[Dhāraṇā 6]

VERSE 29

उद्गच्छन्तीं तडिद्रूपां प्रतिचक्रं क्रमात्क्रमम् ।
ऊर्ध्वं मुष्टित्रयं यावत् तावदन्ते महोदयः ॥ २९ ॥

Udgacchantīṃ taḍitrūpām praticakraṃ kramāt kramam/
Ūrdhvam muṣṭitrayaṃ yāvat tāvad ante mahodayaḥ// 29

TRANSLATION

Meditate on that very lightning-like *śakti* (i.e. *Kuṇḍalinī*), moving upwards successively from one centre of energy (*cakra*) to another upto three fists i.e. *dvādaśānta*.[1] At the end, one can experience the magnificent rise of *Bhairava*.[2]

NOTES

1. This *dvādaśānta* also refers to *Brahmarandhra*.

2. This refers to the rise of *kuṇḍalinī* piercing successively through all the *cakras* or centres of energy till at last, it dissolves in *Brahmarandhra*. This is known as *prāṇa-kuṇḍalinī*. The difference between this *dhāraṇā* and the previous one consists in the fact that, in this dhāraṇā the *kuṇḍalinī* moves successively through the *cakras* and then finally dissolves in *Brahmarandhra*, whereas in the previous *dhāraṇā*, the *Kuṇḍalinī* shoots forth from *mūlādhāra* directly in *Brahmarandhra* and gets dissolved in it without passing through the intervening *cakras*. Jayaratha quotes it in his commentary on Tantrāloka (v.88). This is *Śāktopāya*.

[Dhāraṇā 7]

VERSE 30

क्रमद्वादशकं सम्यग् द्वादशाक्षरभेदितम् ।
स्थूलसूक्ष्मपरस्थित्या मुक्त्वा मुक्त्वान्ततः शिवः ॥ ३० ॥

Kramadvādaśakaṃ samyag dvādaśākṣarabheditaṃ /
Sthūlasūkṣmaparasthityā muktvā muktvāntataḥ Śivaḥ // 30

TRANSLATION

Twelve successively higher centres of energy[1] associated with twelve successive letters[2] should be properly meditated on. Each of them should at first be meditated on in a gross phase, then leaving that in a subtle phase and then leaving that also in the supreme phase till finally the meditator becomes identified with *Śiva*. 30

NOTES

1. The twelve successively higher centres of energy (*krama-dvādaśakam*) are: 1. *janmāgra*, 2. *mūla*, 3. *Kanda*, 5. *nābhi*, 5. *hṛdaya*, 6. *Kaṇṭha*, 7. *tālu*, 8. *bhrūmadhya*, 9. *lalāṭa*, 10. *brahmarandhra*, 11. *śakti*, 12. *vyāpinī*.

These are known as *dvādaśasthāna* or twelve stations.

These are stages of the rising *kuṇḍalinī*. They are correlatives of twelve vowels. The first four stages or stations or centres of energy are lower (*apara*) and concern *bheda* or difference.

i. *Janmāgra* is at the level of the generative organ. Since the generative organ is concerned with *janma* or birth of individuals, therefore the centre of energy at this level is known as *janma*, or *janmādhāra* (basis of generation) or *janmasthāna* (the station which is involved in generation) or *janmāgra* (*janmāgra* means the point or head of the generative organ.)

ii. *Mūla*, generally known as *mūlādhāra* or the root centre. This is in the spinal centre of region below the genitals.

iii. *Kanda*, a bulbous or tuberous root, so called, because it is a tangle of many nerves.

iv. *Nābhī* or navel. The *Maṇipūra cakra* is situated near it.

After this, the following five are concerned with subtler energies known as *bhedābheda* or *parāpara*.

v. *Hṛd* or heart.

vi. *Kaṇṭha*—the cavity at the base of the throat.

vii. *Tālu*—palate

viii. *Bhrūmadhya*—centre between the eye-brows.

ix. *Lalāṭa*—Forehead.

In the following three stages, the energy is of the form of *para* or *abheda*.

x. *Brahmarandhra*—The apex of the cranium.

xi. *Śakti*—pure energy which is not a constituent of the body.

xii. *Vyāpinī*—the energy which appears when *Kuṇḍalinī* finishes its journey.

2. The twelve successive letters are the following twelve vowels;

1. a, 2. ā, 3, i, 4. ī, 5. u, 6. ū, 7. e, 8. ai, 9, o, 10. au, 11. aṃ, 12. aḥ. These vowels have to be meditated on in the above twelve stages of the kuṇḍalinī.

This *dhāraṇā* in the gross form consists of *āṇava upāya,* and in the subtle and supreme form, it consists of *śāktopāya.*

[Dhāraṇā 8]

VERSE 31

तयापूर्याशु मूर्धान्तं भङ्क्त्वा भ्रूक्षेपसेतुना ।
निर्विकल्पं मनः कृत्वा सर्वोर्ध्वे सर्वगोद्गमः ॥ ३१ ॥

Tayāpūryāśu mūrdhāntaṃ bhaṅktvā bhrūkṣepasetunā /
Nirvikalpaṃ manaḥ kṛtvā sarvordhve sarvagodgamaḥ // 31

TRANSLATION

Having filled the *mūrdhānta*[1] with the same *prāṇic* energy quickly and having crossed it with the help of the bridge-like contraction of the eye-brows[2], one should free one's mind of all dichatomizing thought-constructs. His consciousness will then rise higher than *dvādaśānta* and then there will appear the sense of omnipresence.

NOTES

1. *Mūrdhānta* here means *dvādaśānta* i.e. *Brahmarandhra,* a space covered by twelve fingers from the middle of eye-brows.

2. Just as a river is crossed by means of a bridge, even so the prāṇic energy has to be crossed over by an esoteric technique of *bhrūkṣepa*. Then that prāṇic energy will be converted into *cit-śakti,* and the aspirant's consciousness will rise higher than that of the *Brahmarandhra* and he will have a feeling of omnipresence. The esoteric technique of *bhrūkṣepa* was a closely guarded secret among the mystics and is now practically lost.

This is *Śāktopāya.*

[Dhāraṇā 9]

VERSE 32

शिखिपक्षैश्चित्ररूपैर्मण्डलैः शून्यपञ्चकम् ।
ध्यायतोऽनुत्तरे शून्ये प्रवेशो हृदये भवेत् ॥ ३२ ॥

Śikhipakṣaiś citrarūpair maṇḍalaiḥ śūnyapañcakam /
Dhyāyato' nuttare śūnye praveśo hṛdaye bhavet // 32

TRANSLATION

The *yogī* should meditate in his heart on the five voids[1] of the five senses which are like the five voids appearing in the circles[2] of motley feathers of peacocks. Thus will he be absorbed in the Absolute void.[3]

NOTES

1. Five voids or *śūnya-pañcakam*. This means that the *yogi* should meditate on the five ultimate sources of the five senses, i.e. the five *tanmātras*, sound as such, form as such, etc. which have no concrete appearance and are mere voids.

There is also a *double entendre* in *śūnyapañcakam*. Just as there are five holes in the circles of the feathers of the peacocks —one above, one below, one in the middle, and one on each side, even so the *yogī* should meditate on the five ultimate sources of the sense i.e. the five *tanmātras* as five voids.

2. Circles—*maṇḍalas*. There is a *double entendre* in the word *maṇḍala* also. In the case of the peacock, it means the circles in the feather; in the case of the *yogī*, it means the senses. (*maṇḍaṃ rasasāraṃ lānti iti maṇḍalāni*—those that carry the quintessence of the five objects of sense are *maṇḍalas*, i.e. the five senses).

3. The Absolute void is *Bhairava* who is beyond the senses and the mind, beyond all the categories of these instruments. From the point of view of the human mind, He is most void. From the point of view of Reality, He is most full, for He is the source of all manifestation.

[Dhāraṇā-10]

VERSE-33

ईदृशेन क्रमेणैव यत्र कुत्रापि चिन्तना ।
शून्ये कुड्ये परे पात्रे स्वयं लीना वरप्रदा ॥ ३३ ॥

Īdṛśena krameṇaiva yatrakutrāpi cintanā /
Śūnye kuḍye pare pātre svayaṃ līnā varapradā // 33

TRANSLATION

In this way, successively.[1], wherever there is mindfulness on whether void, on wall, or on some excellent person[2], that mindfulness is absorbed by itself in the supreme and offers the highest benefaction.[3]

NOTES

1. Just as there is concentration in successive steps on *gudādhāra* (*mūlādhāra*), *janma*, *kanda*, *nābhi*, *hṛdaya*, *kaṇṭha*, *tālu*, *bhrūmadhya*, *lalāṭa*, *brahmarandhra*, *śakti and vyāpinī* in one's own body, so concentration in successive steps may be practised outside one's body also e.g. on some vast empty space, on some high wall, etc.

2. *Parepātre – pātre* here means fit, competent person, *pare pātre* means on some excellent competent person, e.g. on a pureminded competent pupil.

3. The highest spiritual experience is here said to be the highest benefaction.

The above *dhāraṇā* begins with *Āṇava upāya* and finally merges in *Śāktopāya*.

[Dhāraṇā 11]

VERSE 34

कपालान्तर्मनो न्यस्य तिष्ठन्मीलितलोचनः ।
क्रमेण मनसो दार्ढ्यात् लक्षयेल्लक्ष्यमुत्तमम् ॥ ३४ ॥

Kapālāntarmano nyasya tiṣṭhan mīlitalocanaḥ /
Krameṇa manaso dārḍhyāt lakṣayet lakṣyam uttamam // 34

TRANSLATION

Fixing one's attention on the interior[1] of the cranium (kapāla) and seated with eyes closed,[2] with the stability of the mind,[3] one gradually discerns that which is most eminently discernible.[4]

The word *kapāla* means 'cranium.' There is also an esoteric meaning of his word. Śivopādhyāya quotes the following verse from Tantrakośa in this connexion.

"Kaśabdena parāśaktiḥ pālakaḥ Śivasaṃjñayā /
Śiva-Śakti-samāyogaḥ kapālaḥ paripaṭhyate" //

"The word *ka* signifies *parāśakti* or the supreme divine Energy, and the word *pāla* meaning 'protector' signifies *Śiva.* The whole word *kapāla* is therefore, used in the sense of union between *Śiva* and *Śakti.*" *Śiva* and *Śakti* in other words, stand for *prakāśa* and *vimarśa* i.e. Light of Consciousness and its awareness. According to this interpretation the translation of the above verse would stand thus:

"Having fixed one's mind inwardly on the union of Śiva and Śakti,[5] and seated with eyes closed, gradually with the stability of the mind, one discerns what is most eminently discernible."

NOTES

1. 'On the interior means 'on the Light that is ever present inside'.

2. 'With eyes closed' means 'detached from the external world and completely introverted.'

3. The mind is, at first, very fickle, but by constant practice, it acquires stability and then one can concentrate with steadiness.

4. This means that one becomes aware of the Highest spiritual Reality.

By this practice, the sense of difference gradually diminishes; and one begins to view the entire universe as an expression of Śiva.

This *dhāraṇā* comes under *Śāktopāya.*

[Dhāraṇā 12]

VERSE 35

मध्यनाडी मध्यसंस्था बिससूत्राभरूपया ।
ध्यातान्तर्व्योमया देव्या तया देवः प्रकाशते ॥ ३५ ॥

Madhyanāḍī madhyasaṃsthā bisasūtrābharūpayā |
Dhyātāntarvyomayā devyā tayā devaḥ prakāśate || 35

TRANSLATION

The medial *nāḍī*[1] is situated in the middle. It is as slender as the stem of a lotus. If one meditates on the inner vacuity of this *nāḍī*, it helps in revealing the Divine.[2]

NOTES

1. *Nāḍī* here means the '*prāṇic* channel'

2. *Prāṇaśakti* exists in *Suṣumnā* or the medial *nāḍī*. If one meditates on the inner vacuity existing in this medial *nāḍī* the *prāṇa* and *apāna* currents get dissolved in the *Suṣumnā*, the *udāna* current becomes active. Thus the *kuṇḍalinī* rises, passes through *suṣumnā*, and piercing the various centres of energy (*cakras*), finally merges in *Sahasrāra*. There the *yogī* experiences spiritual light with which he feels identified. This is what is meant by saying that the Divine is revealed by the aid of the interior *prāṇic* force residing in *Suṣumnā*. The same idea has been expressed in the following verse of *Spandakārikā*:

Tadā tasmin mahāvyomni pralīnaśaśibhāskare.
Sauṣuptapadavanmūḍhaḥ prabuddhaḥ syādanāvṛtaḥ.
(Verse 25)

When the moon (*apāna* current of vital energy) and sun (*prāṇa* current of vital energy) get dissolved and the *yogī* enters the *Suṣumnā*, the *yogī* who is after supernormal powers becomes befuddled like one who is fast asleep, but the one who is not under such an influence is wide awake and experiences spiritual Light.

This begins with *Āṇava upāya* and ends in *Śāktopāya*.

[Dhāraṇā 13]

VERSE 36

करुद्धदृगस्त्रेण भ्रूभेदाद् द्वाररोधनात् ।
दृष्टे बिन्दौ क्रमाल्लीने तन्मध्ये परमा स्थितिः ॥ ३६ ॥

Kararuddhadṛgastreṇa bhrūbhedād dvārarodhanāt /
Dṛṣṭe bindau kramāt līne tanmadhye paramā sthitiḥ //36

TRANSLATION

By stopping the openings (of the senses) with the weapon (*astra*) in the form of the hands,[1] by which are blocked the eyes (and other openings in the face) and thus by breaking open (the knot in the centre of the eye-brows)[2] the *bindu* is perceived[3] which (on the development of one-pointedness) gradually disappears (in the ether of consciousness)[4]. Then (in the centre of the ether of consciousness), the *yogī* is established in the highest (spiritual) state.

NOTES

1. 'Kararuddhadṛgastra' is a kind of *karaṇa* used in *āṇava upāya*. *Karaṇa* is thus defined *Karaṇaṃ dehasanniveśa-viśeṣ-ātmā mudrādivyāpāraḥ*. i.e. 'disposition of the limbs of the body in a particular way, usually known as mudrā i.e. control of certain organs and senses that helps in concentration'. Here the *karaṇa* specified is by means of the hands. The ten fingers of the two hands are used in this *mudrā*. The ears are closed with the two thumbs: the eyes are closed with the index fingers: the two nostrils are closed with the two middle fingers; the mouth is closed with the ring-fingers and the little fingers. This is what is meant by saying "By stopping (the openings of the sense) with the weapon in the form of the hands." The openings of all the *jñānendriyas* or organs of sense are closed.

By this device consciousness is closed to all exterior influences. and the vital energy is confined within.

2. The vital energy, by closing the various openings of the senses, rises up towards the centre of the eye-brows and reach-

ing there ruptures the knot or tangle of nerves in which a very significant energy is locked up.

3. When the centre of the eye-brows is ruptured by the vital energy that rises up from within, a point of brilliant light is perceived. This is the *bindu* or *vindu* which means a dot, a globule, a drop, a point. It is written both as *bindu* and *vindu*.

4. As soon as the *bindu* is perceived, the *yogī* has to concentrate on it. When the concentration develops, the *bindu* begins to disappear gradually and finally vanishes in the ether of universal consciousness (*cidākāśa*). This is said to be *paramā sthitiḥ*, the highest state of the *yogī*.

There are five stages in this *dhāraṇā*, viz. (1) *dvāra-rodhanaṃ* or stopping the openings of the senses with the fingers of the two hands, (2) *bhrūbhedaḥ*—by closing the openings of the senses, the vital energy that is pent up within rises to the centre of the eye-brows, and ruptures the tangle of nerves situated in that centre; (3) *bindudarśanam*—when the centre of the eye-brows is pierced by the vital energy, then a *bindu* or point of light that is imprisoned within it is released and the *yogī* perceives it mentally (4) *Kramāt-ekāgratāprakarṣāt līne saṃvidgagane* i.e. when the *bindu* is concentrated upon, it gradually begins to disappear and finally vanishes in the ether of consciousness, (5) *tanmadhye yoginaḥ paramā sthitiḥ-bhairavābhivyaktiḥ*—in that ether of consciousness, the *yogī* realizes the highest state, that is to say, in that is revealed the essential nature of *Bhairava*.

Svāmī Lakṣmaṇa Joo, however, gives a different interpretation of this *dhāraṇā*. He maintains that bhrūbhedāt is *lyablope pañcamī* which means 'after having ruptured the tangle of nerves in the middle of the eye-brows'. This is to be achieved by concentration on the central spot of the eye-brows. When this is effected, a drop of light will be visible there. After achieving this result, the openings of the senses have to be blocked by the above *mudrā*, then *prāṇa śakti* will arise in the *suṣumnā* which will mount up towards *Brahmarandhra*. This will hasten the dissolution of the drop of light in *Brahmarandhra* and in that state the *yogī* will realize his essential Self. This is an *āṇava upāya* ending in *śāktopāya*.

[Dhāraṇā 14]

VERSE 37

धामान्तःक्षोभसंभूतसूक्ष्माग्नितिलकाकृतिम् ।
बिन्दुं शिखान्ते हृदये लयान्ते ध्यायतो लयः ॥ ३७ ॥

Dhāmāntaḥ-kṣobhasambhūtasūkṣmāgnitilakākṛtim /
Binduṁ śikhānte hṛdaye layānte dhyāyato layaḥ // 37.

TRANSLATION

The *yogī* should meditate either in the heart or in *dvādaśānta*[1] on the *bindu* which is a subtle spark of fire resembling a *tilaka*[2] produced by pressure on the *dhāma* or *teja* (light existing in the eyes).[3] By such practice the discursive thought (*vikalpa*) of the *yogī* disappears, and on its disappearance, the *yogī* is absorbed in the light of supreme consciousness.

NOTES

1. The word *śikhānta* (end of the tuft of hair on the head) here means *dvādaśānta* or *brahmarandhra*.

2. *Tilaka*—a small round dot of sandalwood paste applied on the forhead by the Hindus as a mark of devotion to a deity.

3. When the eyes are pressed, certain sparks appear. The *yogī* should mentally seize the *bindu* (point) which is one of the sparks appearing in the eye by pressure, and should meditate on that *bindu* either in the heart or dvādaśānta. By this practice, his habit of dichotomising thought (*vikalpa*) will disappear, and when that disappears, he will be established in the essential nature of *Bhairava*.

The word *dhāma* in this context means the light in the eye, or the word *dhāma* may be interpreted as the subtle sparks of light of a lamp that appear at the time of the extinction of its light.

This is an *Āṇava upāya*.

[Dhāraṇā 15]

VERSE 38

अनाहते पात्रकर्णेऽभग्नशब्दे सरिद्द्रुते ।
शब्दब्रह्मणि निष्णातः परं ब्रह्माधिगच्छति ॥ ३८ ॥

Anāhate pātrakarṇe' bhagnaśabde sariddrute /
Śabdabrahmaṇi niṣṇātaḥ param brahmādhigacchati //38

TRANSLATION

One who is deeply versed and deeply bathed[1] or steeped in *Nāda* which is *Brahman* in the form of sound (*śabdabrahmaṇi niṣṇātaḥ*), which is vibrating inside without any impact (*anāhate*),[2] which can be heard only by the ear that becomes competent by *yoga* (*pātrakarṇe*),[3] which goes on sounding uninterruptedly (*abhagnaśabde*) and which is rushing headlong like a river (*sariddrute*) attains to Brahman (*brahmādhigacchati*).

NOTES

1. There is a *double entendre* in *niṣṇāta*. It means both well-versed and well bathed (*ni-snāta*) i.e. deeply steeped.

2. *Anāhata nāda* literally means unstruck sound. It is a sound that goes on vibrating within spontaneously without any impact. About ten such kinds of *nāda* (sound) that vibrate within growing subtler and subtler are referred to in books on *Yoga*. Here the reference is to the subtlest *nāda* that vibrates in *prāṇaśakti* present in *suṣumnā*. Prāṇaśakti is, in the universe, representative of *parāśakti*, the *śakti* of *Parama Śiva*. It is the eternal energy of consciousness, the spiritual *spanda*.

When *Kuṇḍalinī* rises, one is able to hear this. The *yogī* has to concentrate on this sound which is at first like that of a hand-bell, then subtler like that of a flute, then subtler still like that of *vīṇā*, and then subtler like that of the buzz of a bee. When the *yogī* concentrates on this *nāda*, he forgets everything of the external world, is gradually lost in the internal sound and is finally absorbed in *cidākāśa* i.e. in the vast expanse of consciousness. This is what is meant by saying that he attains to *Brahman*. This kind of yoga is known as *varṇa* in *Āṇava upāya* of *Śaiva yoga*, as *nādānusandhāna* in some of the older *upaniṣads* and *Nātha* tradition, and *surati śabda yoga* in Kabīra and other mediaeval saints.

3. *Pātrakarṇe* means that this inner spontaneous sound is not audible to every ear but only to the ear that is made competent to hear it under the guidance of a *guru.*

This is an *Āṇava upāya.*

[Dhāraṇā 16]

VERSE 39

प्रणवादिसमुच्चारात् प्लुतान्ते शून्यभावनात् ।
शून्यया परया शक्त्या शून्यतामेति भैरवि ॥ ३९ ॥

Praṇavādisamuccārāt plutānte śūnyabhāvanāt/
Śūnyayā parayā śaktyā śūnyatām eti bhairavi. 39//

TRANSLATION

O Bhairavi, by perfect recitation of *praṇava* or the sacred syllable *Auṁ*, etc and by contemplating over the void at the end of the protracted phase[2] of it and by the most eminent energy of the void,[3] the *yogī* attains the void.[4]

NOTES

1. Et cetera refers to other *praṇavas*. There are chiefly three *praṇavas*—(1) the Vedic praṇava, *Auṁ*. (2) the *Śaiva praṇava, Hūm* and (3) the *Śākta praṇava, Hrīm.*

2. *Pluta* or the protracted form is an utterance of three *mātrās* or moras. Just as the crow of the cock is at first short, then long and then protracted, even so there are three phases of the recitation of *Auṁ*-short (*hrasva*), then long (*dīrgha*) and then protracted (*pluta*).

The usual practice in the recitation of *Auṁ* is contemplation of *ardhacandra, bindu,* etc. upto *unmanā* after the protracted phase. In the present verse, *Bhairava* is referring to a different practice. He says that at the end of the protracted phase of the recitation, do not contemplate over *ardhacandra, bindu,* etc., but over *śūnya* or void. *Śūnya* or void here means free of all external or internal objective support, of all *tattvas*, and of all residual traces of *kleśas*. Gross objects like jar, cloth etc. are external support of the mind, pleasure, pain, etc. are the internal support of the mind, and residual traces are the *vāsanās* of *avidyā*, *asmitā*, *rāga*, *dveṣa* and *abhiniveśa*.

Śūnya or void means that which is free of the above conditions. In other words, the mind has to be made *nirvikalpa*, free of all *vikalpas*, of all thoughts.

3. The most eminent energy of the void is the energy of the *parāśakti*.

4. Attaining the void means attaining the nature of Bhairava, which is free of difference, duality and *vikalpa*.

This begins with *Āṇava upāya* and ends in *Śāktopāya*.

[Dhāraṇā 17]

VERSE 40

यस्य कस्यापि वर्णस्य पूर्वान्तावनुभावयेत् ।
शून्यया शून्यभूतोऽसौ शून्याकारः पुमान्भवेत् ॥ ४० ॥

Yasya kasyápi varṇasya pūrvāntāv anubhāvayet /
Śūnyayā śūnyabhūto' sau śūnyākāraḥ pumān bhavet // 40

TRANSLATION

The *Yogī* should contemplate over the previous condition of any letter whatsoever before its utterance and its final condition after its utterance as mere void. He will, then with the help of the power of the void,[1] become of the nature and form of the void.[2]

NOTES

1. Power of the void is the power of *parāśakti*.

2. Of the nature and form of the void means that the *yogī* will become completely freed from identification with the *prāṇa*, body, etc. as the Self.

This is *Śāktopāya* ending in *Śāmbhava upāya*.

[Dhāraṇā 18]

VERSE 41

तन्त्र्यादिवाद्यशब्देषु दीर्घेषु क्रमसंस्थितेः ।
अनन्यचेताः प्रत्यन्ते परव्योमवपुर्भवेत् ॥ ४१ ॥

Tantryādivādyaśabdeṣu dīrgheṣu kramasaṃsthiteḥ/
Ananyacetāḥ pratyante paravyomavapur bhavet // 41

TRANSLATION

If one listens with undivided attention to sounds of stringed and other musical instruments which on account of their (uninterrupted) succession are prolonged,[1] he will, at the end,[2] be absorbed in the ether of consciousness (and thus attain the nature of *Bhairava*).

NOTES

1. The resonance of musical notes lasts for a long time and being melodious it attracts the attention of the listener. Even when it stops, it still reverberates in the mind of the listener. The listener becomes greatly engrossed in it. A musical note, if properly produced, appears to arise out of eternity and finally to disappear in it.

2. When the music stops, it still vibrates in the memory. If the *yogī* does not allow his mind to wander to something else, but concentrate on the echo of the music, he will be absorbed in the source of all sound, viz; *parāvāk* and thus will acquire the nature of *Bhairava*.

[Dhāraṇā 19]

VERSE 42

पिण्डमन्त्रस्य सर्वस्य स्थूलवर्णक्रमेण तु ।
अर्धेन्दुबिन्दुनादान्तःशून्योच्चाराद्भवेच्छिवः ॥ ४२ ॥

Piṇḍamantrasya sarvasya sthūlavarṇakrameṇa tu /
Ardhendubindunādāntaḥśūnyoccārād bhavec chivaḥ // 42.

TRANSLATION

By the *uccāra*[1] of all *piṇḍamantras*[2] which are arranged in an order of gross letters and which go on vibrating in subtle forms beginning from *bindu*, *ardhacandra*, *nādānta*, etc. and ending in *śūnya* or *unmanā* one verily becomes *Śiva* or it may mean that by *parāmarśa* or reflection on the *piṇḍamantras* which are arranged in the order of gross letters as *Śūnya* or void up to *samanā*, one attains *unmanā* state i.e. *Śiva*.

NOTES

1. *Uccāra* here does not mean uttering or muttering but moving upward from gross utterance, to subtle *spandana* (vibration) and finally to mental reflection.

2. *Piṇḍamantra* is that in which each letter is separately arranged and in which usually there is a connecting vowel at the end. *Aum̐* is *piṇḍamantra*, *Navātma* or the following mantra consisting of nine letters is a *piṇḍamantra*.

H, R, Kṣ, M, L, V, Y, Ṇ, Ūṁ (ह्, र्, क्ष्, म्, ल्, व्, य्, ण्, ऊँ (णूँ)

3. In a *piṇḍamantra*, there is first the muttering of the gross letters, e.g. *aum̐* (in case of *praṇava*), and 'h' to *ṇūṁ* in case of *navātma mantra*, then reflection on the subtle *spandana* in the form of *bindu*, *ardhacandra*, etc. and finally contemplation on *śūnya* or *unmanā*. When by this process the *yogi*'s mind finally attains to *unmanā*, he becomes identified with *Śiva*.

Taking the *mantra aum̐* for example, Śivopādhyāya in his commentary shows how its recitation points to the mounting of *prāṇaśakti* step by step from the navel upto *dvādaśānta*.

'A' (अ) of *Aum̐* has to be contemplated on in the navel, 'U'(उ) in the heart i.e. the centre, 'm' (म्) in the mouth (or according to some in the palate or roof of the mouth), *bindu* in the centre of the eye-brows, *ardhacandra* in the forehead, *nirodhinī* in the upper part of the forehead, *nāda* in the head, *nādānta* in *Brahmarandhra*, *śakti* in the skin, *vyāpinī* in the root of the *śikhā* (tuft of hair on the top of the head), *samanā* in the *śikhā*, and *unmanā* in the top of the *śikhā*. Beyond this, there is the vast expanse of consciousness which is *Bhairava*. The *yogī* is now identified with *Bhairava*.

In the navel, centre and mouth, a, u, ṃ, are recited in their gross form. The time taken in the recitation of each of these is one *mātrā* or mora (time occupied in uttering one short syllable). From *bindu* upto *samanā*, the time occupied is *ardhamātrā* or half a mora. *Unmanā* is beyond time.

This is *Āṇava upāya* leading to *Śāmbhava state.*

[Dhāraṇā 20]

VERSE 43

निजदेहे सर्वदिक्कं युगपद्भावयेद्वियत् ।
निर्विकल्पमनास्तस्य वियत्सर्वं प्रवर्तते ॥ ४३ ॥

Nijadehe sarvadikkaṃ yugapad bhāvayed viyat /
Nirvikalpamanās tasya viyat sarvam pravartate // 43.

TRANSLATION

If in one's body, one contemplates over *śūnya* (spatial vacuity) in all directions simultaneously (i.e. without succession) without any thought-construct, he experiences vacuity all round (and is identified with the vast expanse of consciousness).

NOTES

Two conditions are laid down for this contemplation, viz. (1) *yugapat* and (2) *nirvikalpamanāḥ*. The contemplation on the void in all directions has to be done simultaneously and the mind has to be stilled completely. If the Yogī succeeds in fulfilling these two conditions, he will attain to the *śūnyātiśūnya* plane, to the plane of absolute void in which all differences and distinctions are totally absent.

This is *Śākta upāya.*

[Dhāraṇā 21]

VERSE 44

पृष्ठशून्यं मूलशून्यं युगपद्भावयेच्च यः ।
शरीरनिरपेक्षिण्या शक्त्या शून्यमना भवेत् ॥ ४४ ॥

Pṛṣṭhaśūnyaṃ[1] mūlaśūnyaṃ yugapad bhāvayec ca yaḥ /
Śarīranirapekṣiṇyā śaktyā[2] śūnyamanā bhavet // 44

TRANSLATION

He who contemplates simultaneously on the void above and the void at the base becomes, with the aid of the energy that is independent of the body, void-minded (i.e. completely free of all *vikalpas* or thought-constructs).

NOTES

1. *Pṛṣṭhaśūnyaṃ* here means the void above.
2. *Śarīranirapekṣiṇyā śaktyā* means with the aid of *prāṇa-śakti.*

This *dhāraṇā* is *Śāktopāya.*

[Dhāraṇā 22]

VERSE 45

पृष्ठशून्यं मूलशून्यं हृच्छून्यं भावयेत्स्थिरम् ।
युगपन्निर्विकल्पत्वान्निर्विकल्पोदयस्ततः ॥ ४५ ॥

Pṛṣṭhaśūnyam mūlaśūnyaṃ hṛcchūnyam bhāvayet sthiram/
Yugapan nirvikalpatvānnirvikalpodayas tataḥ ṭ/ 45.

TRANSLATION

In him who firmly contemplates over the void above, the void at the base and the void in the heart, there arises at the same time, because of his being free of all *vikalpas*, the state of *Śiva* who is above all *vikalpas* (*nirviklpodayaḥ*).

NOTES

In his commentary on the verse 45, Śivopādhyāya says that *pṛṣṭhaśūnyaṃ* suggests that the *yogī* should contemplate over the *pramātā* or the subject as void, *mūlaśūnyaṃ* suggests that he should contemplate over the *prameyas* or objects as void, and *hṛc-chūnyaṃ* suggests that he should contemplate over *pramāṇa* or knowledge as void.

This *dhāraṇā* is also *Śāktopāya.*

[Dhāraṇā 23]

VERSE 46

तनूदेशे शून्यतैव क्षणमात्रं विभावयेत् ।
निर्विकल्पं निर्विकल्पो निर्विकल्पस्वरूपभाक् ॥ ४६ ॥

Tanūdeśe śūnyataiva kṣaṇamātraṁ vibhāvayet /
Nirvikalpaṃ nirvikalpo nirvikalpasvarūpabhāk // 46

TRANSLATION

If a yogi contemplates over his body believed to be the limited empirical subject as void even for a while with an attention freed of all *vikalpas* (thought-constructs), he becomes liberated from *vikalpas* and finally acquires the state of *Bhairava* who is above all *vikalpas*.

NOTES

This verse points to three stages of the *yogī*. Firstly, he contemplates over his body in a *vikalpa*-free way, secondly, by this practice he develops the tendency of being usually free of *vikalpas* (*nirvikalpaḥ*). Lastly, if this tendency is prolonged, he enters the state of *Bhairava* who is above all *vikalpas*, whose very nature is *nirvikalpa* (*nirvikalpasvarūpabhāk*).

This is *Śākta upāya* leading to *Śāmbhava state.*

[Dhāraṇā 24]

VERSE 47

सर्वं देहगतं द्रव्यं वियद्व्याप्तं मृगेक्षणे ।
विभावयेत्ततस्तस्य भावना सा स्थिरा भवेत् ॥ ४७ ॥

Sarvaṃ dehagataṃ dravyaṃ viyadvyāptam mṛgekṣaṇe /
Vibhāvayet tatas tasya bhāvanā sā sthirā bhavet // 47

TRANSLATION

O gazelle-eyed one, (if the aspirant is incapable of śūnyabhāva immediately), let him contemplate over the constituents of his body like bone, flesh, etc. as pervaded with mere vacuity. (After this practice), his *bhāvanā* (contemplation) of vacuity will become steady, (and at last he will experience the light of consciousness).

NOTES

This contemplation is also *Śāktopāya*.

[Dhāraṇā 25]

VERSE 48

देहान्तरे त्वग्विभागं भित्तिभूतं विचिन्तयेत् ।
न किञ्चिदन्तरे तस्य ध्यायन्नध्येयभाग्भवेत् ॥ ४८ ॥

Dehāntare tvagvibhāgam bhittibhūtaṁ vicintayet /
Na kiñcid antare tasya dhyāyann adhyeyabhāg bhavet // 48

TRANSLATION

The yogī should contemplate over the skin-part in his body like (an outer, inconscient) wall. "There is nothing substantial inside it (i.e. the skin)"[1]; meditating like this, he reaches a state which transcends all things meditable.[2]

NOTES

1. Every man is habitually identified with his body. When the *yogī* develops the practice of detaching his consciousness from the limits of the body, he develops a sense of all-pervasiveness.

2. When by the above practice, the *yogī* attains cosmic consciousness, then he experiences *Śiva-Vyāpti;* he is completely identified with *Śiva*. The sense of a separate limited experient disappears. Now there is no object for him to meditate on. The very distinction between subject and object disappears. In the words of *Bhairava* Himself *Evaṃvidhe pare tattve kaḥ pūjyaḥ kaśca tṛpyati* (Verse 16) "When the Highest Reality is realized, who is the object of worship; who is to be satisfied with worship."

This is *Śāktopāya* leading to the state of *Śiva*, leading from *śūnya* (void) to *mahāśūnya* (the vast void).

[Dhāraṇā 26]

VERSE 49

हृद्याकाशे निलीनाक्षः पद्मसम्पुटमध्यगः ।
अनन्यचेताः सुभगे परं सौभाग्यमाप्नुयात् ॥ ४९ ॥

Hṛdyākāśe nilīnākṣaḥ padmasampuṭamadhyagaḥ /
Ananyacetāḥ subhage paraṃ saubhāgyam āpnuyāt // 49.

TRANSLATION

He whose mind together with the other senses is merged in the interior space of the heart,[1] who has entered mentally into the centre of the two bowls of the heartlotus,[2] who has excluded everything else from consciousness[3] acquires the highest fortune[4], O beautiful one.

NOTES

1. The word *hṛt* or heart does not mean the physical heart. It means the central spot in the body above the diaphragm. It is an etheric structure resembling lotus, just as the physical heart resembles a lotus. In the centre of this etheric heart resides *cit* — the consciousness which is always a *pramātā* or subject, never a *prameya* or object. It is this centre which is the essential Self of man and macrocosmically the centre of all manifestation. The word used in the original is *hṛdya* which means both 'pertaining to the heart', and 'pleasant'.

2. The lotus is like two hemispherical bowls blended into one. Śivopādhyāya says in his commentary that the upper bowl of the heart lotus represents *pramāṇa* or knowledge and the lower bowl represents *prameya* or object. The *madhya* or centre of this heart-lotus represents the *pramātā* or knower, the Self. It is in this centre or the Self into which the *yogi* has to plunge mentally.

3. This means who is one-pointed.

4. Śivopādhyāya explains *paraṃ saubhāgyam* (highest fortune) as *viśveśvaratā - svarūpam paramānandam* which means the highest bliss consisting in the lordship of the universe'. Kṣemarāja has quoted this verse in his commentary on *sūtra* 15 of Section I of *Śiva-sūtras.* He also explains *saubhagyaṃ* as *viśvesvaratāpattiḥ* or acquisition of the lordship of the universe. This is *Śāktopāya.*

[Dhāraṇā 27]

VERSE 50

सर्वतः स्वशरीरस्य द्वादशान्ते मनोलयात् ।
दृढबुद्धेर्दृढीभूतं तत्त्वलक्ष्यं प्रवर्तते ॥ ५० ॥

Sarvataḥ svaśarīrasya dvādaśānte manolayāt /
Dṛḍhabuddher dṛḍhībhutaṃ tattvalakṣyam pravartate// 50

TRANSLATION

When the body of the *yogī* is penetrated by consciousness in all parts and his mind which has become firm by one-pointedness (dṛḍhībhūtāṃ) is dissolved in the *dvādaśānta* situated in the body, then that *yogī* whose intellect has become firm experiences the characteristic of Reality.

NOTES

It is not quite clear what exactly is meant by the *dvādaśānta* of the body. In the body the dvādaśāntas (a distance of 12 fingers) are from the navel to the heart, from the heart to the throat, from the throat to the forehead and from the forehead to the top of the cranium. Probably, it refers to *Brahmarandhra*, the *dvādaśānta* from the forehead to the top of the cranium.

Ānandabhaṭṭa says in his commentary *Vijñānakaumudī* that 'dvādaśānta' may mean *śūnyātiśūnya* or the cosmic void or it may mean the *madhya nāḍī* of the body i.e. *suṣumnā.*

The *dhāraṇā* is one of *āṇavopāya* leading to *Śāktopāya.*

[Dhāraṇā 28]

VERSE 51

यथा तथा यत्र तत्र द्वादशान्ते मनः क्षिपेत् ।
प्रतिक्षणं क्षीणवृत्तेर्वैलक्षण्यं दिनैर्भवेत् ॥ ५१ ॥

Yathā tathā yatra tatra dvādaśānte manaḥ kṣipet /
Pratikṣaṇaṃ kṣīṇavṛtter vailakṣaṇyam dinair bhavet // 51

TRANSLATION

If one fixes one's mind at *dvādaśānta*[1] again and again (pratikṣaṇaṃ) howsoever and wheresoever, the fluctuation of his mind will diminish and in a few days, he will acquire an extraordinary status.[2]

NOTES

1. The mind has to be fixed at any *dvādaśānta* from the body whether it is the superior or *ūrdhva dvādaśānta* or *Brahmarandhra* or *bāhya dvādaśānta* i.e. in exterior space at a distance of 12 fingers from the nose, or *āntara dvādaśānta* i. e. the interior dvādaśānta in the centre of the body, etc.

2. Śivopādhyāya explains this as *asāmānyaparabhairava-rūpatā* i.e. the incomparable and ineffable state of Bhairava.

This is *Āṇavopāya*.

[Dhāraṇā 29.]

VERSE 52

कालाग्निना कालपदादुत्थितेन स्वकं पुरम् ।
प्लुष्टं विचिन्तयेदन्ते शान्ताभासस्तदा भवेत् ॥ ५२ ॥

Kālāgninā kālapadād utthitena svakam puraṃ /
Pluṣṭam vicintayed ante śāntābhāsas tadā bhavet // 52.

TRANSLATION

(Uttering the formula *aum ra-kṣa-ra-ya-ūṃ tanuṃ dāhayāmī namaḥ*), one should contemplate in the following way "My body has been burnt by the fire of *kālāgni*[1] rising from the toe of my right foot."[2] He will then experience his (real) nature which is all peace.[3]

1. Kālāgni Rudra is the universal destroyer. The aspirant should imagine that his whole body is being burnt by the flames of Kālāgni Rudra. The idea is that all the impurities that are due to the limitation of the body have to be destroyed by Kālāgni Rudra who destroys all impurities, sins, etc.

2. *Kālapada* is a technical term for the toe of the right foot.

3. By this practice, the aspirant feels that his impurities have been burnt away and thus he experiences his essential Self which is all peace and joy.

This is an *Āṇava upāya*.

[Dhāraṇā 30]

VERSE 53

एवमेव जगत्सर्वं दग्धं ध्यात्वा विकल्पतः ।
अनन्यचेतसः पुंसः पुंभावः परमो भवेत् ॥ ५३ ॥

Evam eva jagat sarvaṃ dagdhaṃ dhyātvā vikalpataḥ /
Ananyacetasaḥ puṃsaḥ pumbhāvaḥ paramo bhavet //53.

TRANSLATION

In this way, if the aspirant imagines that the entire world is being burnt by the fire of *Kālāgni*[1] and does not allow his mind to wander away to anything else, then in such a person, the highest state of man appears.[2]

NOTES

1. In the previous *dhāraṇā*, it was one's own body that had to be imagined as being burnt by *kālāgni*; in the present *dhāraṇā*, it is the entire world that has to be imagined as being burnt by *Kālāgni*.

2. The highest state of man is as Śivopādhyāya puts it in his commentary, *aparimitapramātṛbhairavatā*—'the nature of Bhairava that is the Infinite Subject.' It is this nature that the aspirant will acquire by this *dhāraṇā*.

This *dhāraṇā* is *Śāktopāya*.

[Dhāraṇā 31]

VERSE 54

स्वदेहे जगतो वापि सूक्ष्मसूक्ष्मतराणि च ।
तत्त्वानि यानि निलयं ध्यात्वान्ते व्यज्यते परा ॥ ५४ ॥

Svadehe jagato vāpi sūkṣmasūkṣmatarāṇi ca /
Tattvāni yāni nilayaṃ dhyātvānte vyajyate parā //54

TRANSLATION

If the *yogī* thinks deeply that the subtle and subtler constitutive principles of one's own body or of the world are being absorbed in their own respective causes,[1] then at the end, *parā devī* or the supreme goddess is revealed.[2]

NOTES

1. This verse refers to the technique of *vyāpti* or fusion by which the gross *tattva* (constitutive principle of manifestation) is reabsorbed into the subtle, the subtle into the subtler, the subtler into the subtlest, e.g. the *pañca-mahābhūtas*—the five gross material principles are to be contemplated as being absorbed into the *tanmātrās* (primary subtle elements of perception),) the *tanmātrās* into *ahaṃkāra* (the I or ego-making principle), this into *buddhi*, this again into *prakṛti* and so on till all are finally reabsorbed into *Sadāśiva*. Then *Śakti* or what has been designated as *parā devī* (the supreme goddess) is revealed. This kind of *vyāpti* or fusion which has been described in this verse is known as *ātmavyāpti*.

There is another stage of *vyāpti*, known as *Śivavyāpti* which will be described in verse 57.

2. At the appearance of *parā devī*, the entire cosmos appears as nothing but the expression of that universal Divine Energy. Everything is surrendered unto Her and the sense of difference disappears.

This verse refers to *Śāktopāya*.

[Dhāraṇā 32]

VERSE 55

पीनां च दुर्बलां शक्तिं ध्यात्वा द्वादशगोचरे ।
प्रविश्य हृदये ध्यायन् मुक्तः स्वातन्त्र्यमाप्नुयात् ॥ ५५ ॥

Pīnāṃ ca durbalāṃ śaktiṃ dhyātvā dvādaśagocare /
Praviśya hṛdaye dhyāyanmuktaḥ svātantryam āpnuyāt //55

TRANSLATION

If *prāṇaśakti* which is gross and thick, is made frail and subtle (by *yogic* discipline, particularly *prāṇāyāma*) and if a *yogī* meditates on such *śakti* either in *dvādaśānta* or in the heart (i.e. the centre of the body) by entering mentally into it, he is liberated and he gains his (natural) sovereign power.

NOTES

The reading of the last line as given by Abhinavagupta in Tantrāloka (Ā XV, verses 480-81) is different. It is *suptaḥ svācchandyam āpnuyāt*. Kṣemarāja reads the last line in Spandanirṇaya (p. 56) as *svapnasvātantryam āpnuyāt* which is practically the same as Abhinavagupta's.

According to Svāmi Laksmaṇa Joo, the traditional interpretation of this verse is the following:

Pīnām indicates that the breath has to be inhaled or exhaled in a gross way i. e. with sound and *durbalām* indicates that the inhalation or exhalation has to be done slowly. According to the above reading the meaning of the verse would be "If the *yogī* practises breathing (both inhalation and exhalation) with sound and slowly meditating in *dvādaśānta* and in the heart (centre), goes to sleep, he will acquire the freedom to control his dream i.e. he will have only the dream that he desires to have."

This is *Āṇava upāya* leading to *Śāmbhava* state.

[Dhāraṇā 33]

VERSE 56

भुवनाध्वादिरूपेण चिन्तयेत्क्रमशोऽखिलम् ।
स्थूलसूक्ष्मपरस्थित्या यावदन्ते मनोलयः ॥ ५६ ॥

Bhuvanādhvādirupeṇa cintayet kramaśo'khilam /
Sthūlasūkṣmaparasthityā yāvadante manolayaḥ //56.

TRANSLATION

One should contemplate step by step on the whole universe under the form of *bhuvana* and other *adhvas*[1] (courses) as being dissolved successively from the gross state into the subtle and from the subtle state into the supreme state till finally one's mind is dissolved in *Cinmātra* (pure consciousness).[2]

NOTES

1. According to Trika philosophy the whole universe consisting of subjective and objective aspects is a proliferation of the *svātantrya śākti* or *parāvāk* under six forms known as *ṣaḍadhvā* which means six routes or courses (ṣaṭ=six) *adhvā* =route, course). Three of them are under the *vācaka* (indicator) side which is the subjective or *grāhaka* aspect of manifestation ; the other three are under the *vācya*, the indicated or objective side.

At the level of *parāvāk*, *vācaka* and *vācya*, *śabda* and *artha*, word and object are in a state of indistinguishable unity. In manifestation, these begin to differentiate. The first *adhvā* or step of this differentiation is the polarity of *varṇa* and *kalā*. *Varṇa* at this stage, does not mean letter, or colour, or class. It means a measure index of the function-form associated with the object, and *kalā* means an aspect of creativity. *Varṇa* is the function-form and *kalā* is predicable. This is the first *adhvā* of the polarisation of *parāvāk*. This *adhvā* is known as *para* (supreme) or *abheda*, for at this stage, there is no difference between *varṇa* or *kalā*, the creative aspect.

The next *adhvā* or step in the creative descent is the polarity of *mantra* and *tattva*. This level of creativity is known as *parāpara* or *bhedābheda* (identity in difference) or *sūkṣma* (subtle). *Mantra* is the basic formula of *tattva* : *tattva* is the principle or source and origin of the subtle structural forms.

The third and final polarity is that of *pada* and *bhuvana*. This level of manifestation is known as that of *apara* (inferior) or *bheda* (total difference between the *vācaka* and *vācya*) or *sthūla* (gross). *Bhuvana* is the universe as it appears to apprehending centres like ourselves. *Pada* is the actual formulation of that universe by mind reaction and speech.

The *trika* or triad on the *vācaka* side is known as *kālādhvā* i.e. of temporal order, and the *trika* or triad on *vācya* side is known as *deśādhvā* or of spatial order.

The *ṣaḍadhvā* may be arranged in the following tabular form :—

	VĀCAKA OR ŚABDA	*VĀCYA OR ARTHA*
	The subjective order; the temporal order, phonematic manifestation.	The objective order; the spatial order; cosmogonic manifestation.
Para or *abheda* level.	Varṇa	kalā
Parāpara or bhedābheda or sūkṣma level.	Mantra	tattva
Apara or *bheda* or *sthūla* level.	pada	bhuvana

Of these, each preceding *adhvā* is *vyāpaka* i.e., pervasive, inhering (in the succeeding one) and each succeeding *adhvā* is *vyāpya* i.e. capable of being pervaded by the preceding one. So there is *vyāpyavyāpaka* relationship among these.

2. The *dhāraṇā* or the yogic practice recommended here is that the *yogī* should practise the *bhāvanā* or imaginative contemplation of the succeeding gross (*sthūla*) *adhvā* being dissolved in the preceding subtle (*sūkṣma*) *adhvā*. The gross (*sthūla*) manifestation, viz., *pada* and *bhuvana* should be earnestly imagined as being dissolved in their preceding subtle (*sūkṣma*) origins, viz., *mantra* and *tattva*; *mantra* and *tattva*, the subtle *adhvā*, should in turn, be earnestly imagined as being dissolved in their preceding supreme (*para*) origin *varṇa* and *kalā*. Finally these should be imagined as being dissolved in *parāvāka* or *parāśakti*, and *parāvāk* in *Śiva* i.e. *cinmātra* or *vijñāna* (pure consciousness) which alone is *Bhairava* or the ultimate Divine principle.

Kramaśaḥ in the verse means step by step, i.e. the first step should consist of the practice of the *bhāvanā* of the *sthūla* or gross manifestation being dissolved into the subtle (*sūkṣma*) one. When by sufficient practice of this *bhāvanā*, the *yogī* is fully convinced that this solid seeming world (*bhuvana*) and gross speech (*pada*) are only an appearance of a much subtler process of *mantra* and *tattva*, he should take the next step which would consist of the *bhāvanā* of the subtle (*sūkṣma*) *mantra* and *tattva* as being dissolved into the supreme (*para*) aspects of *varṇa*, *kalā*, and so on.

When the *yogī* has sufficiently practised the *bhāvanā* of the dissolution of the entire manifestation into *cit* or *vijñāna*, he will attain to the plane of *Bhairava* and his *manas* or *citta* will be automatically dissolved into *cit* (pure consciousness). This is known as *laya bhāvanā* (creative contemplation pertaining to dissolution). This ascent to the Divine is known as *āroha* or *adhyāroha krama*, the process of ascent. The 13th *sūtra* of *Pratyabhijñāhṛdayam* expressly says that *citta* finally becomes *citi*. This is known as *cittapralaya* or the dissolution of the empirical individual mind into the Divine.

The difference between this *dhāraṇā* and *dhāraṇā* No. 30 in verse 54 consists in the fact that the *dhāraṇā* described in verse 54 leads the *yogī* only upto the subtle *śakti* where *parā devī* reveals Herself, but this leads the *yogī* upto the utmost plane of Śiva where the individual mind completely dissolves into the universal consciousness. In verse 54, the aim was the realization of the Supreme Power that is the source of the gross manifestation of the universe. In verse 56, the emphasis is on the transformation of the individual consciousness by its dissolution into the universal Divine Consciousness (*Manolaya* or *cittapralaya*). So, this is *Śāktopāya* leading to *Śāmbhava* state.

[Dhāraṇā 34]

VERSE 57

अस्य सर्वस्य विश्वस्य पर्यन्तेषु समन्ततः ।
अध्वप्रक्रियया तत्त्वं शैवं ध्यात्वा महोदयः ॥ ५७ ॥

Asya sarvasya viśvasya paryanteṣu samantataḥ /
Adhvaprakriyayā tattvaṃ śaivaṃ dhyātvā mahodayaḥ //57

TRANSLATION

If one meditates on the *Śaiva* tattva[1] (which is the quintessence) of this entire universe on all sides and to its last limits by the technique of ṣaḍadhvā[2] he will experience great awakening.[3]

NOTES

1. *Śiva* is both *prakāśa* and *vimarśa,* both the light of Consciousness and the consciousness or awareness of that consciousness. *Śaiva tattva* is the *svarūpa* or essential nature of *Śiva.* Meditating on *Śaiva tattva* means meditating on the *svarūpa* (own form, essential nature) of *Śiva* who is both *prakāśa* and *vimarśa.*

2. The *ṣaḍadhvā* has two sides— *Vācaka* and *vācya.* The *vācaka* side—*varṇa, mantra* and *pada* are an expression of *prakāśa,* the *vācya* side—*kalā tattva*, and *bhuvana* are an expression of *vimarśa.*

In the previous *dhāraṇā* No. 32 in verse 56, the technique of the *ṣaḍadhvā* was used for tracing back the entire universe of subjects and objects to its source, the Central Reality. Here the technique of *ṣaḍadhvā* is to be used for realizing the *svarūpa* or essential nature of this Central Reality. The technique of *ṣaḍadhvā* is incomplete if it simply ends in re-integrating the universe to its source. It has still to realize the *śaiva tattva,* the nature of the Central Reality which is both *prakāśa* and *vimarśa* in one and the source of both the *vācaka* and *vācya* of the *ṣaḍadhvā.*

Again in *dhāraṇā* No. 30 (verse 54), the technique of tracing back the constitutive principles was used for *ātmavyāpti,* for the fusion of manifestation into the essential Self which, according to the Trika system, is a lower ideal. *Ātmavyāpti* emphasizes *prakāśa* which does not necessarily include the universe. In verse 57, the ideal of realization that is emphasized is *Śiva-vyāpti,* fusion into Śiva who is both *prakāśa* and *vimarśa.* It is the Reality that is inclusive of the universe. In this realization, the universe is not negated but seen *sub specie eternitatis*, under the form of the Eternal, as an expression of the *vimarśa* aspect of *Śiva*.

3. This great awakening is the realization of the *svarūpa* or essential nature of *Śiva* who is both *prakāśa* and *vimarśa*.

The difference between the previous *dhāraṇā* (in verse 56) and this one (verse 57) lies in the fact that in the previous *dhāraṇā* the dissolution of both the objective and subjective order was to be contemplated one by one successively (*kramaśaḥ*) i.e. first the dissolution of the gross into the subtle, and then of the subtle into the supreme, whereas in the present *dhāraṇā* (verse 57) the dissolution of the entire world (*asya sarvasya viśvasya*) has to be contemplated simultaneously and integrally into *Śiva tattva*. As Śivopādhyāya puts it, *Bhuvanādiadhvaparyanteṣu jagataḥ Śivāt vinā na kiñcit iti jagad rūpam tyaktvā, śivameva dhyāyato mahodayaḥ syāt*. The reality of this world is nothing apart from Śiva. Therefore this world should be viewed not as the world (i.e. as something different from *Śiva*) but as the modality of *Śiva*. Therefore it is *Śiva* alone who has to be contemplated on. Thus there will be *mahodaya* i.e. great spiritual Awakening. This *dhāraṇā* is *Śāktopāya*.

[Dhāraṇā 35]

VERSE 58

विश्वमेतन्महादेवि शून्यभूतं विचिन्तयेत् ।
तत्रैव च मनो लीनं ततस्तल्लयभाजनम् ॥ ५८ ॥

Viśvam etan mahādevi śūnyabhūtaṃ vicintayet /
Tatraiva ca mano līnaṁ tatas tallayabhājanam //58

TRANSLATION

O great goddess, the *yogī* should concentrate intensely on the idea that this universe is totally void. In that void, his mind would become absorbed. Then he becomes highly qualified for absorption i.e. his mind is absorbed in *śūnyātiśūnya*, the absolute void i.e. *Śiva*.

NOTES

This *dhāraṇā* is the first of a number of *dhāraṇās* on *śūnya* (void) which will come later on in the book. This is *Śāktopāya* leading to *Śāmbhava* state.

[Dhāraṇā 36]

VERSE 59

घटादिभाजने दृष्टिं भित्तीस्त्यक्त्वा विनिक्षिपेत् ।
तल्लयं तत्क्षणाद्गत्वा तल्लयात्तन्मयो भवेत् ॥ ५९ ॥

Ghaṭādibhājane dṛṣṭim bhittīs tyaktvā vinikṣipet /
Tallayaṃ tatkṣaṇād gatvā tallayāt tanmayo bhavet //59

TRANSLATION

A *yogī* should cast his eyes in the empty space inside a jar or any other object leaving aside the enclosing partitions. His mind will in an instant get absorbed in the empty space (inside the jar) When his mind is absorbed in that empty space, he should imagine that his mind is absorbed in a total void. He will then realize his identification with the Supreme.

NOTES

Casting one's gaze into the empty space inside a jar is a device for preparing the mind for getting absorbed in total void. When the mind is absorbed in the empty space of the jar, the aspirant should imagine that the empty space has extended into a total void. Thus his mind will be absorbed in the absolute void i.e. *Śiva*.

This is *Śāmbhava upāya*.

[Dhāraṇā 37]

VERSE 60

निर्वृक्षगिरिभित्त्यादि-देशे दृष्टिं विनिक्षिपेत् ।
विलीने मानसे भावे वृत्तिक्षीणः प्रजायते ॥ ६० ॥

Nirvṛkṣagiribhittyādideśe dṛṣṭiṃ vinikṣipet /
Vilīne mānase bhāve Vṛttikṣīṇaḥ prajāyate //60

TRANSLATION

One should cast his gaze on a region in which there are no trees, on mountain, on high defensive wall[1] His mental state being without any support will then dissolve and the fluctuations of his mind will cease.[2]

NOTES

1. The idea is that when the mind dwells on a vast vacant space, then being without the support of any definite concrete object, the mind gets absorbed in that void.

2. When the mind is absorbed in a vast open space, its *vikalpas* or thought-constructs come to a dead stop. That is the moment when the Light within makes its presence felt and the aspirant realizes that there is a deeper Reality than what is open to the senses.

Abhinavagupta quotes the first line of this verse in his Parātriṃśikā (on p. 136) and confirms that, in such a moment, there is *Bhairavabodhānupraveśa* (entry into Bhairava-consciousness).

This type of fixed gaze into vast vacant space without any thought-construct or objective support for the mind is known as *dṛṣṭibandhanabhāvanā*. As there is neither meditation nor *japa* (recitation of *mantra*), nor any meditation involved in this *dhāraṇā*, this is *Śāmbhava upāya*.

[Dhāraṇā 38]

VERSE 61

उभयोर्भावयोर्ज्ञाने ध्यात्वा मध्यं समाश्रयेत् ।
युगपच्च द्वयं त्यक्त्वा मध्ये तत्त्वं प्रकाशते ॥ ६१ ॥

Ubhayor bhāvayor jñāne dhyātvā madhyaṃ samāśrayet /
Yugapac ca dvayaṁ tyaktvā madhye tattvam prakāśate //61

TRANSLATION

At the moment when one has perception or knowledge of two objects or ideas, one should simultaneously banish both perceptions or ideas and apprehending the gap or interval between the two, should mentally stick to it (i.e. the gap). In that gap will Reality flash forth suddenly.

NOTES

The reading *jñātvā* instead of *dhyātvā* has been adopted by Jayaratha in Tantrāloka I, p. 127. This reading gives better sense.

The above is *Śākta upāya.* Our mind is always caught up in perceptions or ideas. We are prisoners of our own ideas. Behind all the activities of the mind lies Reality which gives life to our mental activity. That Reality cannot be viewed as an object, for it is the Eternal Subject and ground of all experience. If we do not allow our mind to be carried away by the perceptions or ideas succeeding each other incessantly but rather let our mind dip in the gap between the two perceptions or ideas without thinking of any thing, we will, to our surprise, be bathed in that Reality which can never be an object of thought.

This is known as *nirālamba bhāvanā* or creative contemplation without any object as support for the mind. This verse has been quoted as an example of *nirālamba bhāvanā* in Netra Tantra (pt.I.p.201). This is also *Śūnya bhāvanā*—an example of the mind sounding its plummet in the depth of the void.

The sudden flash of Reality by this practice has been designated *unmeṣa* or opening out in *Spanda-Kārikā.* Abandonment of the two perceptions or ideas that precede and succeed the gap is known as *anālocana* or non-observation. The two ideas have not to be pushed aside by effort but have to be abandoned by a smooth, gentle non-observation. This is a very important and unfailing *dhāraṇā* for the grasp of Reality or nature of Bhairava.

[Dhāraṇā 39]

VERSE 62

भावे त्यक्ते निरुद्धा चिन् नैव भावान्तरं व्रजेत् ।
तदा तन्मध्यभावेन विकसत्यति-भावना ॥ ६२ ॥

Bhāve' tyakte niruddhā cin naiva bhāvāntaraṃ vrajet /
Tadā tanmadhyabhāvena vikasatyati bhāvanā //62

TRANSLATION

When the mind of the aspirant that comes to quit one object is firmly restrained (*niruddha*) and does not move towards any other object, it comes to rest in a middle position between the two and through it (i.e. the middle position) is unfolded intensely the realization of pure consciousness in all its intensity.

NOTES

The previous *dhāraṇā* advises the aspirant to reject two positive objects, perceptions or thoughts (*ubhayor bhāvayoḥ*) and contemplate on the middle i.e. the gap between the two. In the present *dhāraṇā*, the aspirant is advised to contemplate on the middle or gap between one positive *bhāva* or object and another negative *bhāva* i.e. another *bhāva* which the aspirant has not allowed to arise in the mind. This is the main difference between the two *dhāraṇās*. The result is the same, viz.; the emergence of the essential Self or the nature of *Bhairava*.

Abhinavagupta refers to this in verse No. 84 in Tantrāloka pt. I

आत्मैव धर्मः इत्युक्तः शिवामृतपरिप्लुतः ।
प्रकाशावस्थितं ज्ञानं भावाभावादिमध्यतः ॥

It is *ātmā* (self) alone who is the essential nature, full of the ambrosia of *Śiva*. The knowledge that one derives by contemplation on the middle between two objects or between one positive and another negative object abides in the light of the self.

The following commentary of Jayaratha leaves no room for doubt that the above verse of Abhinavagupta refers to the two *dhāraṇās* mentioned in Verse No. 61 and 62 of Vijñānabhairava.

"भावद्वयस्य भावाभावयोर्वा प्रतीतिकाले मध्यं तद्द्वयावच्छेदहेतुं शून्यमुपलभ्य तद्भावाभावादि युगपत्त्यक्त्वा तत्रैव सावधानस्य परमोपेये शिवामृतपरिप्लुते परमात्मनि वृत्तिर्जायते इति" ॥

"The middle state i.e. the gap between two positive objects or between one positive and another negative object is *śūnya* or void which is the ground of the determination of both. In him who apprehends that void and abandoning simultaneously both positive perceptions or positive and negative perceptions fixes his attention on that alone arises that stability in the Highest Self (*paramātmani*) who is the highest objective and who is full of the ambrosia of *Śiva.* In confirmation of the above explanation Jayaratha quotes the verses 61 and 62 of Vijñānabhairava.

Like the previous one, this *dhāraṇā* is also *Śāktopāya.*

The reading adopted by the text printed in the Kashmir Series is *bhāve nyakte*, which means 'when the mind is fixed on an object which was never seen previously like *Śiva* with three eyes, *Viṣṇu* with four arms'. *Bhāve tyakte* is, however, a better and more authentic reading as is evident from Jayaratha's commentary quoted above.

[Dhāraṇā 40]

VERSE 63

सर्वं देहं चिन्मयं हि जगद्वा परिभावयेत् ।
युगपन्निर्विकल्पेन मनसा परमोदयः ॥ ६३ ॥

Sarvaṃ dehaṃ cinmayaṃ hi jagad vā paribhāvayet /
Yugapan nirvikalpena manasā paramodayaḥ //63.

TRANSLATION

When an aspirant contemplates with mind unwavering and free from all alternatives his whole body or the entire universe simultaneously as of the nature of consciousness, he experiences Supreme Awakening.

NOTES

There are two important conditions in this contemplation. Firstly, it should be done *nirvikalpena manasā*, with an unhesitating, unwavering mind free from all doubts and alternatives. Secondly, it should be yugapat i.e. simultaneously, in one sweep, not in succession, not in bits.

Paramodayaḥ or the Supreme Awakening referred to means that he realizes that the entire universe is enveloped in Divine Light.

This is a *Śākta upāya.*

[Dhāraṇā 41]

VERSE 64

वायुद्वयस्य संघट्टादन्तर्वा बहिरन्ततः ।
योगी समत्वविज्ञानसमुद्गमनभाजनम् ॥ ६४ ॥

Vāyudvayasya saṃghaṭṭād antarvā bahir antataḥ /
Yogī samatvavijñānasamudgamanabhājanam // 64

TRANSLATION

By the fusion (*saṃghaṭṭa*) of the two breaths, viz., *prāṇa* (expiration) rising inwardly in the centre and *apāna* (inspiration) rising externally in *dvādaśānta*, there arises finally a condition in which there is complete cessation of both whether in the centre or in the *dvādaśānta*. By meditating over that condition of void in which there is no feeling of either *prāṇa* or *apāna*, the *yogī* becomes so competent that there arises in him the intuitive experience of Equality (*samatva-vijñāna-samudgamana*)

NOTES

This is an *Āṇava upāya* leading to *Śāktopāya.*

[Dhāraṇā 42]

VERSE 65

सर्वं जगत्स्वदेहं वा स्वानन्दभरितं स्मरेत् ।
युगपत्स्वामृतेनैव परानन्दमयो भवेत् ॥ ६५ ॥

Sarvaṃ jagat svadehaṃ vā svānandabharitaṃ smaret /
Yugapat svāmṛtenaiva parānandamayo bhavet // 65.

TRANSLATION

The *yogī* should contemplate the entire universe or his own body simultaneously[1] in its totality as filled with his (essential, spiritual) bliss.[2] Then through his own ambrosia-like bliss,[3] he will become identified with the supreme bliss.

NOTES

1. Simultaneously (*yugapat*) means 'with totality of attention,' in one sweep of attention, not in bits.

2. 'His own bliss' means 'his own essential spiritual or divine bliss' (*cidānanda*), not the pleasure derived from sense-objects.

3. The word *mṛtena* or ambrosia points to the fact that there is no change in this bliss. It is eternal.

Kṣemarāja has quoted this verse in Śiva-Sūtra vimarśinī at two places, in I, 18, and III, 39.

According to Svāmī Lakṣmaṇa Joo, the word 'vā' occurring in this verse should not be taken in the sense 'or' but in the sense of 'ca' i.e. 'and' (*samuccaya*). So the first line of the verse would mean 'The yogi should contemplate the entire universe and his body simultaneously in totality as filled with his spiritual bliss'.

This *dhāraṇā* is also *Śāktopāya.*

[Dhāraṇā 43]

VERSE 66

कुहनेन प्रयोगेण सद्य एव मृगेक्षणे ।
समुदेति महानन्दो येन तत्त्वं प्रकाशते ॥ ६६ ॥

Kuhanena prayogeṇa sadya eva mṛgekṣaṇe /
Samudeti mahānando yena tattvaṃ prakāśate // 66.

TRANSLATION

O gazzelle-eyed one, by the employment of magic, supreme delight arises (in the heart of the spectator) instantaneously. (In this condition of the mind), Reality manifests itself.

NOTES

When a spectator beholds some wonderful magical performance, his ordinary normal consciousness is raised to a plane where there is no distinction between subject and object, where it is freed of all thought-constructs and is filled with reverential awe, with mute wonder and ineffable joy. At that plane of consciousness is revealed the essential nature of *Bhairava*. This is only one example. When by contemplating on any scene—vast, awe-inspiring, deeply moving, the mind is thrown into ecstasy and mute wonder, it passes into *nirvikalpa* state, then that is the moment when suddenly and instantaneously Supreme Reality reveals itself.

This is an example of *Śākta upāya*.

According to Svāmī Lakṣmaṇa Joo, this verse can have another meaning also. The word 'kuhana' also means 'tickling the arm-pit'. So the verse would mean, "O gazelle-eyed one, by tickling the arm-pit, there occurs instantaneously a great joy. If one contemplates over the essential nature of joy, Reality manifests itself."

[Dhāraṇā 44]

VERSE 67

सर्वंस्त्रोतोनिबन्धन प्राणशक्त्योर्ध्वया शनैः ।
पिपीलस्पर्शवेलायां प्रथते परमं सुखम् ॥ ६७ ॥

Sarvasrotonibandhena prāṇaśaktyordhvayā śanaiḥ /
Pipīlasparśavelāyāṃ prathate paramaṃ sukham // 67

TRANSLATION

When by stopping the opening of all the senses the current of all sensory activity is stopped, the *prāṇaśakti* moves slowly upward (in the middle *nāḍī* or *suṣumnā* from *mūlādhāra* towards *Brahmarandhra*), then in the upward movement of *prāṇaśakti*, there is felt a tingling sensation (at the various stations in the middle *nāḍī*) like the one created by the movement of an ant (over the body). At the moment of that sensation, there ensues supreme delight.

NOTES

The main point in this *dhāraṇā* is that when *prāṇaśakti* moves upward, there is the awakening of *Kuṇḍalinī* which moves upward towards *dvādaśānta* i.e. towards *Brahmarandhra*. This slow and gradual movement of *prāṇaśakti* or of *kuṇḍalinī* gives a sensation like that of the movement of an ant over the body. This sensation at the time of the ant-like movement of *prāṇaśakti* is very pleasant.

Śivopādhyāya says that the upward movement of *prāṇaśakti* can be achieved by *kumbhaka prāṇāyāma*. He quotes Patañjali's *Yoga-sūtras* (II,49-50) which say that *prāṇa* can be made *dīrgha-sūkṣma* (prolonged and subtle) by *kumbhaka prāṇāyāma* (restraint of breath). This would be *āṇava upāya*. But Patañjali does not refer to Kuṇḍalinī yoga. Śivopādhyā's quotation from Patañjali in this context is irrelevant.

What the *dhāraṇā* actually means to say is that when the openings of all the senses are stopped and the mind is kept free of all thought-constructs (*nirvikalpa*) the *prāṇaśakti*, becomes active in the *suṣumnā*, and as the *kuṇḍalinī* rises slowly towards *Brahmarandhra*, one feels like the sensation of an ant creeping over the body. At that time, the *yogī* experiences the movement of *kuṇḍalinī* from one station to another and is overjoyed.

[Dhāraṇā 45]

VERSE 68

वह्नेर्विषस्य मध्ये तु चित्तं सुखमयं क्षिपेत् ।
केवलं वायुपूर्णं वा स्मरानन्देन युज्यते ॥ ६८ ॥

Vahner viṣasya madhye tu cittaṃ sukhamayaṃ kṣipet /
Kevalaṃ vāyupūrṇaṃ vā smarānandena yujyate // 68

TRANSLATION

One should throw (i.e. concentrate) the delightful *citta* in the middle of *vahni* and *viṣa* bothways whether by itself or permeated by *vāyu* (*prāṇic breath*), one would then be joined to the bliss of sexual union.

NOTES

Vahni and *viṣa* are technical terms of this *yoga*. *Vahni* stands for *saṅkoca* (contraction) by the entrance of *prāṇa* (in *meḍhrakanda* which is near the root of the rectum), *Viṣa* connotes *vikāsa* or expansion. *Vahni* refers to *adhaḥ kuṇḍalinī*, and *viṣa* to *ūrdhvakuṇḍalinī*. *Ūrdhva kuṇḍalinī* is the condition when the *prāṇa* and *apāna* enter the *suṣumnā* and the *kuṇḍalinī* rises up. *Kuṇḍalinī* is a distinct *śakti* that lies folded up in three and a half *valayas* or folds in *Mūlādhāra*. When she rises from one-three-fourths of the folds, goes up through *suṣumnā*, crosses *Lambika* and pierces *Brahmarandhra*, she is known as *Ūrdhva kuṇḍalinī*, and this pervasion of hers is known as *vikāsa* or *viṣa*.

Adhaḥ kuṇḍalinī—Its field is from *Lambika* down to one-three-fourth of the folds of *kuṇḍalinī* lying folded in the *mūlādhāra*. Prāṇa goes down in *adhaḥ kuṇḍalinī* from *Lambika* towards *mūlādhāra*.

The entrance of *prāṇa* into *adhaḥ kuṇḍalinī* is *saṅkoca* or *vahni;* rising into *ūrdhva kuṇḍalinī* is *vikāsa* or *viṣa*. *Vahnī* is symbolic of *prāṇa vāyu* and *viṣa* of *apāna vāyu*. Entering into the root, middle and tip of *adhaḥ kuṇḍalinī* is known as *vahni* or *saṅkoca*. *Vahni* is derived from the root *vah*—to carry. Since *prāṇa* is carried down up to *mūlādhāra* in this state, it is called *vahni*.

The word *viṣa* does not mean poison here. It is derived from the root *viṣ* 'to pervade.' *Viṣa*, therefore, refers to *prasara* or *vikāsa* (expansion).

When the *prāṇa* and *apāna* enter the *suṣumnā*, the *citta* or the individual consciousness should be stopped or suspended between the *vahni* and *viṣa* or in other words between the *adhaḥ kuṇḍalinī* and the *ūrdhva kuṇḍalinī*.

Vāyupūrṇa or full of *vāyu* means that the *citta* should be restrained in such a way that *vāyu* may neither pass out through the nostrils nor through the male organ and the anus. *Citta* and *vāyu* are inter-connected. Restraint of the one brings about the restraint of the other.

Smarānanda or bliss of sexual union : When the *citta* can be restrained between the *adhaḥ* and *ūrdhva kuṇḍalinī*, one has the joy of sexual union. This is inverted union. Sexual union is external; this union is internal.

This *dhāraṇā* is *Āṇava upāya*.

[Dhāraṇā 46]

VERSE 69

शक्तिसङ्गमसंक्षुब्ध-शक्त्यावेशावसानिकम् ।
यत्सुखं ब्रह्मतत्त्वस्य तत्सुखं स्वाक्यमुच्यते ॥ ६९ ॥

Śaktisaṅgamasaṃkṣubdhaśaktyāveśāvasānikam /
Yat sukham brahmatattvasya tat sukhaṃ svākyam ucyate // 69

TRANSLATION

At the time of sexual intercourse with a woman, an absorption into her[1] is brought about by excitement, and the final delight that ensues at orgasm betokens the delight of Brahman. This delight is (in reality) that of one's own Self.

NOTES

1. This absorption is only symbolic of the absorption in the Divine Energy. This illustration has been given only to show that the highest delight ensues only at the disappearance of duality. Sivopādhyāya quotes a verse which clarifies the esoteric meaning of this union.

जायया संपरिष्वक्तो न बाह्यं वेद नान्तरम् ।
निदर्शनं श्रुतिः प्राह मूर्खस्तं मन्यते विधिम् ॥

"Just as being locked in embrace with a woman, one is totally dissolved in the feeling of one-ness (unity) and one loses all sense of anything external or internal, even so when the mind is dissolved in the Divine Energy, one loses all sense of duality and experiences the delight of unity-consciousness. The *Śruti* (scripture) speaks of the union with a woman only to illustrate the union with the Divine. It is only a fool who takes this illustration as an injunction for carnal pleasure.

2. The delight is that of one's own Self. It does not come from any external source. The woman is only an occasion for the manifestation of that delight.

This *dhāraṇā* is *Śāktopāya.*

[Dhāraṇā 47]

VERSE 70

लेहनामन्थनाकोटैः स्त्रीसुखस्य भरात्स्मृतेः ।
शक्त्यभावेऽपि देवेशि भवेदानन्दसंप्लवः ॥ ७० ॥

Lehanāmanthanākoṭaiḥ strīsukhasya bharāt smṛteḥ /
Śaktyabhāve'pi deveśi bhaved ānandasamplavaḥ // 70

TRANSLATION

O goddess, even in the absence of a woman, there is a flood of delight, simply by the intensity of the memory of sexual pleasure in the form of kissing, embracing, pressing, etc.

NOTES

Since the sexual pleasure is obtained simply by memory even in the absence of a woman, it is evident that the delight is inherent within. It is this delight apart from any woman that one should meditate on in order to realize the bliss of the divine consciousness.

This *dhāraṇā* is *Śāktopāya.*

[Dhāraṇā 48]

VERSE 71

आनन्दे महति प्राप्ते दृष्टे वा बान्धवे चिरात् ।
आनन्दमुद्गतं ध्यात्वा तल्लयस्तन्मना भवेत् ॥ ७१ ॥

Ānande mahati prāpte dṛṣṭe vā bāndhave cirāt /
Ānandam udgataṃ dhyātvā tallayas tanmanā bhavet // 71

TRANSLATION

On the occasion of a great delight being obtained, or on the occasion of delight arising from seeing a friend or relative after a long time, one should meditate on the delight itself and become absorbed in it, then his mind will become identified with it.

NOTES

On the occasion of such great delight or intensive experience, one should lay hold of the source of such experience, viz, the *spanda* or the pure spiritual throb and meditate on it till his mind is deeply steeped in it. He will then become identified with the Spiritual Principle. Such an experience vanishes quickly, therefore, one should seize it mentally as soon as the experience occurs.

This *dhāraṇā* is *Śāktopāya.*

[Dhāraṇā 49]

VERSE 72

जग्धिपानकृतोल्लास-रसानन्दविजृम्भणात् ।
भावयेद्भरितावस्थां महानन्दस्ततो भवेत् ।। ७२ ।।

Jagdhipānakṛtollāsarasānandavijṛmbhaṇāt /
Bhāvayed bharitāvasthām mahānandas tato bhavet // 72

TRANSLATION

When one experiences the expansion of joy of savour arising from the pleasure of eating and drinking, one should meditate on the perfect condition of this joy, then there will be supreme delight.

NOTES

If the *yogī* meditates on the perfect condition of the joy that arises even from the satisfaction of physical needs, he will feel that the source of this joy is also the divine *spanda*, and being absorbed in it, he will experience supreme spiritual bliss.

This *dhāraṇā* is also *Śāktopāya*.

[Dhāraṇā 50]

VERSE 73

गीतादिविषयास्वादा-समसौख्यैकतात्मनः ।
योगिनस्तन्मयत्वेन मनोरूढेस्तदात्मता ॥ ७३ ॥

Gītādiviṣayāsvādāsamasaukhyaikatātmanaḥ /
Yoginas tanmayatvena manorūḍhes tadātmatā // 73

TRANSLATION

When the *yogī* mentally becomes one with the incomparable joy of song and other objects, then of such a *yogī*, there is, because of the expansion of his mind, identity with that (i.e. with the incomparable joy) because he becomes one with it.

NOTES

In verses 69-73, Bhairava says that one can turn even a sensuous joy into a means of *yoga*. In the above verses examples of all sorts of sensuous joy have been given. Joy of sexual intercourse is an example of the pleasure of *sparśa* (contact); joy at the sight of a friend is an example of the pleasure of *rūpa* (visual perception); joy of delicious food is an example of *rasa* (taste); joy derived from song is an example of the pleasure of sound (*śabda*).

In each of these, the emphasis is on the meditation of the source of the joy which is spiritual. Leaving aside the various sensuous media, the aspirant should meditate on that fountain of all joy which only trickles in small drops in all the joys of life.

In verses 69-72, the examples given are only those of physical delight. In verses 73, the main example is of aesthetic rapture that one feels in listening to a melodious song. According to *Śaiva* aesthetics, there can be aesthetic rapture only when the person experiencing that rapture has *samid-viśrānti* i.e. when his mind is withdrawn from everything around him and reposes in his essential Self. Aesthetic delight is, therefore, a greater source of the experience of the spiritual Self.

This is *Śāktopāya* leading to *Śāmbhava* state.

[Dhāraṇā 51]

VERSE 74

यत्र यत्र मनस्तुष्टिर्मनस्तत्रैव धारयेत् ।
तत्र तत्र परानन्दस्वरूपं सम्प्रवर्तते ॥ ७४ ॥

Yatra yatra manas tuṣṭir manas tatraiva dhārayet /
Tatra tatra parānandasvarūpaṃ sampravartate // 74

TRANSLATION

Wherever the mind of the individual finds satisfaction[1] (without agitation), let it be concentrated on that. In every such case the true nature of the highest bliss will manifest itself.[2]

NOTES

1. *Tuṣṭi,* lit., satisfaction indicates deep, moving joy, not agitation of the mind. *Tuṣṭi* refers to that deep delight in which (1) one forgets every thing external, in which all thought-constructs (*vikalpas*) disappear (2) and in which there is no agitation (*kṣobha*) in the mind.

2. One has to plunge in the source of the delight. One will then find that it is the Divine, the Essential Self of all.

This is *Śāktopāya*.

[Dhāraṇā 52]

VERSE 75

अनागतायां निद्रायां प्रणष्टे बाह्य गोचरे ।
सावस्था मनसा गम्या परा देवी प्रकाशते ॥ ७५ ॥

Anāgatāyāṃ nidrāyām praṇaṣṭe bāhyagocare /
Sāvasthā manasā gamyā parā devī prakāśate // 75

TRANSLATION

When sleep has not yet fully appeared i.e. when one is about to fall asleep, and all the external objects (though present) have faded out of sight[1] then the state (between sleep and waking) is one on which one should concentrate. In that state the Supreme Goddess will reveal Herself.[2]

NOTES

1. The intermediate state between sleep and waking is the *nirvikalpa* state, i. e. a state in which all thought-constructs have disappeared. This is the *turīya* or transcendental state of consciousness.

2. By concentrating on this thought-free state of consciousness, one will have an experience of the essential nature of Self which transcends all thought-constructs. Thus one will have an experience of the divine nature. It is this Divine nature which has been called *parā devī*, the Supreme Goddess.

This is also *Śāktopāya*.

[Dhāraṇā 53]

VERSE 76

तेजसा सूर्यदीपादेराकाशे शबलीकृते ।
दृष्टिर्निवेश्या तत्रैव स्वात्मरूपं प्रकाशते ।। ७६ ।।

Tejasā sūryadīpāderākāśe śabalīkṛte /
Dṛṣṭir niveśyā tatraiva svātmarūpam prakāśate // 76

TRANSLATION

One should fix one's gaze on a portion of the space that appears variegated with the rays of the sun, lamp, etc. At that very place, the nature of one's essential Self will manifest itself.[2]

NOTES

1. Etcetera includes moon with whose light the sky appears variegated at night.

2. Under such circumstances, the *yogī* casts off the limitation of the objective consciousness and experiences the infinity of the spiritual consciousness.

This is *Aṇava upāya*.

[Dhāraṇā 54]

VERSE 77

करङ्किण्या क्रोधनया भैरव्या लेलिहानया ।
खेचर्या दृष्टिकाले च परावाप्तिः प्रकाशते ॥ ७७ ॥

Karaṅkiṇyā krodhanayā bhairavyā lelihānayā /
Khecaryā dṛṣṭikāle ca parāvāptiḥ prakāśate // 77

TRANSLATION

At the moment of the (intuitive) perception (of the universe), there is manifested the supreme attainment through the *Karaṅkiṇī*, *Krodhanā*, *Bhairavī*, *Lelihānā* and *Khecarī mudrās*.

NOTES

Dṛṣṭi-kāle is explained by Svāmī Lakṣmaṇa Joo as 'on the occasion of the *yogic practice*.' *Mudrā* (posture) is a technical term meaning a particular disposition and control of the organs of the body as a help in concentration. It is called *mudrā* because it gives the joy of spiritual consciousness.

Karaṅkiṇī mudrā is so-called, because by it the *yogī* views the world as mere *karaṅka* or skeleton. It views the physical body as dissolved in the highest ether. It is the *mudrā* of *jñāna-siddhas* i.e. of those who have become perfect in *jñāna* or spiritual insight.

Krodhanā is a *mudrā* expressive of *krodha* or anger. It assumes a tense, tight posture. It gathers up all the twentyfour *tattvas* from the earth upto *prakṛti* into the corpus of *mantra*. It is the *mudrā* of *mantra-siddhas* i.e. of those who have become perfect in *mantra*.

Bhairavī mudrā consists in keeping the eyes fixed externally without blinking but making the gaze turned towards the inner Reality.

It withdraws everything into the inner Self, and is the *mudrā* of the *melāpasiddhas*. *Melāpa* means the 'supernatural power of the union of the energies of the various organs'. It also means the meeting of the *siddhas* and *Yoginīs*. Those who have become perfect in this matter are known as *Melāpa-siddhas.*

Lelihānā is the *mudrā* in which the *yogī* tastes the entire universe in his nature of essential I-consciousness. It is the *mudrā* of the *Śākta-siddhas.*

Khecarī literally means that which moves in the sky or empty space. *Kha* or 'empty-space' is a symbol of consciousness. There are four kinds of *Khecarī mudrā*. One kind is the *mudrā* referred to in *Haṭha-yoga-pradīpikā*. It consists in turning the tongue backward towards the palate inside the cranium. The second kind is the one described by Kṣemarāja in *Śiva-Sūtra-vimarśinī* under *sūtra* 5 of the 2nd section.

"A *yogī* should be seated in the *padmāsana* (lotus posture) erect like a stick and should then fix his mind on the navel and should lead the mind upto *kha-trayas* or the three *śaktis* (*śakti, vyāpinī*, and *samanā*), situated in the space in the head. Holding the mind in that state, he should move it forward with the above triad. Putting himself in this condition, the great *yogī* acquires movement in the head."

The third kind of *khecarī* is as described in *Viveka-mārtaṇḍa*. 'The tongue should be turned back inside the cranium. The gaze should be directed towards the centre in between the eye-brows'.

The fourth or the highest kind of *Khecarī mudrā* is that state in which the *yogī* remains in Śiva-consciousness all the while, in which his consciousness moves in all beings.

This is the *mudrā* of the *Śāmbhava-siddhas.*

This *dhāraṇā* is *Śāmbhava upāya.*

[Dhāraṇā 55]

VERSE 78

मृद्वासने स्फिजैकेन हस्तपादौ निराश्रयम् ।
निधाय तत्प्रसङ्गेन परा पूर्णा मतिर्भवेत् ॥ ७८ ॥

Mṛdvāsane sphijaikena hastapādau nirāśrayam /
Nidhāya tatprasaṅgena parā pūrṇā matirbhavet // 78

TRANSLATION

The aspirant should seat himself on a soft (cushioned) seat, placing only one of the buttocks on the seat and leaving the hands and the feet without any support.[1] By maintaining himself in this position, his intelligence will become highly *sāttvika* and endowed with plenitude.[2]

NOTES

1. He should sit in a very relaxed position.

2. His mind will acquire perfect ease in this position and therefore *rajas* (agitation of the mind) and *tamas* (cloth) will disappear. His mind will experience perfect equilibrium (*sattva*). This is an *Āṇava upāya.*

[Dhāraṇā 56]

VERSE 79

उपविश्यासने सम्यक् बाहू कृत्वार्धकुञ्चितौ ।
कक्षव्योम्नि मनः कुर्वन् शममायाति तल्लयात् ।। ७९ ।।

Upaviśyāsane samyag bāhū kṛtvārdhakuñcitau /
Kakṣavyomni manaḥ kurvan śamam āyāti tallayāt // 79

TRANSLATION

Sitting comfortably on his seat and placing the two arms in the form of an arch overhead, the aspirant should fix his gaze in the arm-pits. As the mind gets absorbed in that posture of repose, it will experience great peace.

NOTES

This posture has been recommended for making the mind at ease. In this posture, one feels great peace. This is an *Āṇava upāya.*

[Dhāraṇā 57]

VERSE 80

स्थूलरूपस्य भावस्य स्तब्धां दृष्टिं निपात्य च ।
अचिरेण निराधारं मनः कृत्वा शिवं व्रजेत् ।। ८० ।।

Sthūlarūpasya bhāvasya[1] stabdhāṃ dṛṣṭiṃ nipātya ca /
Acireṇa nirādhāram manaḥ kṛtvā śivaṃ vrajet // 80

TRANSLATION

Having fixed his gaze without blinking on a gross object, (and directing his attention inward), and thus making his mind free of all prop[2] of thought-constructs, the aspirant acquires the state of *Śiva* without delay.

NOTES

1. The word *upari* meaning 'on' is understood after *bhāvasya*. So this means fixing one's gaze on a gross object.

2. *Nirādhāra* or without a prop means free of all thought constructs (*vikalpas*). It is these *vikalpas* that serve as a prop for the mind.

This is *Bhairavī mudrā* and the upāya is *Śāmbhava*.

[Dhāraṇā 58]

VERSE 81

मध्यजिह्वे स्फारितास्ये मध्ये निक्षिप्य चेतनाम् ।
होच्चारं मनसा कुर्वंस्ततः शान्ते प्रलीयते ।। ८१ ।।

Madhyajihve sphāritāsye madhye nikṣipya cetanām /
Hoccāram manasā kurvaṃs tataḥ śānte pralīyate // 81

TRANSLATION

If one maintains the mouth widely open, keeping the inverted tongue at the centre[1] and fixing the mind in the middle of the open mouth, and voices vowel-less *ha* mentally, he will be dissolved in peace.

NOTES

1. This refers to *Khecarī mudrā* which is described in the following way in Vivekamārtaṇḍa:

कपालकुहरे जिह्वा प्रविष्टा विपरीतगा ।
भ्रुवोरन्तर्गता दृष्टिर्मुद्रा भवति खेचरी ॥

When the inverted tongue is made to enter the cavity of the cranium touching the palate and the gaze is fixed between the eye-brows, it is *khecarī mudrā.*

2. After effecting this *mudrā*, one should keep his mind fixed on the middle of the open mouth.

Prāṇa goes on sounding *haṃsaḥ* inwardly automatically without cessation. When the tongue is inverted and stuck to the palate, the palatal *sa* cannot be pronounced: *ha* alone of the formula 'haṃsa' remains. This *ha* has to be voiced in a vowel-less manner. Since it is not possible to utter vowel-less (*anacka*) *ha* physically, the *dhāraṇā* says that it should be uttered mentally. As the vowel-less *ha* symbolizes *prāṇaśakti*, its mental repetition develops *prāṇa śakti* or *madhya daśā* and thus one attains the state of his essential Self and experiences peace.

This is *Āṇava upāya.*

[Dhāraṇā 59]

VERSE 82

आसने शयने स्थित्वा निराधारं विभावयन् ।
स्वदेहं मनसि क्षीणे, क्षणात् क्षीणाशयो भवेत् ॥ ८२ ॥

Āsane śayane sthitvā nirādhāraṃ vibhāvayan /
Svadeham, manasi kṣīṇe, kṣaṇāt kṣīṇāśayo bhavet // 82.

TRANSLATION

Seated on a (soft) seat or bed, one should contemplate one's body as without support. By this contemplation when all props of one's thought vanish i.e. when one's mind becomes free of thought-constructs, then in an instant, all his old (undesirable) mental dispositions (lying in the unconscious) will also vanish.

NOTES

Though seated on a soft seat or bed, the aspirant should contemplate with firm belief that his body is without the support of any seat or bed whatsoever. In this way his mind will become free of thought-constructs which act like props, and when his mind becomes thought-free, then his habitual tendencies of thought (*vāsanās*) lying in the unconscious will also vanish.

This is *Śāktopāya*.

[Dhāraṇā 60]

VERSE 83

चलासने स्थितस्याथ शनैर्वा देहचालनात् ।
प्रशान्ते मानसे भावे देवि दिव्यौघमाप्नुयात् ॥ ८३ ॥

Calāsane sthitasyātha śanair vā dehacālanāt /
praśānte mānase bhāve devi divyaughamāpnuyāt // 83

TRANSLATION

O goddess, owing to the swinging of the body of a person seated on a moving vehicle or owing to self-caused swinging of his body slowly,[1] his mental state becomes calmed. Then he attains *divyaugha*[2] and enjoys the bliss of supernal consciousness.

NOTES

1. If one is seated in a cart or on horse-back, or an elephant or in any other moving vehicle, then owing to the movement of the vehicle, his body begins to swing to and fro, or he may himself make his body swing. In such a condition, he experiences a peculiar kind of joy, and his mind becomes introverted. Owing to the introversion of the mind, he experiences great peace which may give him a taste of divine bliss.

2 The word *augha* literally means flood, stream. In the context of *yoga*, it means 'continuous tradition of wisdom'. Three kinds of *augha* are mentioned in the tantras—

Mānavaugha siddhaugha divyaugha.

The traditional *jñāna* (spiritual insight) obtained through human *gurus* (spiritual directors) is known as *mānavaugha*, that obtained through *siddhas* (perfect masters who have gone beyond human condition) is known as *siddhaugha*, and that obtained through *devas* (gods) is known as *divyaugha*.

This again is *Śāktopāya.*

[Dhāraṇā 61]

VERSE 84

आकाशं विमलं पश्यन् कृत्वा दृष्टिं निरन्तराम् ।
स्तब्धात्मा तत्क्षणाद्देवि भैरवं वपुराप्नुयात् ॥ ८४ ॥

Ākāśaṃ vimalam paśyan kṛtvā dṛṣṭiṃ nirantarām /
Stabdhātmā tatkṣaṇād devi bhairavaṃ vapur āpnuyāt // 84

TRANSLATION

If one making himself thoroughly immobile[1] beholds the pure (cloudless) sky[2] with fixed eyes,[3] at that very moment, O goddess, he will acquire the nature of Bhairava.

NOTES

1. This means that the sense of the body should vanish and all thoughts and emotions should be completely arrested.
2. Looking at the sky has been recommended, because on account of the vastness of the sky, the beholder is apt to be lost in a sense of infinity.
3. With fixed eyes means without blinking.

This is *Śāmbhavopāya.*

[Dhāraṇā 62]

VERSE 85

लीनं मूर्ध्नि वियत्सर्वं भैरवत्वेन भावयेत् ।
तत्सर्वं भैरवाकार–तेजस्तत्त्वं समाविशेत् ॥ ८५ ॥

Līnam mūrdhni viyat sarvam bhairavatvena bhāvayet /
Tat sarvaṃ bhairavākāratejastattvaṁ samāviśet // 85

TRANSLATION

The *yogī* should contemplate the entire open space (or sky) under the form of the essence of Bhairava and as dissolved in his head. Then the entire universe will be absorbed in the light of Bhairava.

NOTES

If the *yogī* by *bhāvanā* (creative contemplation) imagines the vast sky as expression of Bhairava and as being dissolved in the space inside his head, the space in his head will become the symbol of the infinity of Bhairava and he will feel that the entire universe is bathed in the Light of Bhairava.

This is *Śāktopāya*.

[Dhāraṇā 63]

VERSE 86

किंचिज्ज्ञातं द्वैतदायि बाह्यालोकस्तमः पुनः ।
विश्वादि, भैरवं रूपं ज्ञात्वानन्तप्रकाशभृत् ॥ ८६ ॥

Kiñcij jñātaṃ dvaitadāyi bāhyālokas tamaḥ punaḥ /
Viśvādi bhairavaṃ rūpaṁ jñātvānantaprakāśabhṛt // 86

TRANSLATION

When the *yogī* knows the three states of consciousness, viz. *viśva* (waking) in which there is limited knowledge productive of duality, (2) *taijas* (dream) in which there is perception of the impressions of the exterior, (3) *prājña* (deep sleep) in which it is all darkness as (only) the form of Bhairava[1] (*bhairavaṃ rūpam*), he is then filled with the splendour of infinite consciousness.[2]

NOTES

1. As (only) the form of Bhairava means as the expression of the *turīya* or the fourth state of consciousness which is Bhairava.

2. In ordinary life, there is always subject-object duality. In the *turīya* or the fourth state of consciousness, the sense of duality disappears. It is the Light of the Essential Self or Bhairava. That is why it is said to be the splendour of infinite consciousness.

When the *yogī* knows all the three states as only the expression of the fourth state which is the state of Bhairava, he is filled with the Infinite Light of Bhairava.

This is *Āṇava upāya* leading to *Śāmbhava* state.

[Dhāraṇā 64]

VERSE 87

एवमेव दुर्निशायां कृष्णपक्षागमे चिरम् ।
तैमिरं भावयन् रूपं भैरवं रूपमेष्यति ॥ ८७ ॥

Evam eva durniśāyāṃ kṛṣṇapakṣāgame ciram /
Taimiram bhāvayan rūpam bhairavaṃ rūpam eṣyati // 87

TRANSLATION

In the same way, at (completely) dark night in the dark fortnight, by contemplating for long over the (terrible) circumambient darkness, the *yogī* will attain the nature of Bhairava.

NOTES

Contemplation over darkness at dark night in the dark fortnight has been recommended, because in such darkness, distinct objects are not visible. So there is nothing to distract the attention.

When one contemplates over darkness for long, one is filled with a sense of awe and uncanny mystery and easily slips into the mystic consciousness. It is at such an hour that the Light of Bhairava makes its appearance and one acquires the nature of Bhairava.

This is *bāhya timirabhāvanā* or contemplation over external darkness with open eyes. This *dhāraṇā* pertains to *Śāktopāya.*

[Dhāraṇā 65]

VERSE 88

एवमेव निमील्यादौ नेत्रे कृष्णाभमग्रतः ।
प्रसार्य भैरवं रूपं भावयंस्तन्मयो भवेत् ॥ ८८ ॥

Evam eva nimīlyādau netre kṛṣṇābham agrataḥ /
Prasārya bhairavaṃ rūpam bhāvayaṃs tanmayo bhavet //88

TRANSLATION

Similarly, (even during the absence of dark fortnight), the aspirant should at first contemplate over terrible darkness in front of him by closing his eyes, then later should contemplate over the dark, terrible form of Bhairava in front with eyes wide open. Thus will he become identified with Him.

NOTES

This verse points to the transition from *nimīlana* to *unmīlana samādhi*. If after the *nimīlana samādhi*, the aspirant goes into *unmīlana samādhi* i.e. contemplates over the form of Bhairava with eyes wide open, he will find his mind swallowed up in the nature of *Bhairava* and will realize his identity with Him.

This is *Śāktopāya* again.

[Dhāraṇā 66]

VERSE 89

यस्य कस्येन्द्रियस्यापि व्याघाताच्च निरोधतः ।
प्रविष्टस्याद्वये शून्ये तत्रैवात्मा प्रकाशते ॥ ८९ ॥

Yasya kasyendriyasyāpi vyāghātāc ca nirodhataḥ /
Praviṣṭasyādvaye śūnye tatraivātmā prakāśate // 89

TRANSLATION

When some organ of sense is obstructed in its function by some external cause or in the natural course or by self-imposed device, then the aspirant becomes introverted, his mind is absorbed in a void that transcends all duality and there itself his essential Self is revealed.

NOTES

As the particular organ of sense is unable to establish contact with the external world, there arises a feeling of vacuity in that organ. Then the aspirant becomes introverted. He gets absorbed in that void where the duality of subject and object does not exist, and forthwith the essential Self of the aspirant is revealed.

This *dhāraṇā* pertains to *Śāktopāya*.

[Dhāraṇā 67]

VERSE 90

अबिन्दुमविसर्गं च अकारं जपतो महान् ।
उदेति देवि सहसा ज्ञानौघः परमेश्वरः ॥ ९० ॥

Abindum avisargaṃ ca akāraṃ japato mahān /
Udeti devi sahasā jñānaughaḥ parameśvaraḥ // 90

TRANSLATION

If one recites the letter *a* without *bindu* or *visarga* then, O goddess, *Parameśvara*—a magnificent torrent of wisdom appears suddenly.

NOTES

Bindu in this context indicates the *anusvāra* or dot on a letter which is the symbol of nasal pronunciation. *Visarga* indicates two dots placed one upon the other immediately after a letter which symbolize the articulation of a letter with *ḥ* sound. Thus अ (a) with *bindu* would be अं (aṃ), and अ (a) with *visarga* would be अः (aḥ).

In sounding 'a' with *anusvāra* i. e. as *aṃ* there will be inhalation (*pūraka*) and in sounding 'a' with *visarga* i. e. as *aḥ* there will be exhalation (*recaka*). The above *dhāraṇā* says that the letter अ 'a' should be recited without a *bindu* i. e. without an *anusvāra*, and also without a *visarga* (without the *ḥ* sound) i. e. neither with inhalation nor with exhalation (neither with *pūraka* nor with *recaka*). This implies that the letter 'a' (अ) should be recited in a *kumbhaka* state i.e. in a state of the retention of the breath as 'a' (अ).

Svāmī Lakṣmaṇa Joo interprets *kumbhakasthasya* occurring in the commentary in a different way. According to him *kumbhakasthasya* here means *cakitamudrāyāṃ sthitasya* i.e. in the posture of *cakitamudrā*. In this posturc, the mouth is wide open and the tongue is held back. In this posture 'a' (अ) can neither be recited with *anusvāra* nor with *visarga*. The aspirant will be automatically compelled to contemplate over 'a' only mentally.

In sounding 'a' with *anusvāra* i.e. as *aṃ* there will be inhalation (*pūraka*, and in sounding 'a' with *visarga* i.e. as 'aḥ', there will be exhalation (*recaka*). The above *dhāraṇā* says that the letter अ (a) should be recited without a *bindu* i.e. without an *anusvāra*, and also without a *visarga* (without the *ḥ* sound) i.e. neither with inhalation nor with exhalation (neither with *pūraka*, nor with *recaka*). This implies that the letter 'a' (अ) should be recited in a *kumbhaka* state i.e. in a state of the retention of the breath as 'a' (अ).

Why of all letters has particularly 'a' (अ) been selected for recitation ? The reason is firstly that the lettter 'a' (अ) is the initial letter of the alphabet; it is the source and origin of all other letters; it is neither generated out of any other letter, nor is it dissolved in any other letter. Secondly, it symbolizes *anuttara* the absolute, the state which is beyond description, the state in which *Śiva* and *Śakti* are in indistinguishable unity. The recitation of 'a' (अ), therefore, betokens the longing of the soul for *Śiva-śakti-sāmarasya* (the state of the harmonious fusion of Śiva-śakti) a nostalgia for its ultimate source.

Thirdly 'a' (अ) represents *aham*, the perfect I-consciousness of the Absolute. Therefore, the contemplation of *a* establishes one in the absolute I-consciousness of *Śiva*.

Lastly the recitation of 'a' (अ) without *anusvāra* or *visarga* in a *kumbhaka* state or in *cakita mudrā* makes the mind *nirvikalpaka* i.e. freed of all dichotomizing thought-constructs and suddenly in this state appears *Parameśvara* (the highest Lord), the flood of divine wisdom.

This is *Āṇava upāya*.

[Dhāraṇā 68]

VERSE 91

वर्णस्य सविसर्गस्य विसर्गान्तं चितिं कुरु ।
निराधारेण चित्तेन स्पृशेद्ब्रह्म सनातनम् ॥ ९१ ॥

Varṇasya savisargasya visargāntaṃ citiṃ kuru /
Nirādhāreṇa cittena spṛśed brahma sanātanam //91

TRANSLATION

When one fixes his mind freed of all props on the end of the visarga of a letter coupled with visarga, then (being completely introverted), he enters the eternal Brahman.

NOTES

Abhinavagupta says that *visarga* connotes the creative power of the Supreme:

अनुत्तरं परं धाम तदेवाकुलमुच्यते ।
विसर्गस्तस्य नाथस्य कौलिकी शक्तिरुच्यते ॥

(Tantrāloka, III, 143)

"Anuttara is the highest plane of Reality. That is known as *akula*. His state of manifestation or emanation (*visarga*) is the *kaulikī* power *kaulikī śakti* of the Supreme Lord.

Śivopādhyāya quotes another verse to show that *visarga* is the creative power of the Supreme and it is out of this *visarga* that the entire cosmos emerges:

अकुलस्य परा येयं कौलिकी शक्तिरुत्तमा ।
स एवायं विसर्गस्तु तस्मात् जातमिदं जगत् ॥

"The highest *Śakti* of *Akula* (*śiva*) is known as *Kaulikī*. The *kaulikī śakti* is the same as *visarga*. It is from *visarga* that the entire world has emanated.

Visarga is represented in writing by two dots placed perpendicularly one upon the other immediately after a letter and in speech it is represented by the sound *ḥ*. The sound *ḥ* represents the creative energy.

Now when the aspirant fixes his mind on the end of the *visarga* which is the symbol of manifestation, his mind is detached from all manifestation and easily slips into the void. He is now steeped in the silence of Brahman.

This *dhāraṇā* starts in *Āṇava* and ends in *Śāktopāya*.

[Dhāraṇā 69]

VERSE 92

व्योमाकारं स्वमात्मानं ध्यायेद्दिग्भिरनावृतम् ।
निराश्रया चितिः शक्तिः स्वरूपं दर्शयेत्तदा ॥ ९२ ॥

Vyomākāraṃ svam ātmānaṃ dhyāyed digbhir anāvṛtam /
Nirāśrayā citiḥ śaktiḥ svarūpaṃ darśayet tadā // 92

TRANSLATION

When one concentrates on one's self in the form of a vast firmament, unlimited in any direction whatsoever[1], then the *citi śakti* freed of all props reveals[2] herself (which is the essential Self of the aspirant).

NOTES

1. One has to concentrate on one's Self as a vast sky unlimited by any form, adjunct or direction.

2. In such a frame of mind, the *citi śakti*—the divine power of consciousness is freed of all thought-constructs and shines in its *nirvikalpa* state which is the essential nature of Self. Thus the aspirant is established in his essential Self.

This is *Śāktopāya*.

[Dhāraṇā 70]

VERSE 93

किञ्चिदङ्गं विभिद्यादौ तीक्ष्णसूच्यादिना ततः ।
तत्रैव चेतनां युक्त्वा भैरवे निर्मला गतिः ॥ ९३॥

Kiñcid aṅgaṃ vibhidyādau tīkṣṇasūcyādinā tataḥ /
Tatraiva cetanāṃ yuktvā bhairave nirmalā gatiḥ // 93

TRANSLATION

If one pierces at first any limb (of one's body) with sharp-pointed needle etcetera, and then concentrates on that very spot, then (owing to the intensity of one-pointed awareness) one has access to the pure nature of *Bhairava.*

NOTES

In intensity of attention whether due to pleasure or pain, there is one-pointedness of the mind and in that state the nature of the essential Self is revealed.

This *dhāraṇā* starts with *Āṇava upāya* and ends in *Śāmbhava* state.

[Dhāraṇā 71]

VERSE 94

चित्ताद्यन्तःकृतिर्नास्ति ममान्तर्भावयेदिति ।
विकल्पानामभावेन विकल्पैरुज्झितो भवेत् ॥ ९४ ॥

Cittādyantaḥkṛtir nāsti mamāntar bhāvayed iti /
Vikalpānām abhāvena vikalpair ujjhito bhavet // 94

TRANSLATION

One should contemplate thus : "Within me the inner psychic apparatus consisting of *citta*, etc. does not exist". In the absence of thought-constructs, he will be (completely) rid of all thought-constructs (*vikalpas*) and will abide as pure consciousness (*śuddha caitanya*) which is his essential Self.

NOTES

When one becomes fully convinced by *bhāvanā* (contemplation) that he is not his psychic apparatus consisting of *manas*, *buddhi*, *ahaṁkāra* (mind, the ascertaining intellect, and the ego) with which he is always identified, then his mind ceases to form *vikalpas* (thought-constructs) and his essential nature which transcends all *vikalpas* is revealed.

This is *Śāktopāya.*

[Dhāraṇā 72]

VERSE 95

माया विमोहिनी नाम कलायाः कलनं स्थितम् ।
इत्यादिधर्मं तत्त्वानां कलयन्न पृथग्भवेत् ॥ ९५ ॥

Māyā vimohinī nāma kalāyāḥ kalanaṃ sthitam /
Ityādidharmaṃ tattvānāṃ kalayan na pṛthag bhavet //95

TRANSLATION

"Māyā is delusive, the function of *kalā* is limited activity (of vidyā, it is limited knowledge, etc)," considering the functions of the various *tattvas* (constitutive principles) in this way, one does not remain separate any longer.

NOTES

Abhinavagupta thus defines Māyāśakti:

"Sarvathaiva svarūpaṃ tirodhatte āvṛṇute vimohinī sā"

I.P.VI.II,17.

"She veils the essential Self and thus proves delusive."

"भेदे त्वेकरसे भातेऽहन्तयानात्मनीक्षिते ।
शून्ये बुद्धौ शरीरे वा मायाशक्तिर्विजृम्भते ॥"

I.P.V.III. 1, 8

"The power of Māyā shows itself in manifesting undiluted diversity and in bringing about the identity of Self with the not-Self such as *śūnya* (void), *buddni* and the body."

The yogi fully understands that Māyā subjects every one to her charm. She brings about a sense of difference in life which is essentially one whole, and through her *kañcukas* (coverings). viz. *kalā*, *vidyā*, *rāga*, *kāla*, and *niyati*, effects limitation in respect of activity, knowledge, desire, time, causality and space.

Being fully aware of the limited functions of the *tattvas* and the delusive power of *Māyā*, the *yogī* does not lose sight of the wholeness of Reality and, therefore, does not cut himself adrift from it. Rather by *unmīlana samādhi*, he views the entire manifestation as the expression of *Śiva* and is thus chockful of a deep sense of relatedness.

If the reading *Kalayan nā pṛthag bhavet* is adopted, the meaning would be "(such a) person (*nā*) becomes isolated (*pṛthak*) and is established in his essential Self."

This is *Śāktopāya*.

[Dhāraṇā 73]

VERSE 96

झगितीच्छां समुत्पन्नामवलोक्य शमं नयेत् ।
यत एव समुद्भूता ततस्तत्रैव लीयते ॥ ९६ ॥

Jhagitīcchāṃ samutpannām avalokya śamaṃ nayet /
Yata eva samudbhūtā tatas tatraiva līyate // 96

TRANSLATION

Having observed a desire that has sprung up, the aspirant should put an end to it immediately. It will be absorbed in that very place from which it arose.

NOTES

When the mind of the aspirant becomes introverted, and he considers his essential Self as completely separate from desire which is only a play of the mind which is not-self, then desires dissolve in the mind even as waves rising on the surface of the sea dissolve in the sea itself.

If another desire arises, the best means of putting an end to the desire is to shift the attention from the desire to the underlying spiritual Reality, the creative moment between the two desires, known as *unmeṣa*.

This is *Śāktopāya* leading to *Śāmbhavopāya*.

[Dhāraṇā 74]

VERSE 97

यदा ममेच्छा नोत्पन्ना ज्ञानं वा, कस्तदास्मि वै ।
तत्त्वतोऽहं तथाभूतस्तल्लीनस्तन्मना भवेत् ॥ ९७ ॥

Yadā mamecchā notpannā jñānaṃ vā, kas tadāsmi vai /
Tattvato'haṃ tathābhūtas tallīnas tanmanā bhavet // 97

TRANSLATION

When desire or knowledge (or activity) has not arisen in me, then what am I in that condition ? In verity, I am (in that condition) that Reality itself (i.e. *cidānanda* or consciousness-bliss). (Therefore the aspirant should always contemplate "I am *cidānanda* or consciousness bliss"). Thus, he will be absorbed in that Reality (*tallīnas*) and will become identified with it (*tanmanā*).

NOTES

The desire, knowledge and activity of the ego are not the desire, knowledge and activity of the essential Self. When the aspirant realizes and practises the *bhāvanā* of the essential Self who is always pure consciousness-bliss, he will rise above his ego and will be dissolved in his essential Self.

This is *Śāktopāya*.

[Dhāraṇā 75]

VERSE 98

इच्छायामथवा ज्ञाने जाते चित्तं निवेशयत् ।
आत्मबुद्ध्यानन्यचेतास्ततस्तत्त्वार्थदर्शनम् ॥ ९८ ॥

Ichhāyām athavā jñāne jāte cittaṃ niveśayet /
Ātmabuddhyānanyacetās tatas tattvārthadarśanam // 98

TRANSLATION

When a desire or knowledge (or activity) appears, the aspirant should, with the mind withdrawn from all objects (of desire, knowledge, etc.) fix his mind on it (desire, knowledge, etc.) as the very Self, then he will have the realization of the essential Reality.

NOTES

When the mind is withdrawn from the object of desire, knowledge, etc. and is fixed on the desire, knowledge as the very Self, as a *śakti* of the divine, then the mind is rid of *vikalpas*, and the aspirant has the realization of Reality.

This is *Śāmbhava upāya.*

[Dhāraṇā 76]

VERSE 99

निर्निमित्तं भवेज्ज्ञानं निराधारं भ्रमात्मकम् ।
तत्त्वतः कस्यचिन्नैतदेवंभावी शिवः प्रिये ९९ ॥

Nirnimittam bhavej jñānaṃ nirādhāram bhramātmakam /
Tattvataḥ kasyacin naitad evambhāvī śivaḥ priye // 99

TRANSLATION

All knowledge is without cause, without base and deceptive. From the point of view of absolute Reality, this knowledge does not belong to any person. When one is given wholly to this contemplation, then, O dear one, one becomes *Śiva.*

NOTES

This *bhāvanā* is the device for entering the heart i.e. the mystic centre of reality. Abhinavagupta designates it as *Sarvātma-saṅkoca* in Tantrāloka (V, 71) and Jayaratha in his commentary, quotes this verse as an example of *sarvātma-saṅkoca.* This consists in rejecting everything external and entering completely within oneself by means of *nimīlana samādhi*—'ecstasy with closed eyes.' The reality of every object is rejected and also its association with the subject (*kasyacin naitad*).

In this way, both *jñātā* (knower, subject) and *jñeya* (known, object) are rejected. Only *jñāna* or *vijñāna* remains which is *Bhairava. Vijñāna* is the base of everything subjective or objective and that is the sole Reality.

This is *Śāktopāya.*

[Dhāraṇā 77]

VERSE 100

चिद्धर्मा सर्वदेहेषु विशेषो नास्ति कुत्रचित् ।
अतश्च तन्मयं सर्वं भावयन्भवजिज्जनः ॥ १०० ॥

Ciddharmā sarvadeheṣu viśeṣo nāsti kutracit /
Ataśca tanmayaṃ sarvam bhāvayan bhavajij janaḥ // 100

TRANSLATION

The same Self characterized by consciousness is present in all the bodies; there is no difference in it anywhere. Therefore, a person realizing that everything (in essence) is the same (consciousness) triumphantly rises above transmigratory existence.

NOTES

Kṣemarāja has quoted this verse in his commentary on the first *sūtra* of *Śiva sūtras* and has aptly pointed out that *caitanya* or consciousness does not mean simply *jñāna* or knowledge but also *kriyā* or autonomous activity.

A person who realizes that the Self characterized by consciousness is the same in all from *Sadāśiva* down to the tiniest worm has become identified with that essential Self and acquires the consciousness of *samatā* (essential oneness). He is, therefore, liberated and is no longer subject to birth and death.

This is *Śāmbhavopāya*.

[Dhāraṇā 78]

VERSE 101

कामक्रोधलोभमोहमदमात्सर्यगोचरे ।
बुद्धिं निस्तिमितां कृत्वा तत्तत्त्वमवशिष्यते ॥ १०१ ॥

Kāmakrodhalobhamohamadamātsaryagocare /
Buddhiṃ nistimitāṃ kṛtvā tat tattvam avaśiṣyate // 101

TRANSLATION

If one succeeds in immobilizing his mind (i.e. in making it

one-pointed) when he is under the sway of desire, anger, greed, infatuation, arrogance and envy, then the Reality underlying these states alone subsists.

NOTES

When an aspirant is under the domination of any strong emotion, he should dissociate his mind from the object of the emotion and concentrate deeply on the emotion itself, without either accepting it or rejecting it. He should withdraw his mind from everything external and turn it within even as a tortoise withdraws its limbs within its shell on the occasion of a great danger. When he is thus intensely introverted, the passion becomes calmed like a charmed snake; all *vikalpas* are shed like leaves in autumn. Such abrupt introversion puts the aspirant in contact with the infinite spiritual energy surging within known as *spanda* and then he is filled with the bliss of divine consciousness (*cidānanda*). This means is known as *ātma-saṅkoca* or *śakti-saṅkoca*. Thus even a strong passion may lead a cautious *yogī* to spiritual bliss.

This is *Śāmbhavopāya*.

[Dhāraṇā 79]

VERSE 102

इन्द्रजालमयं विश्वं व्यस्तं वा चित्रकर्मवत् ।
भ्रमद्वा ध्यायतः सर्वं पश्यतश्च सुखोद्गमः ॥ १०२ ॥

Indrajālamayaṃ viśvaṃ vyastaṃ vā citrakarmavat /
Bhramad vā dhyāyataḥ sarvam paśyataśca sukhodgamaḥ // 102

TRANSLATION

If one perceives the cosmos as mere jugglery conjured up by some magician or as the configuration of a painting, or as illusory as the movement of trees, etc. (appearing to people seated on a moving boat), and contemplates deeply over this fact, then he will experience great happiness.

NOTES

Jayaratha, in his commentary on V. 71, in Tantrāloka, quotes this verse also as an example of *śarvātmasaṅkoca*.

This is *Śāktopāya*.

[Dhāraṇā 80]

VERSE 103

न चित्तं निक्षिपेद्दुःखे न सुखे वा परिक्षिपेत् ।
भैरवि ज्ञायतां मध्ये किं तत्त्वमवशिष्यते ॥ १०३ ॥

Na cittaṃ nikṣiped duḥkhe na sukhe vā parikṣipet /
Bhairavi, jñāyatām madhye kiṃ tattvam avaśiṣyate // 103

TRANSLATION

Neither should one dwell on suffering nor on pleasure. O goddess Bhairavi, it should be known what Reality subsists in the middle of both (the opposites).

NOTES

Both pleasure and suffering are the characteristics of *antaḥ-karaṇa* or the inner psychic apparatus. That which is beyond the pair of opposites like suffering and pleasure, which abides unaffected by both, which witnesses both without being involved in them—that is Reality, that is the essential Self. One should concentrate on and be identified with that Reality.

This is *Śāktopāya*.

[Dhāraṇā 81]

VERSE 104

विहाय निजदेहास्थां सर्वत्रास्मीति भावयन् ।
दृढेन मनसा दृष्ट्या नान्येक्षिण्या सुखी भवेत् ॥ १०४ ॥

Vihāya nijadehāsthāṃ sarvatrāsmīti bhāvayan /
Dṛḍhena manasā dṛṣṭyā nānyekṣiṇyā sukhī bhavet // 104

TRANSLATION

After rejecting attachment to one's body, one should, with firm mind and with a vision which has no consideration for any thing else, contemplate thus, "I am everywhere". He will then enjoy (supernal) happiness.

NOTES

In this *dhāraṇā*, there are two main ideas, one negative and another positive. The negative one is, "I am not my body, nor am I confined to any particular place or time". The positive one is, "I am everywhere." By this practice, one becomes identified with *Śiva-śakti* and acquires cosmic consciousness.

In verse hundred, one has to practise the *bhāvanā* of *cit* or consciousness in all bodies, in every form of existence. In the present *dhāraṇā*, one has to practise the expansion of his own consciousness in all forms of being.

Śivopādhyāya points out in his commentary a further difference between the idea contained in verse 100 and the present one. In the present verse, the *bhāvanā* recommended is *sarvam idam aham*—"All this is myself" which is the *parāmarśa* or consciousness of *sadāśiva* or *Īśvara.* In verse 100, it is *cit* or consciousness as such whose omnipresence has been emphasized. In other words, the plane referred to in verse 100 is that of *Śiva*, whereas the plane referred to in the present verse is that of *Sadāśiva* or *Īśvara.*

This is *Śāktopāya.*

[Dhāraṇā 82]

VERSE 105

घटादौ यच्च विज्ञानमिच्छाद्यं वा ममान्तरे ।
नैव सर्वगतं जातं भावयन्निति सर्वगः ॥ १०५ ॥

Ghaṭādau yac ca vijñānam icchādyaṃ vā, mamāntare /
Naiva, sarvagataṃ jātam bhāvayan iti sarvagaḥ // 105

TRANSLATION

"Knowledge, desire, etc. do not appear only within me, they

appear everywhere in jars and other objects." Contemplating thus, one becomes all-pervasive.

NOTES

In this verse, *icchā* or desire has reference to action. This verse points out the fact that *jñāna* and *kriyā* are not the monopoly only of the human being. They are universal i.e. common to everything in the universe. This *dhāraṇā* suggests that if one contemplates over the fact of knowledge and desire being common to every existent in the universe, he will acquire the consciousness of unity. Man usually thinks that there is nothing common between him and a jar or a tree, but if he comes to realize that *jñāna* and *kriyā* are the common characteristics of all manifestation, that all are co-sharers of this divine gift, he will shed his insularity and feel his kinship with all.

This dhāraṇā is *Śāktopāya.*

As Abhinavagupta puts it in Īśvarapratyabhijñāvimarśinī

"प्रकाश एवास्ति स्वात्मनः स्वपरात्मभिः"

(I.P.V.I.1.5)

"It is one and the same Self that shines as one's own self as well as selves of others."

And in this connexion, he quotes the following verse of *Somānanda* from *Śivadṛṣṭi* :

"घटो मदात्मना वेत्ति वेद्म्यहं च घटात्मना ।
सदाशिवात्मना वेद्मि स वा वेत्ति मदात्मना ।।
नाना भावैः स्वमात्मानं जानन्नास्ते स्वयं शिवः" ।

"The jar (is one with myself at the time of my desire to know and therefore) knows as one with myself. I am one with the jar in knowing. I know as *Sadāśiva* and *Sadāśiva* knows as myself. It is *Śiva* alone who abides knowing Himself through all the existents."

After this quotation, Abhinavagupta makes the following concluding remarks :

"तदेवं येषां तार्किकप्रवादपांसुपातधसरीभावो न वृत्तोऽस्मिन् संवेदनपथे, ते इयतैव आत्मानमीश्वरं विद्वांसो घटशरीरप्राणसुखतदभावान तत्रैव निमज्जयन्त ईश्वरसमाविष्टा एव भवन्ति" ।

"Thus those who have not been altogether soiled by the dust of the chatter of logicians in the matter of this knowledge get absorbed in *Īśvara* (the Divine) when they realize through the above the identity of the individual Self with *Īśvara* (the Divine) and merge everything such as jar, body, prāṇa, pleasure and even their non-being in Him."

[The verse 106 does not contain any separate *dhāraṇā*. This only gives the special characteristic of a Yogī and re-inforces the idea contained in the previous *dhāraṇā*.]

VERSE 106

ग्राह्यग्राहकसंवित्तिः सामान्या सर्वदेहिनाम् ।
योगिनां तु विशेषोऽस्ति संबन्धे सावधानता ॥ १०६ ॥

Grāhyagrāhakasaṃvittiḥ sāmānyā sarvadehinām /
Yogināṃ tu viśeṣo'sti sambandhe sāvadhānatā // 106

TRANSLATION

The consciousness of object and subject is common to all the embodied ones. The *yogīs* have, however, this distinction that they are mindful of this relation.

NOTES

The object is always related to the subject. Without this relation to the subject, there is no such thing as an object. Ordinary people get lost in the object; they forget the Self, the knower. The real knower is the witnessing awareness from which the subject arises and in which it rests. The *yogī* is, however, always mindful of that witnessing awareness which alone is the subject of every thing, which is always a subject and never an object.

[Dhāraṇā 83]

VERSE 107

स्ववदन्यशरीरेऽपि संवित्तिमनुभावयेत् ।
अपेक्षां स्वशरीरस्य त्यक्त्वा व्यापी दिनैर्भवेत् ॥ १०७ ॥

Svavad anyaśarīre'pi saṃvittim anubhāvayet /
Apekṣāṁ svaśarīrasya tyaktvā vyāpī dinair bhavet // 107

TRANSLATION

One should, leaving aside the need of his own body (in other cases), contemplate that the (same) consciousness is present in other bodies as in his own. Thus he will become all-pervasive in a few days.

NOTES

A body is not necessary for thinking or for consciousness. Everybody has an experience of consciousness apart from the body. In dream, one has consciousness apart from the gross body; in deep sleep, one has consciousness apart from the subtle body (*sūkṣma-śarīra*); in the fourth state of experience (*turīya*) one has consciousness apart from the causal body (*kāraṇa śarīra*). So it is clear that a body is not a necessary medium for consciousness. Knowing this from his personal experience, the aspirant should contemplate that his consciousness is not confined to his own body, but is all-pervasive. Thus he will realize the all-pervasiveness of consciousness which is the nature of Bhairava.

This is *Śāktopāya*.

[Dhāraṇā 84]

VERSE 108

निराधारं मनः कृत्वा विकल्पान्न विकल्पयेत् ।
तदात्मपरमात्मत्वे भैरवो मृगलोचने ॥ १०८ ॥

Nirādhāram manaḥ kṛtvā vikalpān na vikalpayet /
Tadātmaparamātmatve bhairavo mṛgalocane // 108

TRANSLATION

Having freed the mind of all supports,[1] one should refrain from all thought-constructs.[2] Then, O gazelle-eyed one, there will be the state of *Bhairava* in the Self that has become the absolute Self.

NOTES

1. 'All supports' includes both external support such as perception of objects and internal support such as imagination, fancies, concepts, pleasure, pain, etc.

2. He should be completely rid of *Vikalpas*. *Savikalpa* (activity of mind with thought-constructs) is the state of the psychological individual or the empirical self; *nirvikalpa* (activity of consciousness without dichotomising thought-constructs) is the state of the spiritual Self, the witnessing Consciousness of all the states.

This is *Śāmbhavopāya*.

[Dhāraṇā 85]

VERSE 109

सर्वज्ञः सर्वकर्त्ता च व्यापकः परमेश्वरः ।
स एवाहं शैवधर्मा इति दार्ढ्याद्भवेच्छिवः ॥ १०९ ॥

Sarvajñaḥ sarvakartā ca vyāpakaḥ parameśvaraḥ /
Sa evāhaṃ śaivadharmā iti dārḍhyāc chivo bhavet // 109

TRANSLATION

The Highest Lord is Omniscient, omnipotent, and omnipresent. "Since I have the attributes of *Śiva*, I am the same as the Highest Lord." With this firm conviction, one becomes *Śiva*.

NOTES

This is the *dhāraṇā* of the first phase of *pratyabhijñā* or recognition. Man is *Śiva* already in essence. The essential Reality in him has put on the mask of *jīva*. When the *jīva* intensely recognizes his essential Reality, the mask is thrown off. The stage of *vilaya* or veiling disappears; *anugraha* (grace) is operative now, and the *jīva* becomes *Śiva* (that he was in reality).

This is *Śākta upāya*.

[Dhāraṇā 86]

VERSE 110

जलस्येवोर्मयो वह्नेर्ज्वालाभङ्ग्यः प्रभा रवेः ।
ममैव भैरवस्यैता विश्वभङ्ग्यो विभेदिताः ॥ ११० ॥

Jalasyevormayo vahner jvālābhaṅgyaḥ prabhā raveḥ /
Mamaiva bhairavasyaitā viśvabhaṅgyo vibheditāḥ // 110

TRANSLATION

Just as waves arise from water, flames from fire, rays from the sun, even so the waves (variegated aspects) of the universe have arisen in differentiated forms from me i.e. *Bhairava.*

NOTES

This is the *dhāraṇā* of the second phase of *pratyabhijñā.* The first phase of *pratyabhijñā* (recognition) consists in recognizing the *jīva* (the empirical self) as Śiva, the identity of the individual Self with the Universal Self. The *dhāraṇā* of this phase has been given in the previous verse (109). The second phase consists in recognizing the fact that this glory of manifestation is mine. This consists in recognizing the identity of the universe with the Self. The present verse gives the *dhāraṇā* for this recognition.

This is also *Śāktopāya.*

[Dhāraṇā 87]

VERSE 111

भ्रान्त्वा भ्रान्त्वा शरीरेण त्वरितं भुवि पातनात् ।
क्षोभशक्तिविरामेण परा संजायते दशा ॥ १११ ॥

Bhrāntvā bhrāntvā śarīreṇa tvaritam bhuvi pātanāt /
Kṣobhaśaktivirāmeṇa parā saṃjāyate daśā // 111

TRANSLATION

When one whirls his body round and round and falls down

swiftly on the earth, then on the cessation of the energy of commotion, there appears supreme spiritual condition.

[Dhāraṇā 88]

VERSE 112

आधारेष्वथवाऽशक्त्याऽज्ञानाच्चित्तलयेन वा ।
जातशक्तिसमावेश-क्षोभान्ते भैरवं वपुः ॥ ११२ ॥

Ādhāreṣv athavā' śaktyā'jñānāccittalayena vā /
Jātaśaktisamāveśakṣobhānte bhairavaṃ vapuḥ // 112

TRANSLATION

If on account of lack of power to apprehend objects of knowledge or on account of (sheer) ignorance, there is dissolution of mind leading to absorption in (anāśrita śakti), then at the end of the cessation of commotion brought about by that absorption, there appears the form of *Bhairava* (i.e. His essential nature) 112.

NOTES ON 111 & 112

Both of these verses refer to the condition of mind at the end of some intense commotion. Verse 111 refers to a state of mind brought about by commotion set up by physical condition. Verse 112 refers to a state of mind brought about by commotion set up by intellectual impasse.

When there is a deep stirring of the mind either by some physical condition, or by some obstinate questioning or doubt, then after the momentary commotion has ceased, the normal mind is completely stilled; *vikalpas* (thought-constructs) are laid to rest, and there is an invasion of truth from a higher plane of consciousness. At such a moment is revealed the essential nature of *Bhairava*.

The *Dhāraṇā* in 111 is *Śāmbhavopāya,* that in 112 is *Śāktopāya.*

[Dhāraṇā 89]

VERSES 113-114

संप्रदायमिमं देवि शृणु सम्यग्वदाम्यहम् ।
कैवल्यं जायते सद्यो नेत्रयोः स्तब्धमात्रयोः ॥ ११३ ॥
संकोचं कर्णयोः कृत्वा ह्यधोद्वारे तथैव च ।
अनच्कमहलं ध्यायन्विशेद्ब्रह्म सनातनम् ॥ ११४ ॥

Sampradāyam imam devi ṣṛṇu samyag vadāmyaham /
Kaivalyaṃ jāyate sadyo netrayoḥ stabdhamātrayoḥ // 113
Saṃkocaṃ karṇayoḥ kṛtvā hy adhodvāre tathaiva ca /
Anackam ahalaṃ dhyāyan viśed brahma sanātanam // 114

TRANSLATION

O goddess, listen, I am going to tell you this mystic tradition in its entirety. If the eyes are fixed without blinking (on the reality within), isolation (*kaivalya*) will occur immediately. 113.

Contracting the openings of the ears and similarly the openings of the anus and penis(and then), meditating on (the interior, impactless sound—*anāhata dhvani*) without vowel and without consonant, one enters the eternal Brahman. 114

NOTES

Stabdhamātrayoḥ netrayoḥ refers to *Bhairavī or Bhairava mudrā* in which the eyes are open outside without blinking, but the attention is turned on the Reality within. In such a state one is freed of all *vikalpas* (thought-constructs) and is identified with *Śiva*.

Kṣemarāja has quoted this verse in his Udyota commentary on Svacchanda Tantra (vol. II.p. 283), and interprets it in the following way:

"निर्लक्ष्यस्तब्धदृष्टिबन्धः शान्तो विगलिताभिलाषप्रक्षीणसकलविकल्पजालः।"

"Rejecting the sight of the external world by *Bhairavī mudrā*, the aspirant enjoys peace inasmuch as his desires are abolished and the entire net-work of *vikalpas* is destroyed."

It should be borne in mind that the *kaivalya* (isolation) recommended by the non-dualistic Śaiva philosophy is different from the one advocated by Sāṅkhya yoga. In accordance with its dualistic standpoint, Sāṅkhya-Yoga believes that there is nothing common between *puruṣa* and *prakṛti*, and, therefore, *kaivalya*, according to it, means complete isolation from *Prakṛti*, and, hence, from the universe. In Śaiva philosophy, it means the disappearance of the externality of the world and its contraction in *Śiva* with whom the experient is identified in *Kaivalya*.

The imperceptible, inaudible, unstruck sound without a vowel or consonant would be अं i.e. the bindu (dot) only minus the vowel 'a'. The *bindu* by itself represents *Śiva*. The inaudible sound without consonant or vowel would be pure *visarga* अः i.e. the *visarga* without 'a'. This pure visarga represents *śakti*. Since the interior sound being *anāhata* cannot be heard and being without vowel or consonant cannot be uttered, it can only be meditated upon. Since *bindu*, without vowel or consonant represents *Śiva*, this particular meditation is meant to assist the *jīva* (the empirical soul) to return to *Śiva*.

By the above practice, the *yogī* enters *brahma sanātanam* i.e. the *Śabdabrahman* who, as the origin of all sound and therefore of all manifestation, is eternal and above all difference and manifestation. By practising the above *dhāraṇā*, the *yogī* acquires wonderful vitality which enables him to enter *Brahman* who represents the union of *Śiva* and *Śakti* and thus of *ānanda* (supreme bliss) and *svātantrya* (supreme autonomy). This is what Abhinavagupta says in parātriṃśikā:

parabrahmamaya-śiva-śakti-saṃghaṭṭānandasvātantryasṛṣṭiparā-bhaṭṭārikārupe'nupraveśaḥ (p. 50)

The *dhāraṇā* in 113-114 is of *Śāktopāya*.

[Dhāraṇā 90]

VERSE 115

कूपादिके महागर्ते स्थित्वोपरि निरीक्षणात् ।
अविकल्पमतेः सम्यक् सद्यश्चित्तलयः स्फुटम् ॥ ११५ ।

Kūpādike mahāgarte sthitvopari nirīkṣaṇāt /
Avikalpamateḥ samyak sadyas cittalayaḥ sphuṭam // 115

TRANSLATION

If one stands above a very deep well, etc., and fixes his eyes (on the space inside the well without blinking) his understanding becomes freed of *vikalpas* (thought-constructs) completely, and immediately he definitely experiences dissolution of mind.

NOTES

If the *yogī* fixes his gaze (without the blinking of the eyes) for a long time on the space inside a deep well or on the summit of a mountain, he feels giddiness and has a sense of fear. In this state, *spanda* or the inner dynamic Reality throws him off his normal consciousness and if he has already developed *mati* or intuitive understanding by pure living, it is freed of *vikalpas* and in an instant, his normal consciousness is dissolved in a consciousness of higher dimension, and he experiences surpassing peace.

This is *Śāmbhava upāya.*

[Dhāraṇā 91]

VERSE 116

यत्र यत्र मनो याति बाह्ये वाभ्यन्तरेऽपि वा ।
तत्र तत्र शिवावस्था व्यापकत्वात्क्व यास्यति ॥ ११६ ॥

Yatra yatra mano yāti bāhye vābhyantare'pi vā /
Tatra tatra śivāvasthā vyāpakatvāt kva yāsyati // 116

TRANSLATION

Wherever the mind goes whether towards the exterior or towards the interior, everywhere there is the state of *Śiva*. Since *Śiva* is omnipresent, where can the mind go (to avoid Him).

NOTES

This verse has two aspects, one metaphysical, the other mystic. The metaphysical aspect maintains that everything in the universe-subjective or objective is *Śiva*. The mystic aspect says that since everything is *Śiva*, the aspirant need not be perturbed if he is unable to concentrate on some mysterious Universal Reality. Whatever attracts the mind, whether it is something external like a jar or some colour like blue, yellow, etc. or whether it is something internal—an emotion, a thought, let that be taken as *Śiva* with full conviction and be made an object of meditation. The result will be surprizing. The particular object or emotion or thought being meditated upon as *Śiva* can no longer stand out as something different from *Śiva*, something isolated from the Universal stream of consciousness but is bound to appear as that Universal Consciousness itself in that particular aspect. It will thus drive away from the mind of the aspirant all selfish and sensuous desire, it will free his mind of useless *vikalpas* (thought-constructs) and will ensure his entry into the divine consciousness.

This is *Śāktopāya*.

The same teaching has been emphasized in Spandakārikā (II, 3, 4, 5).

[Dhāraṇā 92]

VERSE 117

यत्र यत्राक्षमार्गेण चैतन्यं व्यज्यते विभोः ।
तस्य तन्मात्रधर्मित्वाच्चिल्लयाद्भरितात्मता ॥ ११७ ॥

Yatra yatrākṣamārgeṇa caitanyaṃ vyajyate vibhoḥ /
Tasya tanmātradharmitvāc cillayād bharitātmatā // 117

TRANSLATION

On every occasion that the consciousness of the Omnipresent Reality (*caitanyaṃ vibhoḥ*) is revealed through the sensory organs since it is the characteristic only of the Universal Consciousness, one should contemplate over the consciousness appearing through the sensory organs as the pure Universal Consciousness. Thus his mind will be dissolved in the Universal Consciousness. He will then attain the essence of plenitude (which is the characteristic of *Bhairava*).

NOTES

Normally, every sensation appearing through a sense organ is considered to be a characteristic function of that sense-organ. This *dhāraṇā* says that every sensation whether external or internal should be considered not merely as a psycho-physical fact but as an expression of the Universal Consciousness. The aspirant should contemplate over every sensation in this light. Just as every reflection or image appearing in a mirror is nothing different from the mirror, even so the whole world that appears in the Light of the Universal Consciousness is nothing different from it. Apart from that Universal Consciousness, it has no being whatsoever. When the *yogī* contemplates over every manifestation in the above light, his mind is dissolved in that Universal Consciousness which is the essential substance of this universe, and thus he attains the nature of *Bhairava*.

This is *Śāktopāya*.

[Dhāraṇā 93]

VERSE 118

क्षुताद्यन्ते भये शोके गह्वरे वा रणाद्द्रुते ।
कुतूहले क्षुधाद्यन्ते ब्रह्मसत्तामयी दशा ॥ ११८ ॥

Kṣutādyante bhaye śoke gahvare vā raṇād drute /
Kutūhale kṣudhādyante brahmasattāmayī daśā // 118

TRANSLATION

At the commencement and end of sneeze, in terror, in sorrow, in the condition of a deep sigh or on the occasion of flight from the battlefield, during (keen) curiosity, at the commencement or end of hunger, the state is like that of *brahma*.

NOTE

The word *gahvara* means both a cavern or deep sigh. As most of the conditions mentioned are psychophysical or emotional the word *gahvara* has been taken in the sense of deep sigh,

Whether it is an insignificant condition like sneeze or hunger or highly significant condition like terror, keen curiosity or flight from the battlefield, whenever the ordinary normal consciousness receives a sudden jolt or shock, it is thrown back to its inmost depth and comes in contact with *spanda*, the pulsation of the deepest consciousness, the source of his being. It is a sudden and momentary state, but if the person is wide awake, he clings to it. From that moment, his life is completely changed. He becomes spiritually oriented; his energies are released from the hold of the trivialities of life and are free to dive into the deeper recesses of consciousness. If one seizes this momentous opportunity, one enters the sanctuary of the higher life. If one simply lets it go by, one has lost the opportunity of his life, for this condition does not usually return.

Spandakārikā has mentioned a similar condition in the following verse:

अतिक्रुद्धः प्रहृष्टो वा, किं करोमीति वा मृशन् ।
धावन्वा यत्पदं गच्छेत्तत्र स्पन्दः प्रतिष्ठितः ॥ (I 22)

"When one is in extreme anger or experiences surpassing joy, or is in a state of impasse, not knowing what to do, or has to flee for his life, then in that (supremely intensive) state (of mind) is established the *Spanda* principle, the creative pulsation of the divine consciousness.

This is *Śāmbhava upāya*.

[Dhāraṇā 94]

VERSE 119

वस्तुषु स्मर्यमाणेषु दृष्टे देशे मनस्त्यजेत् ।
स्वशरीरं निराधारं कृत्वा प्रसरति प्रभुः ॥ ११६ ॥

Vastuṣu smaryamāṇeṣu dṛṣṭe deśe manas tyajet /
Svaśarīraṃ nirādhāraṃ kṛtvā prasarati prabhuḥ // 119

TRANSLATION

At the sight of a land, when one lets go all the thought of the remembered objects (and concentrates only on the experience which was the basis of that memory) and makes his body supportless, then the Lord (who as the experience was the basis of the memory) appears.

NOTES

On remembering a particular object, the aspirant should ignore the memory of the object and fix his mind on the original experience which is the basis of the memory. At the same time, he should detach himself mentally from the body, i.e. the psycho-somatic organism in which the memory and the residual impressions are stored. In this state, his mind will be freed of I-consciousness and the deposit of the residual impressions (vāsanā) and will be restored to its pristine form of pure Experience, pure Consciousness. This pure Consciousness or Experience is the nature of Bhairava.

This is *Śāktopāya*.

[Dhāraṇā 95]

VERSE 120

क्वचिद्वस्तुनि विन्यस्य शनैर्दृष्टिं निवर्तयेत् ।
तज्ज्ञानं चित्तसहितं देवि शून्यालयो भवेत् ॥ १२० ॥

Kvacid vastuni vinyasya śanair dṛṣṭiṃ nivartayet /
Taj jñānaṃ cittasahitaṃ devi śūnyālayo bhavet //120

TRANSLATION

O goddess, if one, after casting one's gaze on some object, withdraws it and slowly eliminates the knowledge of that object along with the thought and impression of it, he abides in the void.

NOTES

The aspirant can eliminate the knowledge of the object along with its impression either (1) by *śūnyabhāvanā* or (2) by *bhairavī mudrā*.

1. *Śūnyabhāvanā* is the imaginative contemplation that the whole world is unsubstantial, mere void. When the whole world

is believed to be void, naturally a particular object in the world will also become void.

2. *Bhairavīmudrā* is a pose in which the eyes are open externally without blinking, but the attention is turned to the inner essential Self. Though the eyes are open, the aspirant sees nothing of the external world.

This *dhāraṇā* teaches that the aspirant should fix his attention only on his essential Self and withdraw it from everything else so that the external world loses its hold on him.

This is *Śāktopāya.*

[Dhāraṇā 96]

VERSE 121

भक्त्युद्रेकाद्विरक्तस्य यादृशी जायते मतिः ।
सा शक्तिः शाङ्करी नित्यं भावयेत्तां ततः शिवः ॥ १२१ ॥

Bhaktyudrekād viraktasya yādṛśī jāyate matiḥ /
Sā śaktiḥ śāṅkarī nityam bhāvayet tām tataḥ śivaḥ // 121

TRANSLATION

The sort of intuition (*mati*) that emerges through the intensity of devotion in one who is perfectly detached is known as the *śakti* of *śaṅkara*. One should contemplate on it perpetually. Then he becomes *Śiva* Himself.

NOTES

One who is perfectly detached i.e. is not attached to sensuous pleasures and is devoted to God develops *mati*. The word *mati* is used in a technical sense here. It means pure spiritual intuition that is dynamic. This *mati* is full of beneficent power (*śāṅkarī śakti*) that can transform and consecrate life. That is why this *dhāraṇā* recommends contemplation on *mati*.

There are four steps in this *dhāraṇā*. (1) one's value of life has to be totally changed. He should be completely detached from sensuous pleasures and trinkets of life. (2) He should be devoted to God. (3) Through the above two, the mind of the aspirant will become purified, and then will emerge *mati* which is spiritual intuition full of the power to transform life. She can remove all obstacles in the path of the aspirant. (4) The aspirant should perpetually contemplate on this *mati* (*nityam bhāvayet tām*). She will completely transform his life, and then his mind will be dissolved in *Śiva* (*tataḥ Śivaḥ*).

It should be borne in mind that *bhakti* or devotion does not mean simply offering of flowers and burning incense. It means viewing God in all life and dedication of oneself to the Divine in word, thought and deed.

This is *Śāmbhava upāya.*

[Dhāraṇā 97]

VERSE 122

वस्त्वन्तरे वेद्यमाने सर्ववस्तुषु शून्यता ।
तामेव मनसा ध्यात्वा विदितोऽपि प्रशाम्यति ॥ १२२ ॥

Vastvantare vedyamāne sarvavastuṣu śūnyatā /
Tām eva manasā dhyātvā vidito'pi praśāmyati // 122

TRANSLATION

When one perceives a particular object, vacuity is established regarding all other objects. If one contemplates on this vacuity with mind freed of all thought, then even though the particular object be still known or perceived, the aspirant has full tranquillity.

NOTES

When the aspirant contemplates on vacuity with mind freed of all thought, there is only the light of consciousness (*cit-prakāśa*) present and nothing else. There is no object to attract his attention. The result is that his differentiation-making mind is now at stand-still. The sense of difference disappears from his mind. So even when the particular object which he had perceived is still present in the field of his consciousness, his differentiation-making mind is dissolved and he experiences wonderful peace.

The present *dhāraṇā* is *Śāktopāya.*

Though there is some similarity between this *dhāraṇā* and the *dhāraṇā* No. 95 described in verse 120, yet there is one particular difference between them. In Dhāraṇā No. 95 when one has known or perceived a particular object, he withdraws his attention from that particular object and contemplates over the *śūnyatā* or vacuity of that particular object and the impression connected with it, whereas in the present *dhāraṇā* No. 97, the aspirant, after perceiving one particular object, contemplates over the vacuity of all other objects.

Both the *dhāraṇās*, however, pertain to *Śāktopāya.*

[Dhāraṇā 98]

VERSE 123

किंचिज्ज्ञैर्या स्मृता शुद्धिः सा शुद्धिः शम्भुदर्शने ।
न शुचिर्ह्यशुचिस्तस्मान्निर्विकल्पः सुखी भवेत् ॥ १२३ ॥

Kiṃcijjñair yā smṛtā śuddhiḥ sā śuddhiḥ śambhudarśane /
Na śucir hy aśucis tasmān-nirvikalpaḥ sukhī bhavet // 123

TRANSLATION

That purity which is prescribed by people of little understanding is considered to be only impurity in the Śaiva system. It should not be considered to be purity; rather it is impurity in reality. Therefore one who has freed himself of *vikalpas* (dichotomizing thought-constructs) alone attains happiness.

NOTES

The purity criticized in this verse refers only to physical purity like washing, bathing, etc. The *Śaiva* system referred to is the Trika system. This system does not lay any special store by external physical purity. It considers only mental purity to be real purity. Physical purity depends only on *vikalpas*—differentiating thought-constructs and is centred round the body. Therefore, the Trika system considers it only an impurity from the higher spiritual point of view. It does not condemn physical purity as such. It condemns it only when it is considered to be a passport to the spiritual life, when it is boosted at the cost of moral and spiritual purity.

In reality, that cannot be considered to be purity at all which is based on *vikalpas* and the body. In the real sense, he alone is pure who has freed himself of *vikalpas* (*nirvikalpaḥ*), and he alone can enjoy real happiness.

According to Svāmī Lakṣmaṇa Joo, the reading of this verse should be "Kiñcijjñair yā smṛtā śuddhiḥ sā śuddhiḥ śambhudarśane. Na śuchir nāśucis tasmān nirvikalpaḥ sukhī bhavet."

"That which is considered to be purity by men of little understanding is in Trika philosophy neither purity nor impurity. One who rises above *vikalpas* (alone) is really happy." The real purity is not of the body. It consists in rising above *vikalpas* and getting absorbed in the supreme I-consciousness.

This *dhāraṇā* is *Śāktopāya.*

[Dhāraṇā 99]

VERSE 124

सर्वत्र भैरवो भावः सामान्येष्वपि गोचरः ।
न च तद्व्यतिरेकेण परोऽस्तीत्यद्वया गतिः ॥ १२४ ॥

Sarvatra bhairavo bhāvaḥ sāmānyeṣv api gocaraḥ /
Na ca tadvyatirekeṇa paro'stīty advayā gatiḥ // 124

TRANSLATION

"The reality of Bhairava is apparent everywhere—even among common folk (who do not possess any particular sense of discrimination). One who knows thus, "There is nothing else than He" attains the non-dual condition.

NOTES

This *dhāraṇā* does not require any particular practice of meditation. *Bhairava* is an ever-present Reality to one who has an intense deep-rooted conviction of two things—viz. (1) every one uses the first personal pronoun 'I'. Even ignormuses are conscious of this 'I'.

As Maheśvarānanda puts it :

"यं जानन्ति जडा अपि जलहार्योऽपि यं विजानन्ति ।
यस्यैव नमस्कारः स कस्य स्फुटो न भवति कुलनाथः ॥"

(Mahārthamañjarī, verse—4)

"He whom even ignormuses know, whom even portresses of water know well enough, to whom alone every one makes a bow, who is Master of śakti (power)—where is the person to whom He is not evident."

How does every person know Him ? He knows Him in the I-consciousness which is common to all. The pseudo-I which every body has to use willy-nilly is only a symbol of the non-dual Eternal 'I' throbbing in the heart of every creature. This Eternal 'I' is *vijñāna* or *cidānanda*—consciousness-bliss. This is *Bhairava*. Thus He is known internally to every body.

2. He is known externally also through His Śakti—power or Energy, His manifestation in the cosmos.

He who thus knows *Bhairava* both internally and externally is fully convinced of the fact that there is nothing else than *Bhairava*. He is a God-intoxicated person. To him, *Bhairava* is an ever-present Reality. He is identified with *Bhairava* and thus enjoys the non-dual state perpetually.

This dhāraṇā is an example of *anupāya*.

[Dhāraṇā 100]

VERSE 125

समः शत्रौ च मित्रे च समो मानावमानयोः ।
ब्रह्मणः परिपूर्णत्वादिति ज्ञात्वा सुखी भवेत् ॥ १२५ ॥

Samaḥ śatrau ca mitre ca samo mānāvamānayoḥ /
Brahmaṇaḥ paripūrṇatvāt iti jñātvā sukhī bhavet // 125

TRANSLATION

Because of the conviction that everything is full of *Brahman* (who is also the essential Self of all), the aspirant has the same attitude towards friend and foe, remains the same both in honour and dishonour, and thus because of this conviction (viz., the conviction of the presence of *Brahman* everywhere), he is perpetually happy.

NOTES

Because of the conviction of the presence of *Brahman* (the Divine Reality) everywhere, the aspirant develops the consciousness of *samatā* (equality), and, therefore, has the same attitude of goodness towards all, is neither elated when he receives honour, nor is depressed when he is subjected to dishonour. The same idea occurs in Gītā-V, 18 and XIV, 25. All mental agitation disappears in his case. Being even-minded, he enjoys perpetual happiness.

This is *Śāktopāya*.

[Dhāraṇā 101]

VERSE 126

न द्वेषं भावयेत्क्वापि न रागं भावयेत्क्वचित् ।
रागद्वेषविनिर्मुक्तौ मध्ये ब्रह्म प्रसर्पति ॥ १२६ ॥

Na dveṣam bhāvayet kvāpi na rāgam bhāvayet kvacit /
Rāgadveṣavinirmuktau madhye brahma prasarpati // 126

TRANSLATION

The aspirant should neither maintain the attitude of aversion nor of attachment towards any one. Since he is freed of both aversion and attachment, there develops *brahmabhāva* or the nature of the divine consciousness (which is also the nature of the essential Self) in his heart.

NOTES

The consciousness of *samatā* (equality) is the main point in both these verses (125 and 126). The only difference between the two is that in *dhāraṇā* No. 125, the aspirant has to acquire *samatā* by contemplating on the positive presence of *Brahman* everywhere, whereas in *dhāraṇā* No. 126, he has to acquire *samatā* by rejecting the attitude of both aversion and attachment.

Both these dhāraṇās are *Śāktopāya.*

[Dhāraṇā 102]

VERSE—127

यदवेद्यं यदग्राह्यं यच्छून्यं यदभावगम् ।
तत्सर्वं भैरवं भाव्यं तदन्ते बोधसंभवः ॥ १२७ ॥

Yad avedyaṃ yad agrāhyaṃ yac chūnyaṃ yad abhāvagam /
Tat sarvam bhairavam bhāvyaṃ tadante bodhasambhavaḥ //127

TRANSLATION

"That which cannot be known as an abject,[1] that which cannot be grasped (i.e. that which is elusive), that which is void,[2] that which penetrates even non-existence[3] all that should be contemplated as Bhairava. At the end of that contemplation will occur Enlightenment.

NOTES

1. The Ultimate Reality has been called avedya or unknowable in the sense that it is *vedaka* i. e. the Eternal and Ultimate Subject of everything and cannot be reduced to *vedya* or object.

2. Void or *śūnya*, Śivopādhyāya in his *vivṛti* (commentary) quotes the following verse to show in what sense the word *śūnya* is taken in Trika philosophy :

"सर्वालम्बनधर्मैश्च सर्वतत्त्वैरशेषतः ।
सर्वक्लेशाशयैः शून्यं न शून्यं परमार्थतः ॥"

"That which is free of all *ālambanas*, of all *tattvas*, of the residual traces of all *kleśas*, that is *śūnya* or void. It is not void as such in its highest sense.

The word *ālambana* means 'support'. It is either an objective existent like a jar or blue colour etc. or an internal existent like pleasure or pain or a thought etc. *Bhairava* or the Highest Reality is called *śūnya* in the sense that He cannot be characterized or limited by any of these objective or subjective characteristics.

He is free of all *tattvas* or constitutive principles. All constitutive principles derive their existence from Him. Therefore, He cannot be characterized by these.

He is free of all *kleśas* and their residual traces. The *kleśas* are *avidyā* or primal ignorance, *asmitā* or ego-sense, *rāga* or attachment, *dveṣa* or aversion, and *abhiniveśa* clinging to particular forms of life, fear of death.

The Highest Reality is called *śūnya* or void, because it is free of all these, not because it is not Real.

3. Both existents and non-existents owe their stance to that Highest Reality. It is the common ground of both existence and non-existence. Śivopādhyāya quotes in this connection the following significant verse from Mahārthamañjarī :

> "कः सद्भावविशेषः कुसुमाद्भवति गगनकुसुमस्य ।
> यत्स्फुरणानुप्राणो लोकः स्फुरणं च सर्वसामान्यम् ॥" (Verse 32)

"What is the difference between an existent flower and a sky-flower (which is non-existent). The universe derives its life from the (divine) creative flash (*sphuraṇa* or *sphurattā*) and that flash is the same everywhere. It is the common ground of both the existent and the non-existent."

The power of the Supreme viz. *svātantrya śakti* known as *sphurattā* or *mahāsattā* is present everywhere and is the common ground of everything existent or non-existent. In the words of Utpaladeva :

> सा स्फुरत्ता महासत्ता देशकालाविशेषिणी ।
> सैषा सारतया प्रोक्ता हृदयं परमेष्ठिनः ॥
> (I. P. I Verse 14)

"This power of Universal Consciousness is the inner, creative flash which, though in itself unchanging, is the source of all change, it is *mahāsattā* or absolute being inasmuch as it is free to be anything, it is the source of all *bhāva* or *abhāva* (existent or non-existent). It is beyond the determinations of space and time. It being the essence of all is said to be the very heart of the Supreme Sovereign."

Abhinavagupta's commentary on this is very enlightening. He says,

सत्ता च भवनकर्तृता सर्वक्रियासु स्वातंत्र्यम् । सा च खपुष्पादि-कमपि व्याप्नोति इति महती ।

The word *sattā* or being is, in this context, used in a technical sense. It does not mean simply being. "It indicates the essential nature of the agent in the act of being i.e. freedom in all actions. It is called *mahāsattā*, because it pervades even the sky-flower (which is non-existent)."

This *dhāraṇā*, therefore, exhorts the aspirant that he should contemplate on *Bhairava* as totally free of all distinctive thought-constructs, as foundational Consciousness whose essential nature is *mahāsattā*, the absolute freedom to appear in any way. He will then have full enlightenment.

This *dhāraṇā* is *Śāmbhavopāya*.

[Dhāraṇā 103]

VERSE 128

नित्ये निराश्रये शून्ये व्यापके कलनोज्झिते ।
बाह्याकाशे मनः कृत्वा निराकाशं समाविशेत् ॥ १२८ ॥

Nityе nirāśraye śūnye vyāpake kalanojjhite /
Bāhyākāśe manaḥ kṛtvā nirākāśaṃ samāviśet // 128

TRANSLATION

One should fix his mind on the external space which is eternal, without support, void, omnipresent, devoid of limitation. (By this practice) he will be absorbed in non-space.

NOTES

Two important points have been made out in this *dhāraṇā*. Firstly, since it is not easy to concentrate on abstract void, the aspirant has been advised to concentrate on the vast, illimitable external space. *Khaṃ* or *ākāśa*, the endless external expanse of vacuity has generally been held to be the symbol of void, *Brahman*, purity, immensity. Therefore, by prolonged practice of concentration on the boundless external space, one acquires the capacity of concentrating on supportless, objectless, vacant reality. After this, one can, with facility, concentrate on the inner, supportless, objectless Reality, the spiritual consciousness, the met-empirical Self or *ātman* and thus can have the *samāveśa* or absorption into the nature of *Bhairava* which transcends all spatial, temporal and empirical modalities.

Secondly, in the previous verse *Bhairava* has been designated as *śūnya* or *śūnya-dhāma*, the very abode of void. In the present verse, He has been designated as 'nirākāśa' transcending all void (*atiśūnya*) or *aśūnya* (non-void), the base and foundation of the void itself and therefore *mahāsāmānya*, *mahāsattā*.

This *dhāraṇā* is *Śāktopāya*.

[Dhāraṇā 104]

VERSE 129

यत्र यत्र मनो याति तत्तत्तेनैव तत्क्षणम् ।
परित्यज्यानवस्थित्या निस्तरङ्गस्ततो भवेत् ॥ १२६ ॥

Yatra yatra mano yāti tattat tenaiva tatkṣaṇam /
Parityajyānavasthityā nistaraṅgas tato bhavet // 129

TRANSLATION

Towards whatever object the mind goes, one should remove it from there immediately by that very mind, and thus by not allowing it to settle down there i.e. by making is supportless, one will be free from agitation (of the mind).

NOTES

The agitation of the mind can be removed by *vairāgya* and *abhyāsa*, i.e. by disinterestedness and practice i.e. by withdrawing one's interest from other things and by repeated concentration on the object of meditation. Both the negative and the positive method should be practised together. The negative method consists in withdrawing the attention from the object that distracts it and the positive method consists in concentrating on the particular object of meditation.

As Bhagavadgītā puts it :

"यतो यतो निश्चरति मनश्चञ्चलमस्थिरम् ।
ततस्ततो नियम्यैतदात्मन्येव वशं नयेत् ॥"
(VI. 26)

"In whichever direction the fluctuating and unsteady mind moves, it should be held back from that direction and brought under the control of the Self."

This is *Śāktopāya.*

[Dhāraṇā 105]

VERSE 130

भया सर्वं रवयति सर्वदो व्यापकोऽखिले ।
इति भैरवशब्दस्य सन्ततोच्चारणाच्छिवः ॥ १३० ॥

Bhayā sarvaṃ ravayati sarvado vyāpako' khile/
Iti bhairavaśabdasya santatoccāraṇāc chivaḥ // 130

TRANSLATION

Bhairava is one who with His luminous consciousness makes every thing resound or who being of luminous consciousness joined with *kriyāśakti* comprehends the whole universe, who gives everything, who pervades the entire cosmos. Therefore by reciting the word *Bhairava* incessantly one becomes *Śiva.*

NOTES

The hermeneutic etymology of the word *Bhairava* has been given in various ways in Trika philosophy. The important interpretations are given below.

The word 'Bhairava' is composed of four letters—'bhā'+ 'ai' + 'ra' + 'va' (भा + ऐ + र + व). 'Bhā' + '*ai*' (भा + ऐ) by the rule of *sandhi* (i.e. euphonic junction of final and initial letters) becomes *bhai* (भै). This *bhai* together with 'ra', 'va' becomes *bhairava* (भैरव). Each of these letters connotes certain important ideas.

Bhā (भा) is a word by itself which means 'light' i.e. the light of consciousness in this context; *ai* (ऐ), according to Trika philosophy is symbolic of *kriyāśakti* (the power of activity);

rava connotes *ravayati* which, in this context, means *vimarśati* i.e. comprehends. So according to this etymoloty *Bhairava* means "He whose light of consciousness joined with his power of activity (*'bhā'* + *ai* i.e. *bhai*) comprehends (*ravayati*) the entire universe is His Self".

In Parātriṃśikā, Abhinvavagupta gives another interpretation of *Bhairava* viz., ' 'Bhairavo bharaṇātmako mahāmantraravātmakaśca" (p.63), i.e. 'Bhairava is one who supports and protects the cosmos and (constantly) sounds the great mantra of 'I' (*aham*)."

In Tantrāloka, Abhinavagupta gives many interpretations of 'Bhairava' of which the main ones are the following three :

1. He supports the cosmos inasmuch as He makes it appear on Himself as substratum and maintains it and also appears in the form of the cosmos (*bhriyate savimarśatayā*). This interpretation is based on the root *bhṛ* which means both *dhāraṇa* and *poṣaṇa* i.e. support and maintenance.

2. He constantly sounds the great mantra of 'I' (*ravarūpataśca*).

3. He offers intrepedity to those who are terrified by the cycle of transmigratory existence (*saṃsārabhīruhitakṛt*).

Each letter of *Bhairava* is symbolic of His three main activities; *Bha* is symbolic of *bharaṇa* or maintenance of the universe; *ra* is symbolic of *ravaṇa* or withdrawal of the universe; *va* is symbolic of *vamana* or projection of the universe.

The two adjectives of 'Bhairava' viz., *sarvadaḥ* (bestower of all) and *vyāpakaḥ*, (all-pervasive) are also connected by implication with two letters of *Bhairava*, viz., *ra* and *va* ; *ra* is symbolic of the root *rā* which means to give, to grant, to bestow. He is called *sarvadaḥ*, because he bestows everything (*sarvaṃ rāti*) 'va' is symbolic of *vā* which means 'to be diffused' *Bhairava* is called *vyāpaka* because of the diffusion of His presence everywhere.

It should be borne in mind that the word *uccāra* in the verse does not mean mechanical repetition of the word *Bhairava*. *Uccāra* in this context denotes the sounding of the interior *prāṇaśakti* which is the representation of *saṃvid* or consciousness.

This *prāṇaśakti* rises from the heart (centre) and through *suṣumna* reaches *dvādaśānta* or *Brahmarandhra* where it is united with *prakāśa* or *Bhairava.*

This Dhāraṇā is *Śāktopāya.*

[Dhāraṇā 106]

VERSE 131

अहं ममेदमित्यादि प्रतिपत्तिप्रसङ्गतः ।
निराधारे मनो याति तद्ध्यानप्रेरणाच्छमी ॥ १३१ ॥

Ahaṃ mamedam ityādi pratipattiprasaṅgataḥ/
Nirādhāre mano yāti taddhyānapreraṇāc chamī // 131

TRANSLATION

On the occasion of the assertion, "I am; this is mine, etc.," the thought goes to that which does not depend on any support. Under the impulsion of the contemplation of that (tat), one attains (abiding) peace.

NOTES

Nirādhāra or supportless is *pūrṇāham,* the absolute 'I' which is *nirvikalpa* (above all thought-constructs). Even when a man considers the pseudo-I to be the Self, there is present behind the pseudeo-I, the absolute 'I', the *nirvikalpaka* or the thought-free Self which is ever-present consciousness—bliss both in the ignorant and the wise. So when a man asserts the pseudo-I to be the Self, his mind sub-consciously reflects the real, the absolute, the thought-free I which is eternally vibrating in him behind his psycho-physical I. The present *dhāraṇā* exhorts the aspirant to lay hold of that absolute, thought-free I, and then by the creative contemplation (*bhāvanā*) of that thought-free I, (*taddhyānapreraṇāt*) his *savikalpaka* mind will ultimately be absorbed in *nirvikalpaka* state, and thus he will attain abiding peace.

The word *dhyāna* (meditation) in this context is equivalant to *bhāvanā* (contemplation). This *dhāraṇā* is, therefore, *Śāktopāya.*

By Śāktopāya, a *śuddha vikalpa* ultimately ends in *nirvikalpa* which is the essential nature of Bhairava. The *tat* (that) in *taddhyāna* refers to *nirādhāra.* This *dhāraṇā* advises the aspirant to lay hold of the *nirādhāra* and contemplate over that (*tat*) as his real Self. Surely this contemplation will also be a *vikalpa* (dichotomizing thought), but it will be *śuddha vikalpa* (pure *vikalpa*) which by *Śākta bhāvanā* will ultimately end in *nirvikalpa.*

In Tantrāloka I (Verses 214-215) Abhinavagupta points out how by *Śākta upāya, savikalpa* is finally transformed in *nirvikalpa.*

शाक्तोऽथ भण्यते चेतो धीमनोहंकृतिस्फुटम् ।
सविकल्पतया मायामयमिच्छादि वस्तुतः ॥ २१४ ॥
अभिमानेन संकल्पाध्यवसायक्रमेण यः ।
शाक्तः स मायोपायोऽपि तदन्ते निर्विकल्पकः ॥ २१५ ॥

."The consciousness of the empirical individual is limited to *buddhi, manas,* and *ahaṃkāra.* Though this functions in thought-forms in the manner of māyā whose main characteristic is the making of differentiation, yet in reality, it is also inspired by will, etc. If the limited ego of the empirical individual *(ahaṃkṛti abhimāna)* adopts a *vikalpa* or thought (function of *manas*) like the following, "I am present everywhere, everything is in me" then *adhyavasāyakrameṇa* by constant, persevering determination (function of *buddhi*), his *vikalpa* though dominated by māyā ultimately ends in *nirvikalpa* (thought-free, intuitive apprehension)."

This *dhāraṇā* pertains to *Śāktopāya.*

[Dhāraṇā 107]

VERSE 132

नित्यो विभुर्निराधारो व्यापकश्चाखिलाधिपः ।
शब्दान् प्रतिक्षणं ध्यायन् कृतार्थोऽर्थानुरूपतः ॥ १३२ ॥

Nityo vibhur nirādhāro vyāpakaś cākhilādhipaḥ /
Śabdān pratikṣaṇaṃ dhyāyan kṛtārtho'rthānurūpataḥ // 132

TRANSLATION

"Eternal, omnipresent, without depending on any support, all-pervasive, lord of all that is "—meditating every instant on these words in conformity with their sense, one attains his object (i.e. has fulfilment)

NOTES

By constantly pondering over the implication of these words, the mind of the aspirant becomes chockful of the essential reality of *Śiva*. By comprehending perfectly the sense of *nitya* and *vibhu*, the aspirant comes to realize that the essential nature of *Bhairava* and so also of his essential Self transcends 'time', and by meditating on the significance of *vyāpaka*, he realizes that it transcends 'space' also. By meditating on *nirādhāra*, he realizes that the nature of *Bhairava* and so also of his essential Self is *nirvikalpa* i.e. 'transcendent to thought'.

So by meditating on these characteristics of *Śiva*, he has Self-realization. Thus he becomes *kṛtārtha*, his aim in life is fulfilled, for knowledge of Self is the highest aim one can entertain.

This *dhāraṇā* pertains to *Śāktopāya*.

[Dhāraṇā 108]

VERSE 133

अतत्त्वमिन्द्रजालाभमिदं सर्वमवस्थितम् ।
किं तत्त्वमिन्द्रजालस्य इति दार्ढ्याच्छमं व्रजेत् ॥ १३३ ॥

Atattvam indrajālābham idaṃ sarvam avasthitam /
Kiṃ tattvam indrajālasya iti dārḍhyāc chamaṃ vrajet //133

[Dhāraṇā 109]

VERSE 134

आत्मनो निर्विकारस्य क्व ज्ञानं क्व च वा क्रिया ।
ज्ञानायत्ता बहिर्भावा अतः शून्यमिदं जगत् ॥ १३४ ॥

Ātmano nirvikārasya kva jñānaṃ kva ca vā kriyā /
Jñānāyattā bahirbhāvā ataḥ śūnyam idaṃ jagat // 134

TRANSLATION OF VERSE 133

This whole universe is without any essential reality like a magical spectacle. What is the reality of a magical spectacle ? If one is fully convinced of the non-essentiality of the universe in this way, he attains to peace.

TRANSLATION OF VERSE 134

In the unchangeable Self, how can there be knowledge or activity ? All external objects are dependent on knowledge; therefore this world is void.

NOTES ON VERSES 133—134

Both the above verses refer to the unreality of the world.

The first one says that the world is like a magic show; therefore, it has no reality. The second one teaches the unreality of the world on the basis of non-knowledge and non-activity. The Self is one mass of consciousness without any division or differentiation. There can be no change in it. Both knowledge and activity are a kind of change. Therefore, knowledge and activity cannot be possible in Self. All external objects of the world are dependent on knowledge (and activity). As knowledge and activity are unreal, so the world that is dependent on these is also unreal, mere void. By contemplating in the above ways, one acquires peace.

It has to be borne in mind that the knowledge and activity mentioned in this verse refer to the knowledge and activity of the limited, empirical individual whose knowledge and activity are permeated by a sense of difference, and pertain to the world full of changes.

In the essential Self there is absolutely no change or difference. Therefore, the knowledge and activity of the empirical individual belong only to the psycho-physical self, not to the essential Self. The knowledge and activity (*jñāna* and *kriyā*) which are the characteristics of the essential Self are *śaktis* (*jñānaśakti* and *kriyā-śakti*) by which alone there can be any knowledge or activity. Secondly, they are not dependent on the *antaḥkaraṇa* (*buddhi*, *manas* and *ahaṃkāra*) and *jñānendriyas* and *karmendriyas* (organs of sense and action) just as the knowledge and activity of the empirical individual are. Thirdly, they are not prompted by any sense of difference.

Both the above *dhāraṇās* are *Śāktopāya*

[Dhāraṇā 110]

VERSE 135

न मे बन्धो न मोक्षो मे भीतस्यैता विभीषिकाः ।
प्रतिबिम्बमिदं बुद्धेर्जलेष्विव विवस्वतः ॥ १३५ ॥

Na me bandho na mokṣo me bhītasyaitā vibhīṣikāḥ /
Pratibimbam idam buddher jaleṣv iva vivasvataḥ // 135

TRANSLATION

There is neither bondage nor liberation for me. These (bondage and liberation) are only bogies for those who are terrified (on account of the ignorance of their essential nature). This (the universe) appears as a reflection in *buddhi* (the intellect) like the image of the sun in water.

NOTES

The Self is pure consciousness (*cinmātram*). It is not limited by space and time. The question of bondage or liberation can arise only in the case of an entity that is limited by space and time.

Just as the image of the sun appears inverted in water, even so it is the limited *buddhi* (in which the Self is reflected) that poses as the Self and considers itself bound or liberated. Both bondage and liberation are the imaginative constructs of *buddhi*. Self which is pure consciousness transcends these imaginative constructs.

Abhinavagupta throws a flood of light on this question in *Īśvarapratyabhijñāvimarśinī* (IV. I,2)

"तत्र स्वसृष्टेदंभागे बुद्ध्यादिग्राहकात्मना ।
अहंकारपरामर्शपदं नीतमनेन तत् ॥"

"In His light of Consciousness, the Lord makes, in the objective world created by Himself, *buddhi* etc. function as subject, i.e. as the substratum of pseudo I-consciousness, because they can function as limited subjects."

Abhinavagupta's gloss on this *Kārikā* runs as follows :

स्वात्मनि महेश्वरे स्थिते तस्मिन्नेव प्रकाशरूपे स्वात्मदर्पणे तेनैव परमेश्वरेण स्वातंत्र्यात् तावत्सृष्टः संकोचपुरःसर इदंभागः, तन्मध्ये यदेतद्बुद्धिप्राणदेहरूपमिदन्तया वेद्यं तद्बुद्ध्यादिभिन्नस्य वेद्यस्य ग्राहकतया समुचितम् इदंभावोभिभवाप्रभविष्णुत्वात् कृतकेनापूर्णेनाहंभावेन परामर्शेन भासमानं चकास्ति "अहं देवदत्तोऽहं चैत्र" इति ।

"The Highest Lord, resting within His own self, in the luminous mirror of His Self manifests within Himself by the power of His perfect freedom, the objective aspect of the world which is limited in its nature. In the midst of this creation, there are the objects, such as *prāṇa*, *buddhi*, body, etc. They are objects and are to be referred to as this. But they can appropriately function as subjects in relation to objects which are separate from them. Therefore, as they cannot completely cast off objectivity, so they shine as illumined with assumed and imperfect self-consciousness, as 'I am Devadatta," "I am Caitra", etc.

When the aspirant is fully convinced that the question of bondage or liberation arises only for the psychophysical self, not for the metaphysical Self, he rises above the *vikalpas* of the psycho-physical self and is immersed in the nature of *Bhairava*.

According to Svāmī Lakṣmaṇa Joo, *jīvasya* (of the empirical subject) in place of *bhītasya* is a better reading, because bondage and liberation are bogies for all empirical subjects.

This *dhāraṇā* pertains to *Śāmbhavopāya*.

[Dhāraṇā 111]

VERSE 136

इन्द्रियद्वारकं सर्वं सुखदुःखादिसङ्गमम् ।
इतीन्द्रियाणि संत्यज्य स्वस्थः स्वात्मनि वर्तते ।। १३६ ।।

Indriyadvārakaṃ sarvaṃ sukhaduḥkhādisaṅgamam /
Itīndriyāṇi saṃtyajya svasthaḥ svātmani vartate // 136

TRANSLATION

All contact with pleasure and pain is through the senses, (knowing this), one should detach oneself from the senses, and withdrawing within should abide in his essential Self.

NOTES

All pleasure, pain, etc, derived through the senses are not the characteristics of the *cidātmā*, the essential met-empirical Self, but only of the empirical, psycho-physical complex miscalled Self. When one is centred in his essential Self, one automatically gets freed from the peremptory demands of the senses.

The previous *dhāraṇā* teaches that it is necessary to rise above the activity of the *buddhi* (the intellect) and be poised in one's essential Self. The *dhāraṇā* mentioned in the present verse teaches that it is necessary to detach oneself from the activities of the senses also which lead us on towards the pleasures of the external world. This is to be effected principally through *śakti-saṅkoca* which has been defined in the following words in Pratyabhijñāhṛdayam.

"शक्तेः सङ्कोचः–इन्द्रियद्वारेण प्रसरन्त्या एव आकुञ्चनक्रमेण उन्मुखीकरणम् ।"

"*Śakti-saṅkoca* consists in turning in towards the Self, by the process of withdrawal, of that consciousness which is spreading externally through the doors of the senses (towards the objects)". *Śakti saṅkoca* is the technique of introversion or interiorization. By this practice, one becomes *svastha*, i.e. poised in oneself and the attractions of the world do not trouble him any longer. He is freed from the opposites of pleasure and pain and abides in his essential Self which is the nature of Bhairava. In the words of Yoga-vāsiṣṭha

"एते हि चिद्विलासान्ता मनोबुद्धीन्द्रियादयः"

(VI. Su, 78, 31) "On the luminous emergence of *cit* (the spiritual consciousness, the essential Self), the wayward activities of the *manas*, *buddhi* and the senses come to an end."

This is *Śāktopāya*.

[Dhāraṇā 112]

VERSE 137

ज्ञानप्रकाशकं सर्वं सर्वेणात्मा प्रकाशकः ।
एकमेकस्वभावत्वात् ज्ञानं ज्ञेयं विभाव्यते ॥ १३७ ॥

Jñānaprakāśakàṃ sarvaṃ sarveṇātmā prakāśakaḥ /
Ekam ekasvabhāvatvāt jñānaṃ jñeyaṃ vibhāvyate // 137

TRANSLATION

All things are revealed by *jñāna* i.e. the knowledge or Self and the Self is revealed by all things. By reason of their nature being the same, one should contemplate on the knower and the known as one and the same.

NOTES

"All things are manifested by knowledge (jñāna)." In this, knowledge or *jñāna* stands for the *jñātā* or the knower. So the verse means to say that all the things known (*jñeya*) are revealed by the *jñāna* or knower (the *jñātā*) and the knower or *ātmā* is revealed by the known.

As Ucchuṣmabhairava puts it :

"यावन्न वेदका एते तावद्वेद्याः कथं प्रिये ।
वेदकं वेद्यमेकं तु तत्त्वं नास्त्यशुचिस्ततः ॥"

"O dear one, so long as there are no knowers (selves, subjects), how can there be the known (object) ? The known and the knower are really the same principle. Therefore, there is nothing which is inherently impure or insentient."

When the aspirant seriously and earnestly contemplates over this fact, he is implanted in the nature of *Bhairava*.

Śivopādhyāya quotes another verse to re-enforce the significance of the present *dhāraṇā* :

"प्रकाशमानं न पृथक् प्रकाशात्
स च प्रकाशो न पृथग् विमर्शात् ।
नान्यो विमर्शोऽहमिति स्वरूपाद्
अहंविमर्शोऽस्मि चिदेकरूपः ।"

"All manifestation is not separate from the light of consciousness. The light of consciousness is never separate from I-consciousness. The I-consciousness is nothing else than Self and Self is simply *cit* or pure consciousness."

Thus contemplating over the fact that the Subject, object and *cit* constitute the same reality, one attains to the nature of *Bhairava*.

This is *Śāktopāya*.

According to Svāmī Lakṣmaṇa Joo, there is another reading of this verse prevalent in the Śaiva tradition :

"Jnānam prakāśakaṃ loke ātmā caiva prakāśakaḥ /
Anayor apṛthagbhāvāt jñāne jñānī vibhāvyate." //

"In the world, *jñāna* or knowledge reveals things and the Self is the source of all revelation. Since there is no difference between the Self and *Jñāna* (knowledge), the *jñānī* (knower or Self) is revealed in the *jñāna* (knowledge)."

CONCLUSION OF THE DHĀRAṆĀS

VERSE 138

मानसं चेतना शक्तिरात्मा चेति चतुष्टयम् ।
यदा प्रिये परिक्षीणं तदा तद्भैरवं वपुः ॥ १३८ ॥

Mānasaṃ cetanā śaktir ātmā ceti catuṣṭayam /
Yadā priye parikṣīṇaṃ tadā tad bhairavaṃ vapuḥ // 138

TRANSLATION

O dear one, when the ideating mind (*manas*), the ascertaining intellect (*buddhi*), the vital energy (*prāṇaśakti*) and the limited empirical I—this set of four dissolves, then the previously described (tat) state of Bhairava appears.

NOTES

Parikṣīṇam or the dissolution of *manas*, *buddhi*, etc. means that they are transformed and appear in the words of Śivopādhyāya *citcamatkāram āpannam* as delightful aspects of the pure, universal consciousness.

This verse sums up the entire cosmic process. There is first gradual *nimeṣa* or evolution of the universal Dynamic Consciousness (*citi*) into inconscient matter. This is the arc of descent (*avaroha*). *Citi* assumes four forms for appearing as limited individual life, viz., (1) *Cetanā*, ascertaining intellect (*buddhi*), (2) *manas*, ideating mind, (3) *prāṇaśakti* or vital energy which keeps the body and the mental faculties in proper form, (4) the ego or the empirical self (designated as *ātmā* in the present verse). All these which form the inner life of the individual are usually summed up under the word *citta*, the individual consciousness. Kṣemarāja maintains very clearly in sūtra 5 of Pratyabhijñāhṛdayam that "*Citi* (universal consciousness) itself descending from the state of *cetana* (uncontracted conscious stage) becomes *citta* (individual consciousness) inasmuch as it becomes contracted (saṅkocinī) in conformity with the object of consciousness."

Gradual *unmeṣa* or evolution begins from the stage of the animal. Here life is mostly *bahirmukhī* or extroverted. There is only slight development of mind. Life at the human stage is on the arc of ascent (*adhyāroha*). Man alone is given the opportunity of mounting to the summit of the spiritual life provided he is prepared to surrender his ego.

The Trika philosophy proclaims that *citta* (individual consciousness) can be transformed into *citi* (universal consciousness). Pratyabhijñāhṛdayam says that *cittameva antarmukhībhāvena cetanapadādhyārohāt citiḥ* (*sūtra*, 13)—"*citta* itself by inward movement becomes *citi* by rising to the status of *cetana*." The status of *cetana* is the nature of *Bhairava* which is our own essential Self. It is for this consummation that the various *dhāraṇās* have been recommended in Vijñānabhairava. When the aspirant has reached a stage where he fully realizes that *buddhi*, *manas*, *prāṇa* and the ego are only formations of *Māyā* for carrying on the individual life, that they are only the instruments of Self and do not constitute his essential Self, then he is poised in his essential Self which is the nature of *Bhairava*, then these instruments reflect the life of the Spirit and can no longer hamper its expression.

VERSES 139-140

निस्तरङ्गोपदेशानां शतमुक्तं समासतः ।
द्वादशाभ्यधिकं देवि यज्ज्ञात्वा ज्ञानविज्जनः ॥१३९॥
अत्र चैकतमे युक्तो जायते भैरवः स्वयम् ।
वाचा करोति कर्माणि शापानुग्रहकारकः ॥ १४० ॥

Nistaraṅgopadeśānāṃ śatam uktaṃ samāsataḥ /
Dvādaśābhyadhikaṃ devi yajjñātvā jñānavij janaḥ // 139
Atra caikatame yukto jāyate bhairavaḥ svayam /
Vācā karoti karmāṇi śāpānugrahakārakaḥ // 140

TRANSLATION

O goddess, I have described hundred and twelve *dhāraṇas* (yogic practices) in which there can be no surge[1] in the mind. Knowing them, one can be a perfect gnostic person-139. If one is established even in one of these practices, he will become Bhairava in himself. He can effect anything by word alone. He will have the power to confer benediction or malediction[2]—140.

NOTES

1. *Nistaraṅga*—without any surge in the mind i.e. in which the mind becomes *nirvikalpaka*—freed of thought-constructs. Jayaratha in his viveka commentary explains it as *svātmamātra-viśrāntyā śāntarūpā* (Tantrāloka III. 5, p. 349). i.e. resting in one's essential Self, full of peace.

2. Since he becomes identified with *Śiva*, the source of all power, he can effect anything he desires.

112 *dhāraṇās* have been described in order that the aspirant may choose any according to his capacity. *Bhairava* says that even if one *dhāraṇā* is properly understood and practised by the aspirant, he will be established in his essential Self and will attain perfect peace.

VERSES 141-144

अजरामरतामेति सोऽणिमादिगुणान्वितः ।
योगिनीनां प्रियो देवि सर्वमेलापकाधिपः ॥ १४१ ॥
जीवन्नपि विमुक्तोऽसौ कुर्वन्नपि न लिप्यते ।

श्रीदेवी उवाच
इदं यदि वपुर्देव परायाश्च महेश्वर ॥ १४२ ॥
एवमुक्तव्यवस्थायां जप्यते को जपश्च कः ।
ध्यायते को महानाथ पूज्यते कश्च तृप्यति ॥ १४३ ॥
हूयते कस्य वा होमो यागः कस्य च किं कथम् ।
श्रीभैरव उवाच
एषात्र प्रक्रिया बाह्या स्थूलेष्वेव मृगेक्षणे ॥ १४४ ॥

Ajarāmaratām eti so'ṇimādiguṇānvitaḥ /
Yoginīnām priyo devi sarvamelāpakādhipaḥ // 141
Jīvann api vimukto'sau kurvannapi na lipyate /
Śrī Devī uvāca
Idaṃ yadi vapur deva parāyāś ca maheśvara // 142.
Evamuktavyavasthāyāṃ japyate ko japaś ca kaḥ /
Dhyāyate ko mahānātha pūjyate kaś ca tṛpyati // 143
Hūyate kasya vā homo yāgaḥ kasya ca kiṃ katham /
Śrī Bhairava uvāca
Eṣātra prakriyā bāhyā sthūleṣv eva mṛgekṣaṇe // 144

TRANSLATION

O goddess, the aspirant (who has become efficient in any one of the above *dhāraṇās*) gains freedom from old age and mortality, and becomes endowed with *aṇimā*[1] and other powers. He becomes the darling of the *yoginīs*[2] and master of all *melāpakas*[3] 141.

He is liberated even while living, and carrying on all the activities (of life), he is not affected by them.

The goddess said "Great lord, if such is the nature of the Supreme Śakti,142 then in the admittedly established rules of spiritual life, who would be invoked in recitation and what will be the recitation? Who, O great lord, would be meditated on, who would be worshipped, who is to be gratified ? 143

To whom is oblation to be offered ? For whom is sacrifice to be performed ?[4] And how is it to be accomplished ?

Bhairava says in reply, O, gazelle-eyed one, this practice (referred to by you) is exterior and pertains only to gross forms. 144.

NOTES

1. Aṇimā and other supernormal powers are the following:

(1) Aṇimā—the power of becoming as small as an atom.

(2) Laghimā—the power of assuming excessive lightness.

(3) Mahimā—the power of increasing the size.

(4) Prāpti—the power of obtaining everything.

(5) Prākāmya—the power of fulfilling one's desire without any resistance; irresistible will.

(6) Vaśitva—the power of bringing all the elements and material objects into subjection.

(7) Īśitṛtva—the power of producing and destroying the elements and material objects.

(8) Yatrakāmāvasāyitva—the power of fulfilling all resolves.

2. Darling of the *yoginīs*—one sense of this expression is that he becomes the master of the *Śaktis* (powers) like *jñāna* (knowledge), *kriyā* (activity), *ānanda* (bliss). According to the Kaula tradition, there is another sense of the *yoginīs*. A male practitioner of *yoga* was known as *vīra* or *siddha* and a female one was known as *yoginī*. From this point of view, the sense of the above would be "He becomes the favourite of the *yoginīs*."

3. Melāpakas—The word *melāpaka* means uniting, conjunction. In this context, Ānandabhaṭṭa interprets it as *sakalasya asya vedya-vedaka-ādi-rāśeḥ khilīkṛtasvabhāvaḥ i. e.* 'one who has risen above all the distinctions of the knower and the known etc., and has thus acquired the nature of *Bhairava*.' According to the Kaula tradition *melāpaka* means the gathering or union of the *siddhas* and the *yoginīs*.

4. The question of Bhairavī was "who is *parā devī* or the highest *śakti* (power) of the divine ?" The answer that Bhairava has given is that *parā devī* is only the *śakti* or nature of *Bhairava* that everything in the universe is only an expression of that nature and that out of the 112 *dhāraṇās* described, if any one masters even one *dhāraṇā*, he would attain that divine nature.

Bhairavī now puts a further question "If every thing in the universe is only an expression of the divine and if the aspirant by practising to perfection any one of the *dhāraṇās* becomes divine, then what becomes of the distinction between the devotee and the object of devotion which is an established tenet and fully accepted by religion ?

The answer to this question of the *devī* is found in the next verse.

VERSE 145

भूयो भूयः परे भावे भावना भाव्यते हि या ।
जपः सोऽत्र स्वयं नादो मन्त्रात्मा जप्य ईदृशः ॥ १४५ ॥

Bhūyo bhūyaḥ pare bhāve bhāvanā bhāvyate hi yā /
Japaḥ so'tra svayaṃ nādo mantrātmā japya īdṛśaḥ // 145

TRANSLATION

That creative contemplation which is practised on the highest Reality[1] over and over again is in this scripture japa[2] (recitation in reality). That which goes on sounding spontaneously (inside) in the form of a *mantra* (mystic formula) is what the japa is about.[3]

NOTES

1. *Pare bhave* (the highest Reality) referred to in this verse is the absolute I-consciousness. The import of this I-consciousness is beautifully expressed in the following verse by Utpaladeva :

प्रकाशस्यात्मविश्रान्तिरहंभावो हि कीर्तितः ।
उक्ता च सैव विश्रान्तिः सर्वापेक्षानिरोधतः ।
स्वातंत्र्यमथ कर्तृत्वं मुख्य ईश्वरतापि च ।

(*Ajaḍapramātṛsiddhi*-22-23)

"Resting of all objective experience within the Self is what is meant by I-feeling. This resting (within the self) is called autonomy of Will, primordial doership and universal sovereignty because of the cancellation of all relational consciousness, and of dependence on anything outside oneself."

2. *Japa* is not the muttering of some sacred formula. *Japa*, in its real sense, is the *bhāvanā* or contemplation on one's

essential Self. Kṣemarāja in his commentary on III, 27 of the Śiva-sūtras puts the idea of *japa* beautifully in the following words : "स्वात्मदेवताविमर्शानवरतावर्तनात्मा जपो जायते"। "*Japa* consists in the repetition of constant contemplation on the deity that is one's own essential Self." In that connexion, he quotes the present verse of Vijñānabhairava.

Abhinavagupta also gives expression to the same idea about *japa* in Tantrāloka (I, 90).

"तत्स्वरूपं जपः प्रोक्तो भावाभावपदच्युतः ।"

"Japa freed of all ideas of ens and non-ens is the constant contemplation of Siva's nature."

Jayaratha commenting on this verse says :

"तस्य शिवस्य स्वरूपं परावाक्स्वभावम् आत्मरूपम् भूयोभूयः परामृश्यमानं जपः । अत एव भावाभावपदच्युतः पूर्वोक्तनीत्या तन्मध्यस्फुरत् परामर्शमात्रसारः इत्यर्थः ।" (I. p. 315).

"Constant mindfulness of the nature of *Śiva* which is *parāvāk* or Self is *japa*, the essence of which consists in the mindfulness of the reality which shines in between both *bhāva* (ens) and *abhāva* (non-ens)". Immediately after this, Jayaratha also quotes the present verse of Vijñānabhairava.

3. *Japa* (recitation) consists in the repetition of *mantra*. What is the *mantra* here. The second half of the verse clarifies what this *mantra* is. It is the *svayaṃnāda*, i.e. it is the *mantra* *so' ham* (I am Śiva) which the inward *prāṇaśakti* ceaselessly goes on sounding by itself in every living creature. It is this automatic *mantra* which has to be contemplated on, and it is this that is real *japa*.

VERSE 146

ध्यानं हि निश्चला बुद्धिर्निराकारा निराश्रया ।
न तु ध्यानं शरीराक्षिमुखहस्तादिकल्पना ॥ १४६ ॥

Dhyānaṃ hi niścalā buddhir nirākārā nirāśrayā /
Na tu dhyānaṃ śarīrākṣimukhahastādikalpanā // 146

TRANSLATION

Unswerving *buddhi*[1] without any image[2] or support[3] constitutes meditation. Concentration on an imaginative representation of the divine with a body, eyes, mouth, hands, etc. is not meditation.

NOTES

1. Buddhi is the immediate and determinative aspect of consciousness.
2. Without any image means without an idol or *yantra* (diagram), etc.
3. *Nirāśrayā* or without support means without the help of a particular spot to meditate on such as *hṛdaya* (centre) *mūlādhāra* or *nābhi* (navel), etc.

Abhinavagupta has defined *dhyāna* (meditation) in a similar strain in Tantrāloka (I, 89). Jayaratha in his commentary on *dhyāyate paramaṃ dhyeyam* occurring in verse 89 says, *paramaṃ dhyeyaṃ śivalakṣaṇam paramakāraṇaṃ dhyāyate svātmābhedena parāmṛśyate* i.e. "the object of meditation is Śiva who is the supreme source of all manifestation and who is to be meditated on as non-different from one's own essential Self." This is what is meant by *dhyāna* or meditation in this system. Immediately after the above comment, Jayaratha quotes the present verse of Vijñānabhairava.

VERSE 147

पूजा नाम न पुष्पाद्यैर्या मतिः क्रियते दृढा ।
निर्विकल्पे महाव्योम्नि सा पूजा ह्यादराल्लयः ।। १४७ ।।

Pūjā nāmạ na puṣpādyair yā matiḥ kriyate dṛḍhā /
Nirvikalpe mahāvyomni sā pūjā hy ādarāt layaḥ // 147

TRANSLATION

Worship does not mean offering of flowers, etc.[1] It rather consists in setting one's heart on that highest ether of consciousness which is above all thought-constructs.[2] It really means dissolution of self with perfect ardour (in the Supreme Consciousness known as *Bhairava*).

NOTES

1. Et cetera includes burning of incense, lighting a candle, blowing of conch and other gross forms of worship.

2. The highest ether of consciousness means *vijñāna* or the supreme spiritual consciousness which is *Bhairava*.

In the same strain, Abhinavagupta gives an excellent description of worship in the following verse in Tantrāloka :

पूजा नाम विभिन्नस्य भावौघस्यापि संगतिः ।
स्वतन्त्रविमलानन्तभैरवीयचिदात्मना ॥ (IV. 121)

Jayaratha elucidates this beautiful verse in the following words :

"विभिन्नस्यापि रूपरसादेर्भावौघस्य देशकालाद्यनवच्छिन्ननिरुपाधिपूर्णपरसंविदात्मना या संगतिः एकीकारः सा पूजा ।"

(IV, p. 123)

"Worship consists in the unification of the different streams of sense experiences like form, colour, savour, etc. with the infinite (*ananta*), free (*svatantra*), immaculate (*vimala*) consciousness of *Bhairava* which is above the limitation of space, time, etc. (*deśakālādyanavacchinna*), entirely unconditioned (*nirupādhi*), perfect and highest consciousness (*pūrṇa—parasaṃvid*)."

Immediately after the above comment, Jayaratha quotes the present verse of Vijñānabhairava.

VERSE 148

अत्रैकतमयुक्तिस्थे योत्पद्येत दिनाद्दिनम् ।
भरिताकारता सात्र तृप्तिरत्यन्तपूर्णता ॥ १४८ ॥

Atraikatamayuktisthe yotpadyeta dinād dinam /
Bharitākāratā sātra tṛptir atyantapūrṇatā // 148

TRANSLATION

By being established in even one of the *yogas* described here, the plenitude of spiritual consciousnesss that goes on developing day after day until it reaches its highest perfection[2] is known here[3] as *tṛpti* (satisfaction).

1. This means the attainment of the essential nature of Self.
2. The highest perfection is the attainment of *Vijñāna* (the supreme spiritual consciousness) which is *Bhairava.*
3. 'Here' means 'in this yogic tradition.'

VERSE 149

महाशून्यालये वह्नौ भूताक्षविषयादिकम् ।
हूयते मनसा सार्धं स होमश्चेतनास्रुचा ॥ १४९ ॥

Mahāśūnyālaye vahnau bhūtākṣaviṣayādikam /
Hūyate manasā sārdhaṁ sa homaś cetanā-srucā // 149

TRANSLATION

When in the fire of Supreme Reality (i. e. *Bhairava*) in which even the highest void is dissolved, the five elements, the senses, the objects of the senses along with the mind (whose characteristic is dichotomizing thought-constructs) are poured, with *cetanā* as the ladle, then that is real oblation (*homa*).

NOTES

Three things are required in a sacrificial oblation (1) fire (2) substances that are poured into the fire (3) a ladle in which the substances to be poured are placed.

In a real spiritual *homa*, (1) the Supreme Reality or Bhairava is the fire. (2) It is into this fire that the body constituted by the five elements, the senses, the objects of the senses together with the *manas* i.e. all that constitutes the Empirical personality is to be poured and sanctified.

(3) *Cetanā* functions as the laddle. That word *cetanā* is untranslatable. It is intermediate between *citi*, the supreme Universal consciousness and *citta*, the individual, empirical mind. *Cetanā* is the intuitive consciousness which serves as *anusandhātrī*—that which leads and unites the *citta* with *citi*.

There is another reading in place of *cetanāsrucā*, viz. *cetanā ca sruk*, adopted by Kṣemarāja which means *cetanā* functions as the laddle. There is no difference of meaning between the two readings.

VERSES 150-151

यागोऽत्र परमेशानि तुष्टिरानन्दलक्षणा ।
क्षपणात्सर्वपापानां त्राणात्सर्वस्य पार्वति ॥ १५० ॥
रुद्रशक्तिसमावेशस्तत्क्षेत्रं भावना परा ।
अन्यथा तस्य तत्त्वस्य का पूजा कश्च तृप्यति ॥ १५१ ॥

Yāgo'tra parameśāni tuṣṭir ānandalakṣaṇā /
Kṣapaṇāt sarvapāpānāṃ trāṇāt sarvasya pārvati // 150
Rudraśaktisamāveśas tat kṣetraṃ bhāvanā parā /
Anyathā tasya tattvasya kā pūjā kaś ca tṛpyati // 151

TRANSLATION

O supreme goddess, sacrifice in this system simply means spiritual satisfaction characterized by bliss. O Pārvati. the absorption into the śakti of Rudras is alone real *kṣetra* (place of pilgrimage) inasmuch as this absorption destroys all sins (*kṣapaṇāt*), and protects all (*trāṇāt*). This constitutes the highest contemplation. Otherwise in the case of the (non-dual)Reality, how can there be any worship and who is it that is to be gratified ?

NOTES

All the rituals of the ordinary religious life are interpreted in Vijñānabhairava in a higher spiritual sense. *Japa* (recitation of *mantras*) has been interpreted as contemplation on the highest Reality (in verse 145). *Dhyāna* (meditation) has been interpreted as unswerving *buddhi* without the aid of any image or support (in verse 146). *Pūjā* (worship) has been interpreted as firm fixation of the mind on *mahāvyoma*(highest Reality)(in verse 147). *Tṛpti* has been interpreted as plenitude of spiritual consciousness (in verse 148). *Homa* (oblation) has been interpreted as pouring of the senses together with their objects in the fire of Supreme Reality (i. e. *Bhairava*) (in verse 149).

Now in verses 150-151 *yāga* or sacrifice has been interpreted as the bliss of spiritual satisfaction. *Kṣetra* or place of pilgrimage has been interpreted in a higher sense. The word *Kṣetra* is composed of two letters *kṣa* and *tra*. *kṣa* symbolizes *kṣapaṇa* or destruction of all sins by absorption in the *śakti* of the Rudras, known as *anāśrita śakti*, and *tra* symbolizes *trāṇa* or protection inasmuch as one who merges himself in this *śakti* receives her protection.

VERSE 152

स्वतंत्रानन्दचिन्मात्रसारः स्वात्मा हि सर्वतः ।
आवेशनं तत्स्वरूपे स्वात्मनः स्नानमीरितम् ॥ १५२ ॥

Svatantrānandacinmātrasāraḥ svātmā hi sarvataḥ /
Āveśanaṃ tatsvarūpe svātmanaḥ snānam īritam // 152

TRANSLATION

The essence of Self consists universally in autonomy, bliss, and consciousness. One's absorption in that essence is said to be (real) bath.

NOTES

Bath is considered to be an important purificatory step in every ritual. Bhairava says that the usual physical bath does not lead to real purification. It is the spiritual bath which consists in a plunge in the essential Self characterized by autonomy, bliss and consciousness that alone can lead to real purification.

Abhinavagupta expresses this mystic bath beautifully in the following lines in Tantrāloka :

उल्लासिबोधहुतभुग्दग्धविश्वेन्धनोदिते ।
सितभस्मनि देहस्य मज्जनं स्नानमुच्यते ॥ (IV, 116-117)

"The intuitive perception of Reality (*jñāna*) that flashes forth by its light is like fire. Both the objective and subjective spheres of experience are like fuel. When this fuel of the objective and subjective spheres of experience is burnt completely by the fire of *jñāna* and the perception of the essential Self results in the form of white ashes, then an immersion of the limited, empirical self in that essential Self is alone said to be the real bath."

VERSE 153

यैरेव पूज्यते द्रव्यैस्तर्प्यते वा परापरः ।
यश्चैव पूजकः सर्वः स एवैकः क्व पूजनम् ॥ १५३ ॥

Yair eva pūjyate dravyais tarpyate vā parāparaḥ /
Yaś caiva pūjakaḥ sarvaḥ sa evaikaḥ kva pūjanam // 153

TRANSLATION

The offerings[1] with which worship is done, the objects[2] with which the Highest Reality (*para*) together with His highest *śakti* (*parā*) is sought to be satisfied, and the worshippers are all (really speaking) one and the same.[3] Whence then this worship ?

NOTES

1. Offerings—like flower, incense, etc.
2. Objects—like milk, honey, sweets, etc.
3. There is only one non-dual Reality. Flower, honey, and the worshipper who worships with these are non-different from Bhairava who is worshipped. When all are one and the same Reality, what is the sense in this so-called worship?

VERSE 154

व्र जेत्प्राणो विशेज्जीव इच्छया कुटिलाकृतिः ।
दीर्घात्मा सा महादेवी परक्षेत्रं परापरा ॥ १५४ ॥

Vrajet prāṇo viśej jīva icchayā kuṭilākṛtiḥ /
Dīrghātmā sā mahādevī parakṣetram parāparā // 154

TRANSLATION

Prāṇa or the breath of exhalation goes out and the breath of inhalation (*jīva*) enters in, in a curvilinear form. They do so of their own accord (*icchayā*). The great goddess (*prāṇaśakti* or *kuṇḍalinī*) stretches up (*dīrghātmā*). Being both transcendent and immanent, she is the most excellent place of pilgrimage.

NOTES

As Kallaṭa puts it *prāk saṃvit prāṇe pariṇatā*. In all living creatures, the divine consciousness is, at first, converted into *prāṇa*. This is known as *prāṇaśakti*. Its two main forms in all living beings are known as *prāṇa* and *apāna*. *Prāṇa* is the breath of exhalation and *apāna* that of inhalation.

In *Śaivāgama*, the letter ह (ha) is the symbol of *prāṇaśakti*. In *Śāradā* script of Kashmir, the letter 'ha' is written in a curvilinear fashion. Both *prāṇa* and *apāna* move in all living beings in a curvilinear way. That is why *prāṇa* and *apāna* have been designated as *kuṭilākṛtiḥ* (of curvilinear form) in the verse. The letter *ha* which is written in a curvilinear fashion, therefore, very correctly represents *prāṇaśakti*.

The *apāna* breath (inhalation) has been very significantly denominated as *jīva* (life). *Apāna* or inhalation is the breath that returns inside after the *prāṇa* or exhalation. If *apāna* or the breath of inhalation does not return, the living being is bound to die.

The word *icchayā* in the verse has been used to signify the fact that *prāṇa* and *apāna* move out and move in, in a curved way of their own accord. This kind of movement is automatic, natural.

Prāṇaśakti lies in three and a half folds round the centre-*mūlādhāra* in a curved way like a sleeping snake. In this form, it is known as *kuṇḍalinī*. When it lies in a dormant way, the *kuṇḍalinī śakti* is known as *aparā*, simply immanent in life, not yet active.

So long as *kuṇḍalinī* is *aparā*, there is always a sense of difference.

Apāna or the breath of inhalation that enters the centre inside produces the sound *ha* automatically, and the breath of exhalation that goes out to *dvādaśānta* produces the sound 'saḥ' automatically. At their junction in the centre an *anusvāra* on *ha* is also added automatically. Thus this *mantra haṃsaḥ* (हंसः) goes on sounding in every round of *prāṇa—apāna* in every living being. This is known as *ajapājapa* (a recitation that goes on automatically in every living being without effort on the part of any one). This *mantra* means 'I am he' i.e. 'I am *Śiva*. When this automatic *mantra* is consciously and repeatedly contemplated on by the aspirant, it automatically becomes *so'ham* (that am I). By constant contemplation of this *mantra*, *Kuṇḍalinī* rises and stretches upward i.e. is elongated. That is why she is called *dīrghātmā* (elongated). Traversing through the intermediate centres, she enters *Brahmarandhra*, and then arises unity consciousness in the aspirant. In this condition, she is known as *parā* (the highest, the most excellent, the transcendent). Since she is both transcendent and immanent, she is called *parāparā*. Because she inheres in the Supreme consciousness and also carries on the life of the world consisting of *pramātā* (subject), *prameya* (object) and *pramāṇa* (the cognitive relation between the two), therefore, she is rightly called *parāparā*. Because she is the *śakti* of Mahādeva (*Śiva*, the great lord), therefore, is she known as *Mahādevī* (the great goddess).

She is called *parakṣetram*, the most holy place of pilgrimage, because she destroys all the sins of the seeker (*kṣapaṇāt*) and because she protects all (*trāṇāt*). It is this mystic holy place that the seeker must resort to and not geographical places like Kurukṣetra or Banārasa.

VERSE 155

अस्यामनुचरन् तिष्ठन् महानन्दमयेऽध्वरे ।
तया देव्या समाविष्टः परं भैरवमाप्नुयात् ॥१५५ ॥

Asyām anucaran tiṣṭhan mahānandamaye'dhvare /
Tayā devyā samāviṣṭaḥ paraṃ bhairavam āpnuyāt // 155

TRANSLATION

In that great goddess there is the great joy (of the conjunction of 'sa' and 'ha' i.e. of the *mantra so'ham*) which is like a *yajña* or sacrifice (of *vimarśa* or I-consciousness). Pursuing it and resting in it (i.e. in the joy of the *mantra* (*anucaran tiṣṭhan*), one becomes identified with the great goddess and thus (through her) one attains to *bhairava*.

NOTES

This verse only completes the sense of the previous one. The importance of the *haṃsaḥ* or *so'haṃ mantra* has already been discussed in the notes on the previous verse. By constant contemplation on this *mantra*, one becomes identified with the goddess *kuṇḍalinī* and thus through her, one attains the nature of *Bhairava*.

VERSES 155 (repeated)—156

सकारेण बहिर्याति हकारेण विशेत् पुनः ।
हंसहंसेत्यमुं मंत्रं जीवो जपति नित्यशः ।। १५५ ।।
षट्-शतानि दिवा रात्रौ सहस्राण्येकविंशतिः ।
जपो देव्याः समुद्दिष्टः सुलभो दुर्लभो जडैः ।। १५६ ।।

Sakāreṇa bahir yāti hakāreṇa viśet punaḥ /
Haṃsahaṃsety amum mantraṃ jīvo japati nityaśaḥ // 155
Ṣaṭ śatāni divā rātrau sahasrāṇyekaviṃśatiḥ /
Japo devyāḥ samuddiṣṭaḥ sulabho durlabho jaḍaiḥ // 156

TRANSLATION

The breath is exhaled with the sound *sa* and then inhaled with the sound *ha*. (Thus) the empirical individual always recites this mantra *haṃsaḥ*. 155

Throughout the day and night, he (the empirical individual) recites this *mantra* 21,600 times. Such a *japa* (recitation) of the goddess is mentioned which is quite easy to accomplish; it is only difficult for the ignorant. 156

NOTES

The present verse 155 is not printed in the edition of Vijñānabhairava published in the Kashmir series of Texts and Studies. But this has been quoted by Kṣemarāja in his commentary on III. 27 of the *Śiva-sūtras*. This is definitely required, for without it, the sense is incomplete. Therefore, with out disturbing the arrangement of the number of verses as given in the available edition of Vijñānabhairava, the verse as quoted by Kṣemarāja has been given above.

In verse No. 156, the reading of the last line as adopted in the available edition of Vijñānabhairava is as follows: *prāṇasyānte sudurlabhaḥ*. In this edition, it is the reading of Kṣemarāja that has been adopted.

The *mantra hamsaḥ* is repeated by every individual automatically in every round of expiration—inspiration as the verse 155 clearly says. "The incoming breath produces the sound *ha* and the outgoing breath produces the sound *saḥ* spontaneously. "It is recited automatically in a natural way without any one's conscious recitation. Hence it is called *ajapā-japa* i.e. automatic recitation. It is also known as *haṃsa mantra*. The *ha* of this *mantra* represents *śakti* and *saḥ* represents *Śiva*; *aṃ* in *haṃsaḥ* represents the living individual (jīva). This is known as *trika mantra* also, as it includes in itself the three realities of *Śiva*, *śakti* and *nara* or *jīva*. The aspirant has to concentrate on *aṃ*, the junction point of *ha* and *saḥ*.

One round of inspiration-expiration takes 4 seconds. So there is automatic japa of *haṃsaḥ* 15 times in a minute. In one hour, there is (15 × 60) 900 repetitions of this *japa*. In a full day and night, there are (900 × 24) 21,600 repetitions of this *japa*.

Kṣemarāja quotes the verse No. 156 in *Svacchandatantra* (VII. p. 20) and there also he adopts the reading given here. He has quoted the verse No. 156 in connexion with the following verse of *Svacchandatantra* :

"प्राणहंसे सदालीनः साधकः परतत्त्ववित् ।
तस्यायं जप उद्दिष्टः सिद्धिमुक्तिफलप्रदः ॥" (Verse 56)

"The advanced aspirant always reposes in *prāṇahaṃsa* i.e. the *prāṇaśakti* in *suṣumnā* and thus realizes the highest Reality. Because this *prāṇa* is associated with the universal I (*ahaṃ*) which is the very quintessence of all the *mantras*, therefore, it is known as *prāṇahaṃsa*. The *japa* or recitation of *haṃsa mantra* is indicated for him i.e. he who is absorbed in this mantra always sounds it automatically. It gives both supernormal powers and liberation."

If the reading *prāṇasyānte sudurlabhaḥ* is adopted, the meaning would be "on the occasion of the last breath i.e. on the occasion of death, one's identification of himself with this *ajapājapa* is difficult i.e. it is only the fortunate few who owing to excess of meritorious acts are able to maintain their identification with the *ajapājapa* at the last moment."

VERSES 157-160

इत्येतत्कथितं देवि परमामृतमुत्तमम् ।
एतच्च नैव कस्यापि प्रकाश्यं तु कदाचन ॥ १५७ ॥
परशिष्ये खले क्रूरे अभक्ते गुरुपादयोः ।
निर्विकल्पमतीनां तु वीराणामुन्नतात्मनाम् ॥ १५८ ॥
भक्तानां गुरुवर्गस्य दातव्यं निर्विशङ्कया ।
ग्रामो राज्यं पुरं देशः पुत्रदारकुटुम्बकम् ॥ १५९ ॥
सर्वमेतत्परित्यज्य ग्राह्यमेतन्मृगेक्षणे ।
किमेभिरस्थिरैर्देवि स्थिरं परमिदं धनम् ॥ १६० ॥

Ityetat kathitaṃ devi paramāmṛtam uttamam /
Etac ca naiva kasyāpi prakāśyaṃ tu kadācana // 157
Paraśiṣye khale krūre abhakte gurupādayoḥ/
Nirvikalpamatīnāṃ tu vīrāṇām unnatātmanām // 158
Bhaktānāṃ guruvargasya dātavyaṃ nirviśaṅkayā /
Grāmo rājyaṃ puraṃ deśaḥ putradārakuṭumbakam // 159
Sarvam etat parityajya grāhyam etan mṛgekṣaṇe /
Kim ebhir asthirair devi sthiram param idaṃ dhanam / 160

TRANSLATION

O goddess, I have explained to you this teaching which leads to the highest immortal state. This should never be revealed to any and every one, particularly to those pupils who belong to another tradition, who are mischievous, cruel, and wanting in devotion to their spiritual teachers.[1] On the contrary, this teaching should be imparted without the least hesitation to those whose minds are free from oscillating opinions,[2] to *vīras*,[3] to magnanimous ones and to those who are devoted to the line of spiritual teachers.

O gazelle-eyed one, renouncing all these, viz., one's village, kingdom, city, and country, son, daughter, and family, one should lay hold of this teaching. What is the good of the above evanescent things? This is the lasting treasure.

NOTES

1. Unworthy pupils may misuse these teachings. So these should not be imparted to them..

2. *Nirvikalpamatīnām* here does not mean 'whose minds are freed of all dichotomizing thought-constructs'. This is the highest stage. If they have already reached that stage, they do not require any teaching. The word *vikalpa* also means alternation, indecision, alternating opinion. It is in this sense that the word has been used here. So, here it means 'those who are free from oscillating opinions'.

3. The word *vīra* does not mean 'hero' here. It means *viśeṣeṇa īrayati ātmānam iti vīraḥ* i.e. 'one who is self-controlled.' According to Śivopādhyāya, it means 'one who has cut asunder all doubts.'

VERSES 161-162

प्राणा अपि प्रदातव्या न देयं परमामृतम् ।
श्रीदेवी उवाच
देवदेव महादेव परितृप्तास्मि शङ्कर ॥ १६१ ॥
रुद्रयामलतन्त्रस्य सारमद्यावधारितम् ।
सर्वशक्तिप्रभेदानां हृदयं ज्ञातमद्य च ॥ १६२

Prāṇā api pradātavyā na deyaṃ paramāmṛtam /
Śrī devī uvāca
Devadeva mahādeva paritṛptāsmi śaṅkara // 161
Rudrayāmalatantrasya sāram adyāvadhāritam /
Sarvaśaktiprabhedānāṃ hṛdayaṃ jñātam adya ca // 162

TRANSLATION

Even life may be renounced, but this teaching which is like most excellent ambrosia should not be imparted (to undeserving one).

The goddess said

O great god, O god of all the gods, O benefactor, I am fully satisfied. Today, I have understood with certainty the quintessence of Rudrayāmalatantra[1], and also the heart of all the grades of śakti[2].

NOTES

1. The *tantra* that teaches the union of *Śakti* with *Śiva.* This is also the name of a book which teaches about the above union but which is now lost to us.

2. The grades of *Śakti* are (1) *parā*—highest, transcendent undifferentiated, (2) *parāparā*, the intermediate, unity in diversity (3) *aparā*, immanent, bringing about a sense of difference.

VERSE 163

इत्युक्त्वानन्दिता देवी कण्ठे लग्ना शिवस्य तु ॥ १६३ ॥

Ity uktvānanditā devī kaṇṭhe lagnā śivasya tu // 163

TRANSLATION

Having said the above, the goddess who was steeped in delight,[1] embraced Śiva.[2]

NOTES

1. She was steeped in delight, because all her doubts were resolved.

2. She was now established in her non-dual state; she became one with Śiva.

GLOSSARY OF TECHNICAL TERMS

A—Ā (अ—आ)

Akula : Śiva.

Aṇu : Infinitesimal point, the limited, empirical individual.

Advaya : One without a second.

Adhvan (Adhvā) : journey, way, course.

Adhaḥ-kuṇḍalinī : The field of kuṇḍalinī from Lambikā to one-three-fourths of its folds, in the Mūlādhāra.

Anacka : Consonant without a vowel.

Anāhata : Interior automatic sound without any impact.

Anugraha : Grace.

Anuttara : The Incomparable, the Highest; the letter 'a' (अ).

Anusvāra : Nasal sound on the top of a letter; representation of Śiva.

Antarvyoma : The interior space where *prāṇa* and *apāna* are dissolved.

Apara : Lower, immanent.

Apāna : The breath of inhalation going down towards the anus. *Soma* and *jīva* are synonyms of *apāna*.

Amṛta : Ambrosia; the spiritual state in which further involution in matter is annulled.

Artha : Object, goal, sense, perfect comprehension of reality.

ardhacandra : Lit., demi-lunar; the second stage in the *ardhamātrā* (half of a mora) in the *japa* or recitation of *Auṁ*; subtle energy of sound.

Ardhendu : -do-

Avasthā : State; condition.

Avikalpa : Intuitive apprehension, free of all thought-construct.

Aśūnya : Non-void.

Aham : I, absolute I.

Ahantā : The state of absolute I; interiority : I-consciousness.

Ahaṃkāra : Ego, ego-hood; the I-making principle.

Ākāśa : Space; ether; the sky; the infinite;

Āgama : Revealed text, traditional knowledge.

Āṇavopāya : The means whereby the *aṇu* or the empirical individual uses his own *karaṇas* or instruments i.e. senses, *prāṇa* and *manas* for self-realization. It includes disciplines concerning the regulation of *prāṇa*, rituals, *japa*, concentration, etc.

Ātman : Self.

Ānanda : Spiritual bliss.

Āveśa : Entry; absorption.

Āśaya : Disposition of mind; *antaḥ-karaṇa* or the psychic apparatus; mental deposits lying in the unconscious.

I—Ī (इ—ई)

Icchā : Will; desire; impulsion, Icchā-śakti—the power of will.

Idam : This, object.

Idantā : Thisness, objectivity.

Indrajāla : Lit., the net of Indra; magic ; Illusion;

Indriya : Organ of sense.

U—Ū (उ—ऊ)

Uccāra : Function of breath that rises up; the upward thrust or buoyancy of breath.

Udaya : Rise; awaking.

Udāna : The *prāṇa* that rises up in the *suṣumnā* at spiritual awakening.

Udyama : Emergence of Spiritual Consciousness.

Unmanā : The supramental śakti, the highest energy of *praṇava*.

Unmeṣa : Unfoldment; *jagadunmeṣa*—unfoldment of the world-process; *svarūpaunmeṣa*—unfoldment of spiritual consciousness.

Unmīlana samādhi : that state of the mind in which, even when the eyes are open, the external world appears as Universal Consciousness or Śiva.

Upādhi : Limiting adjunct or condition.

Ūrdhva kuṇḍalinī : the risen-up *kuṇḍalinī* when the *prāṇa* and *apāna* enter the *suṣumnā*.

Ka (क)

Kañcuka : Covering of Māyā.
Kanda : A bulbous organ, situated near the anus.
Kaṇṭha : The *cakra* at the base of the throat.
Kalā : Energy; creativity; limited agency; phase of manifestation; part of letter or word.
Kāla : Time; the category of time or time-principle.
Kālāgni : Kālāgni Rudra—The Universal Destructive Fire that destroys all impurities, sins, etc.
Kuṇḍalinī : The bio-psychic energy which in its inactive form lies like a snake folded up in three and a half folds round the *mūlādhāra cakra* at the base of the spine.
Kula : Undifferentiated Energy;
Kuṭilākṛti : A curved form in which *prāṇa* flows before the awakening of *Kuṇḍalinī.*
Kumbhaka : Retention of breath.
Kuhana : Magic or tickling of the arm-pit.
Kevala : Alone, isolated.
Kaivalya : Aloneness; isolation; aloofness from the influence of *prakṛti* or *māyā.*
Koṭi : Point, initial or final.
Kramamudrā : A successive occurrence of *nimīlana* and *unmīlana samādhi*; the condition in which the mind by the force of *samāveśa* swings alternately between the internal (essential Self) and the external (the world which now appears as Śiva).
Kriyā : Activity; the power of activity.

Kṣa (क्ष)

Kṣetra : Holy place; place of pilgrimage.
Kṣobha : Agitation.

Kha (ख)

Khecarī mudrā : Vide the note on *Khecarī* under the verse 77.

Ga (ग)

Grāhaka : Knower; subject.
Grāhya : Known; object.

Ca (च)

Cakra : Centre of prāṇic energy. It is through the various *cakras* or centres of prāṇic energy that Kuṇḍalinī passes when she rises from Mūlādhāra and enters Brahmarandhra.

Camatkāra : The bliss of pure I-consciousness.

Cit : Absolute Consciousness.

Cidākāśa : The ether of consciousness.

Cidghana : Mass of consciousness.

Cidānanda : Consciousness-bliss.

Cidānandaghana : Mass of Consciousness-bliss.

Citkalā : Energy of consciousness.

Citprakāśa : Light of consciousness.

Citi : The consciousness-power of the Absolute that brings about the world-process.

Citta : Empirical mind.

Citta viśrānti : Repose of the empirical mind in the higher consciousness.

Citta sambodha : Awakening of the individual mind.

Citta pralaya : Dissolution of the empirical mind in the higher consciousness.

Cintā : Thought, idea.

Cetanā : Consciousness; consciousness intermediate between the highest level and the ordinary empirical consciousness.

Caitanya : Absolute Consciousness characterized by *svātantrya*, absolute autonomy and *jñāna* (knowledge) and *kriyā* (activity).

J (ज)

Jagat : The world process; the universe.

Jagadānanda : The bliss of the Self or the Divine appearing as the universe; the bliss of the Divine made visible.

Japa : Recitation.

Jāgrat : The waking condition.

Jīva : The living being; the individual soul; the empirical self.

Jīvanmukta : One liberated while yet alive.

Jīvanmukti : Liberation while one is alive.

Jñāna : Knowledge; spiritual realization, the Śakti of Śiva; the specific śakti of Īśvara.

Jñānin : The gnostic; one who has obtained spiritual realization.

T (त)

Tattva : Thatness, the very being of a thing; constitutive principle; category of Reality; Ultimate Reality.

Tantra : A scripture in general; Science of the cosmic spiritual forces, revealed work.

Tāntrika : Follower of Tantra; pertaining to Tantra.

Tirodhāna śakti : Power that obscures Reality.

Turya or Turīya : The fourth state of consciousness beyond the state of waking, dream and deep sleep, and stringing together all the states; integral awareness; the metaphysical Self, distinct from the psycho-physical or empirical self; the *śākṣī* or witnessing consciousness.

Turyātīta : The state of consciousness transcending the Turīya state; the state in which the distinctions of the three, viz., waking, dreaming and deep sleep states are annulled; the pure blissful consciousness in which there is no sense of difference, in which the entire universe appears as the Self.

Trika : The system or philosophy of the triad—(1) Śiva, (2) Śakti and (3) Nara—the bound soul, or (1) *para*, the highest, non-different from Śiva, (2) *parāpara*, the intermediate state of identity in difference, (3) *apara*, the state of difference; the lower.

Da (द)

Darśana : Intuitive vision; system of philosophy.

Dārḍhya : Firmness of mind or concentration.

Dṛḍha : Stable in concentration.

Dṛṣṭi : Comprehensive vision.

Diś : Direction.

Deśa : Space; region.

Dvādaśānta : Distance or end of 12 fingers. This is measured in various ways : (1) A distance of 12 fingers from the tip of the nose in outer space is known as *bāhya dvādaśānta*. (2) A distance of 12 fingers from the *bāhya dvādaśānta* to the centre (*hṛdaya*) of the body is known as *āntara dvādaśanta*. (3) A distance of 12 fingers from *hṛdaya* upto *Kaṇṭha*. (4) There is a *dvādaśānta* from the palate to the middle of the eye-brows. (5) There is a *dvādaśānta* from the middle or centre of the eye-brows upto *Brahmarandhra*. This is known as *ūrdhva dvādaśānta*. This distance is of use only when the *kuṇḍalinī* awakens.

Dha (ध)

Dhyāna : meditation.
Dhyānī : meditator.

Na (न)

Navātma : Of nine forms. For details, see note No. 4 under verse 2.
Nāḍī : subtle channel of *prāṇa*.
Nāda : interior spontaneous sound.
Nāda-bindu : The first creative pulsation and its compact mass; the creative sound and light; Śakti and Śiva.
Nādānta : Subtle energy of *praṇava*.
Nibhālana : perception; mental practice.
Nimeṣa : closing of the eye: involution; dissolution of the world.
Nimīlana samādhi : the inward meditative condition in which the individual consciousness gets absorbed in the Universal consciousness.
Niyati: limitation of cause-effect relation; Spatial limitation.
Nirādhāra : without support-objective or subjective.
Nirāśraya : without any prop or base.
Nirodhikā or nirodhinī : a subtle energy of *praṇava*.
Nirvikalpa : higher consciousness free of all thought-constructs.
Niveśa or niveśana : entry into the Universal Consciousness.

Niṣkala : partless; undivided, Śiva above manifestation or creation.

Nistaraṅga : free of undulation or commotion.

Pa (प)

Pati : Śiva; a liberated individual.

Para : the highest; the Supreme.

Para pramātā : the highest experient, *parama Śiva.*

Parama Śiva : the Highest Reality, the absolute.

Paramātmā : the supreme Self.

Paramārtha : highest reality; essential truth: the highest goal.

Parāmarśa : Seizing mentally, experience, comprehension, remembrance; referring or pointing to: a letter; consciousness of a letter.

Parāpara : intermediate stage of śakti; both supreme and non-supreme; both identical and different; unity in diversity.

Parāvāk : the unmanifest Śakti or vibratory moment of the Divine; Logos; cosmic ideation.

Parā-śakti : highest śakti of the Divine; citi.

Paśu : the bound soul; the *jīva;* the empirical self; the individual.

Paśyantī : the Divine view of the universe in undifferentiated form; *vāk śakti*, going forth as seeing, ready to create in which there is no differentiation between vācya (object) and vācaka (word).

Puruṣa : the Self.

Puryaṣṭaka : the city of the group of eight i.e. the subtle body consisting of the five *tanmātras*, *buddhi*, *manas* and *ahaṃkāra.*

Pūrṇa : perfect; full of divine consciousness.

Pūrṇāhantā : the perfect I-consciousness of Śiva; non-relational I-consciousness.

Prakāśa : the light of consciousness, the principle of Self-revelation.

Prakṛti : the primordial source of objectivity from *buddhi* down to earth.

Pratibhā : The illumination of the I-consciousness of Śiva; a synonym of *parāvāk*;

Pratyabhijñā : recognition.
Pramātā : The knower; the subject: the experient.
Pramātṛtā : knowership.
Pramāṇa : means of knowledge; knowledge.
Prameya : Object of knowledge.
Prasara : expansion; manifestation of *Śiva* in the form of the universe through His *Śakti*.
Prāṇa : In general the vital energy; specifically, the vital breath in exhalation.
Prāṇaśakti : Vital energy; bioplasma.
Prāṇana : the animating principle, the principle of all the *prāṇas*.
Prāṇāyāma : breath control.

Ba (ब)

Bindu : written also as vindu—a point, a metaphysical point; concentration of luminous energy; compact mass of śakti gathered into an undifferentiated point ready to create; *paraḥ pramātā*—the highest experient; the *anusvāra* or nasal sound indicated by a dot on a letter indicating the fact that *Śiva* in spite of the manifestation of the universe is undivided; symbol of *Śiva;* a *śakti* of *praṇava*.
Buddhi : the intellect; the ascertaining intelligence; sometimes the higher mind; the super personal mind; intuitive aspect of consciousness by which the essential Self awakens to truth.
Bodha : Enlightenment; spiritual awakening.
Brahma : the highest reality (existence-consciousness-bliss).
Brahmanāḍī : *suṣumnā*, the *madhya nāḍī*, the central subtle channel of *prāṇa*.
Brahmarandhra : *Sahsrāra cakra;* the *prāṇic* centre at the top of the head.

Bha (भ)

Bhakti : Devotion.
Bharitā : plenitude, fulness.
Bhāva : existence—both internal and external; existent; object.

Bhāvanā : Creative contemplation; powerful employment of imagination.

Bhuvana : world.

Bheda : difference.

Bhairava : The Highest Reality, *bha* indicating *bharaṇa* or maintenance of the world, *ra ravaṇa* or withdrawal of the world, and *va*, *vamana* or projection of the world.

Bhairavī : Śakti of Bhairava.

Bhairava or bhairavī mudrā : The posture in which the gaze is turned outwards without the twinkling of the eyes, and the attention is turned inwards.

Bhrūmadhya : the centre or middle of the eye-brows.

Bhoga : experience, sometimes used in the narrow sense of enjoyment.

Bhoktā : experient.

Ma (म)

Mati : understanding; intuitive intelligence.

Madhya : centre; the central consciousness; the pure I-consciousness; the *suṣumnā* or central *prāṇic nāḍī;* internal; gap, middle.

Madhyadhāma : Suṣumnā, also known as *brahmanāḍī.*

Madhyama-pada : the central or middle state.

Madhyamā : Śabda in its subtle form as existing in the mind or *antaḥkaraṇa* prior to its gross manifestation.

Madhyaśakti : *Saṁvit-śakti*, the central consciousness-power.

Manas : the internal sense, the empirical mind.

Mantra : a sacred or mystic formula for recitation.

Mantra-vīrya : the power of *Mantra.*

Marut : Breath (exhalation or inhalation).

Mala : dross; limitation which hampers the free expression of the Spirit.

Mahābodha : the great awakening, the grand illumination.

Mahāmantra : the grand *mantra* of the supreme I-consciousness.

Mahāvyāpti : the grand fusion; the grand pervasion.

Mahāsattā : the Highest Reality which is absolute Light and freedom and the source of all existence.

Mahāśūnya : the great void.

Māyā : the finitizing or limiting principle of the Divine; Illusion.

Māyātattva : the principle of veiling the Infinite and projecting the finite; the source of the five *kañcukas*.

Māyāpramātā : the empirical self, governed by Māyā.

Māyāśakti : the power of Divine for finitizing or limiting.

Māyīya mala : limitation due to Māyā which gives to the soul its gross and subtle bodies.

Mukti : liberation.

Mudrā : Yogic posture as aid in concentration, that which gives the bliss of spiritual consciousness.

Mūlādhāra : the prāṇic centre below the genitals.

Meya : object.

Mokṣa : liberation.

Moha : delusion.

Yugapat : simultaneously.

Yogī : one who is seeking to or has been able to unite with the Universal consciousness.

Yogīndra : the great yogī who has attained the *śāmbhava* state.

Yoginī : the divine energy of Bhairava.

Ra (र)

Rajas: the principle of motion, activity and disharmony, a constituent of *Prakṛti*

Rasa: Flavour; aesthetic rapture

Rāga : Passion; intense desire for and attachment to an object; one of the *kañcukas* of māyā on account of which there is limitation by desire.

Rudrayāmala : intimate union of Rudra and His Śakti.

Rūpa : Form; essence.

La (ल)

Laya-nilaya : absorption.

Līna : absorbed.

Va (व)

Vapus : (bhairavasya) form; the nature of Bhairava, cosmic essence.

Varṇa : letter; sound of letter; subtle energy of speech.

Vahni : a technical word of *Śaiva Yoga,* meaning entering completely into the root and half of the middle of *adhaḥ kuṇḍalinī.*

Vācaka : word; indicator.

Vācya : object; the indicated.

Vāmeśvarī : the divine *śakti* that emits i.e. projects the universe out of the Absolute and produces the reverse consciousness of difference.

Vikalpa : idea, ideation; dichotomising thought-construct.

Vikalpanam : the differentiation-making activity of the mind.

Vikalpa-kṣaya : the dissolution of Vikalpas.

Vikāsa : efflorescence; unfoldment; development.

Vijñāna : consciousness; supreme consciousness.

Vidyā : limited knowledge; pure knowledge (cf. Śuddha *vidyā śakti*).

Vibhūti : splendour: supernormal power.

Vimarśa : experience; the Self-consciousness of the supreme, full of *jñāna* and *kriyā* which brings about the world-process.

Vimarśana : intuitive awareness.

Viyat: space; sky.

Vilaya : concealment.

Viṣa : a technical word of *Śaiva yoga,* meaning entering into the remaining half and wholly into the top of *adhaḥkuṇḍalinī* right upto the portion where *ūrdhva-kuṇḍalinī* ends (from the root *viṣ* to pervade).

Viśrānti : rest; peace.

Viśva : the all; the cosmos; the universe.

Viśvamaya : *viśvātmaka*—immanent.

Viśvottīrṇa : transcendent.

Visarga : *Śiva's* power of projection of the universe; *śakti*; two dots placed perpendicularly one upon the other after a letter, giving the sound *ha.*

Vīrya : virility, vitality; *mantra-vīrya* the virility of *mantra.*

Vaikharī : Śakti as gross word or speech.

Vṛtti : mode, fluctuation.

Vaiṣamya : difference, disquietude of duality.

Vyāna : the pervasive *prāṇa.*

Vyāpta : completely pervaded.

Vyāpti : pervasion; fusion in the whole, in Śiva.
Vyāpinī : all-pervasive energy of *praṇava*.
Vyutthāna : lit.; rising, coming to normal consciousness after trance.
Vyāmohitatā : delusion.
Vyoma : sky; the infinite sky of consciousness; *antar vyoma*, the space in the mystic centre.

Śa (श)

Śakti : Power, identical with Śiva; Śakti as a door of entrance into Śiva (verse, 20); woman (verses 69-70)
Śakti-pāta : descent of the divine *Śakti*, grace.
Śakti-vikāsa : unfoldment of *śakti*;. concentration of attention on the inner consciousness even when the senses are open to their respective objects.
Śakti-saṅkoca : withdrawal of attention from sense activity and turning it towards the inner reality.
Śabda : word; sound.
Śabda brahma : Sound in its absolute state; ultimate Reality in the form of vibration of which human word is a gross representation. In this state, thought and word are one.
Śabda-rāśi : totality of words.
Śāktopāya : the means of approach to the Divine through Śakti, the ever-recurring thought of oneself being essentially Śiva or the supreme I-consciousness.
Śāmbhavopāya : the direct approach to *Śiva*: sudden emergence of Śiva-consciousness without any *vikalpa* by a mere hint that one's essential Self is *Śiva*.
Śikhānta : Brahmarandhra.
Śiva-Vyāpti : fusion with Śiva; absorption of the universe in Śiva.
Śuddha vidyā : the fifth *tattva* counting from *Śiva*, the stage in which there is identity in diversity.
Śuddha adhvā : the pure course; the extra-mundane existence – the first five *tattvas*;
Śūnya : void, the state in which no object is experienced.
Śūnyātiśūnya : absolute void.

Śūnyatā : vacuity.

Śūnyapramātā : the experiencer of the void: pralayākala.

Ṣa (ष)

Ṣaḍadhvā : the six forms of manifestation — three on the subjective side, *varṇa*, *mantra* and *pada* and three on the objective side, *kalā*, *tattva*, *bhuvana*.

Ṣaṣṭha-vaktra : lit. the sixth organ or *meḍhra kanda* near the root of the rectum.

Sa (स)

Saṃkalpa : resolve; the synthetic activity of thought.

Saṅkoca : contraction of *Śakti*, the means to enter the heart or mystic centre.

Saṃvid-saṃvitti : Consciousness; universal consciousness.

Saṃskāra : the residual traces of the mind lying in the unconscious.

Sakala : all the *jīvas* from gods down to the mineral who rest in *māyā tattva*. They have no knowledge of the real Self and their consciousness is only that of diversity.

Sattā : existence; ultimate reality

Sattāmātra : pure existence, mahā sattā—transcendental reality.

Sādāśiva : the third *tattva*, counting from *Śiva*. At this stage the I-experience is more important than the this-experience. Icchā or will is predominant in this *tattva*.

Samatva-samatā : equality, perfect harmony.

Samanā : the energy of *praṇava* below the highest.

Samarasa : one having the same feeling or consciousness, identical.

Saṃhāra : withdrawal, reabsorption.

Saṃsāra : transmigratory existence : world-process.

Saṃsārin : transmigratory being.

Samādhi : collectedness of mind, trance.

Samāna : the vital *vāyu* that helps in assimilation of food, etc. and brings about equilibrium between *prāṇa* and *apāna*.

Samāveśa : total absorption.

Samâpatti : Sometimes synonym of samâdhi, consummation, attainment of psychic at-one-ment.

Sarvakartṛtva : omnipotence.

Sarvaga : omnipenetrant.

Sarvajña : omniscient.

Sarvajñatva : omniscience.

Sâmaraṣya : identity of consciousness—union of *Śiva* and *Śakti.*

Sāra : quintessence.

Siddhi : Supernormal power.

Suṣupti : the condition of dreamless sleep.

Suṣumnā : the middle or central *prāṇic nāḍī* or channel.

Sūkṣma : subtle.

Sṛṣṭi : letting go, manifestation, emanation.

Stabdha : immovable.

Sthiti : maintenance (of the universe); spiritual station.

Sthūla : gross.

Spanda : divine activity, the dynamic aspect of *Śiva*; primordial creative pulsation.

Sphurattā : flashing consciousness.

Svatantra : autonomous; of absolute will.

Svātantrya : the absolute autonomy of the Supreme.

Svapna : the dream condition.

Svarūpa : one's own form; real nature: essence.

Svasthiti or Svasthā : staying in one's essential state.

Svātma : one's own Self.

Svecchā: *Śiva's* or *Śakti's* own Will; synonymous with *svātantrya.*

Ha (ह)

Ha : symbol of śakti; the divine energy as imperceptible, spontaneous sound in the living being.

Haṭhapāka : persistent process of assimilating experience to the consciousness of the experient.

Haṃsa : the *prāṇa* and *apāna* breath—*apāna* sounding inaudibly as 'ha' and *prāṇa* sounding inaudibly as *saḥ* with the *anusvāra* (aṃ) at the junction point forming *haṃsaḥ* which sounds in every living being spontaneously every moment. This is known as *ajapā japa*, because every living being goes on repeating it automatically without any conscious effort on his part. When one consciously observes this process, it is known as *haṃsa mantra*. By conscious repetition it gets converted into *so'ham* (I am He i.e. Śiva).

Haṃsaḥ is also symbol of a jīva, the empirical individual.

Hṛdaya : heart, the mystic centre, the central consciousness.

SUBJECT INDEX

INDEX TO IMPORTANT SANSKRIT WORDS

अ

आ

इ

उ

क

ख

ग

य

र

ल

व

श

AN ALPHABETICAL INDEX

To the first pāda of each Verse